IDENTITY PARADE

Roddy Lumsden's first book *Yeah Yeah Yeah* (1997) was shortlisted for Forward and Saltire prizes. His second collection *The Book of Love* (2000), a Poetry Book Society Choice, was shortlisted for the T.S. Eliot Prize. *Mischief Night: New & Selected Poems* (Bloodaxe Books, 2004) was a Poetry Book Society Recommendation. His latest collection is *Third Wish Wasted* (Bloodaxe Books, 2009).

He is a freelance writer, specialising in quizzes and word puzzles, and has held several residencies, including ones with the City of Aberdeen, St Andrews Bay Hotel, and as "poet-in-residence" to the music industry when he co-wrote *The Message*, a book on poetry and pop music (Poetry Society, 1999). His other books include *Vitamin Q: a temple of trivia lists and curious words* (Chambers Harrap, 2004). His anthology *Identity Parade: new British and Irish poets* was published by Bloodaxe Books in 2010. Born in St Andrews, he lived in Edinburgh before moving to London, where he teaches privately and for The Poetry School.

IDENTITY PARADE

NEW BRITISH & IRISH POETS
EDITED BY RODDY LUMSDEN

BLOODAXE BOOKS

Selection and introduction copyright © 2010 Roddy Lumsden.
Copyright of poems resides with authors as listed.

ISBN: 978 1 85224 839 0

First published 2010 by
Bloodaxe Books Ltd,
Highgreen,
Tarset,
Northumberland NE48 1RP.

www.bloodaxebooks.com
For further information about Bloodaxe titles
please visit our website or write to
the above address for a catalogue.

Supported by
ARTS COUNCIL
ENGLAND

Cover design: Neil Astley & Pamela Robertson-Pearce

Printed in Great Britain by
Bell & Bain Limited, Glasgow, Scotland.

CONTENTS

17   *Introduction*

Patience Agbabi (*b.* 1965)
21   The Wife of Bafa
23   Postmod:
23   The London Eye
24   Josephine Baker Finds Herself

Jonathan Asser (*b.* 1964)
25   Interlude
26   Something To Do
27   The Birdbath's Saying *Dive*
28   No Mercy

Tiffany Atkinson (*b.* 1972)
29   Portrait of the Husband as Farmers' Market
30   Autobiography without pronouns
30   In this one
31   Philology
32   Rain –

Simon Barraclough (*b.* 1966)
33   Frigidaire
34   The Open Road
35   Desert Orchid
35   Los Alamos Mon Amour

Paul Batchelor (*b.* 1977)
36   Keening
37   To a Halver
38   Secret Papers
39   Triage

Kate Bingham (*b.* 1971)
40   The Island-designing Competition
41   The Mouths of Babes
42   Dalby Bush Farm
43   De Beers

Julia Bird (*b.* 1971)
44   Five Years Trying to Win the Flower Show Vegetable Animal Class
45   Your Grandfather Would Have Wanted You to Have This
46   Breathing Pattern

Patrick Brandon (*b.* 1965)

47 Mountain Man
48 Dolphin
49 Higgs Bison
50 Grand Union
50 A Sloping Pitch

David Briggs (*b.* 1972)

51 Asking the Difficult Questions
52 Self-portrait in a Rear-view Mirror
53 Twenty Below Zero
53 Winter Music

Andy Brown (*b.* 1966)

54 The Last Geese
55 A Poem of Gifts
56 As the tide sucks out at daybreak
57 Samhain

Judy Brown (*b.* 1962)

58 The End of the Rainbow
59 Peckham Poem(s)
60 The New Neighbours
61 Unfamiliar Festivals

Colette Bryce (*b.* 1970)

62 The Smoke
63 Line,
64 *Nevers*
64 Self Portrait in a Broken Wing-mirror
66 In Defence of Old Men Dozing in Bookshops

Matthew Caley (*b.* 1959)

67 Acupuncture
68 *King Size Rizlas*
69 Big Sur
69 The Argument
70 For Howard Devoto

Siobhán Campbell (*b.* 1962)

71 Almost in Sight
73 Massy Wood
73 Miner

Vahni Capildeo (*b.* 1973)
75 Lilies
76 White as Jasmine
77 *from* Winter to Winter: August: North
79 Vacant Possession
79 What Is Your Guy Really Like?

Melanie Challenger (*b.* 1977)
81 Sleeping Beauty
82 Blue Whale
83 Stac Pollaidh or *Regret*
83 Pygmalion

Kate Clanchy (*b.* 1965)
85 Patagonia
86 Poem for a Man with No Sense of Smell
87 The Bridge Over the Border
88 Love
89 Dark, Dark
89 Scan

Polly Clark (*b.* 1968)
90 Women
91 South Uist
91 Nibbling
92 Dog Opera
93 Thank You

Julia Copus (*b.* 1969)
94 Love, Like Water
95 In Defence of Adultery
96 Raymond, at 60
97 Topsell's Beasts
97 A Soft-edged Reed of Light

Sarah Corbett (*b.* 1970)
99 Taking the Night Train
100 Shame
101 Kisses
101 The Dog's Kiss

Claire Crowther (*b.* 1947)
103 Investigating the Easter Issue
104 Lost Child
104 Summerhouse

105 Next Door Moon
105 Open Plan

Tim Cumming (*b.* 1963)
107 Snow
108 Days
109 Foreign News
110 Danebury Ring
111 Late Picasso
112 Following the Bloom

Ailbhe Darcy (*b.* 1981)
113 Crossing
114 The Art of Losing
115 The mornings you turn into a grub
116 Swan Song

Peter Davidson (*b.* 1957)
117 The Englishman's Catechism
119 Of Death, Fame and Immortality
120 Concerning Stillness and Distance

Nick Drake (*b.* 1961)
121 Eureka
122 Babylon
122 Sea Change
123 The Hunt By Night (1990)
124 The Ghost Train

Sasha Dugdale (*b.* 1974)
125 Ten Moons
126 Carnation, Bible
127 Maldon
127 Moor
128 *from* The Red House
129 Stolen

Chris Emery (*b.* 1963)
130 The Lermontov
132 Carl's Job
133 The Destroyer's Convention

Bernardine Evaristo (*b.* 1959)
134 *from* Lara
136 *from* The Emperor's Babe

Paul Farley (*b.* 1965)
138   Dead Fish
139   Diary Moon
140   Keith Chegwin as Fleance
140   An Interior
141   Newts
141   North Atlantic Corridor
142   The Scarecrow Wears a Wire

Leontia Flynn (*b.* 1974)
143   The Furthest Distances I've Travelled
144   Airports
145   By My Skin
146   Belfast

Annie Freud (*b.* 1948)
147   The Study of Disease
148   The Symbolic Meaning of Things and Reasons for Not Dying
149   Daube
149   A Scotch Egg
150   A Canaletto Orange

Alan Gillis (*b.* 1973)
151   The Ulster Way
152   Harvest
153   Whiskey

Jane Griffiths (*b.* 1970)
155   Epitaph for X
156   Valediction
157   Clairvoyance
158   Travelling Light
159   On Liking Glass Houses:

Vona Groarke (*b.* 1964)
160   To Smithereens
162   Ghosts
162   Bodkin
163   The Return

Jen Hadfield (*b.* 1978)
164   Melodeon on the Road Home
165   Unfledging
166   Hedgehog, Hamnavoe
166   Prenatal Polar Bear

167   Full Sheeptick Moon
168   Thrimilce – Isbister
168   The Blokes and Beasties

Sophie Hannah (*b.* 1971)

169   Long for This World
170   The Bridging Line
171   'No Ball Games etc'

Tracey Herd (*b.* 1968)

172   Spring in the Valley of the Racehorse
173   Sir Ivor
174   Black Swan
175   Coronach

Kevin Higgins (*b.* 1967)

176   From the future, a postcard home
177   Almost Invisible
177   Shapeless Days Shuffling
178   The Great Depression
178   The Candidate
179   The Couple Upstairs

Matthew Hollis (*b.* 1971)

180   Hedge Bird
181   The Sour House
182   The Diomedes

A.B. Jackson (*b.* 1965)

183   A Ring
184   Lauder's Bar
185   Foxes
185   Star
186   *from* Apocrypha

Anthony Joseph (*b.* 1966)

188   Conductors of His Mystery
190   The Cinema
191   The Myst

Luke Kennard (*b.* 1981)

192   Chorus
193   Daughters of the Lonesome Isle
194   The Forms of Despair
195   Instrumental #3
196   Scarecrow

Nick Laird (*b.* 1975)
197 Adeline
198 Donna
198 Pug
200 The Hall of Medium Harmony
201 The Eventual

Sarah Law (*b.* 1967)
202 Phase Transitions
203 Breathing
204 Parisian
205 *from* Stretch: A Yoga Sequence

Frances Leviston (*b.* 1982)
206 The Zombie Library
207 Sight
207 The Gaps
208 Moon
208 Scandinavia

Gwyneth Lewis (*b.* 1959)
209 Prayer for Horizon
210 A Golf-Course Resurrection
211 Night Passage to Nantucket
212 Memorial Sweater

John McAuliffe (*b.* 1973)
213 Flood
214 You Can See
214 Tinnitus
215 The Electric Jar

Chris McCabe (*b.* 1977)
216 Radio
217 Lemon Blue
218 The Essex Fox
219 Poem in Black Ink

Helen Macdonald (*b.* 1970)
220 Poem
222 MIR
223 Jack
223 Earth Station

Patrick McGuinness (*b.* 1968)

225   Heroes
226   Dust
226   The Age of the Empty Chair
227   Montreal
228   Blue

Kona Macphee (*b.* 1969)

229   Melbourne, evening, summertime –
230   Shrew
230   Pheasant and astronomers
231   Terminus
232   Waltz

Peter Manson (*b.* 1969)

233   Hymn to Light
234   In Vitro
234   Poem
235   Four Darks in Red
236   Familiars

D.S. Marriott (*b.* 1963)

237   The Day Ena Died
238   Tap
240   Over the Black Mountains

Sam Meekings (*b.* 1981)

242   Describing Angels to the Blind
243   Bees
243   Migration
244   Depth

Sinéad Morrissey (*b.* 1972)

245   *from* China
246   Shadows in Siberia According to Kapuściński
247   'Love, the nightwatch...'
248   On Waitakere Dam

Daljit Nagra (*b.* 1966)

250   Look We Have Coming To Dover!
251   This Be the Pukka Verse
252   University
253   Our Town With the Whole of India!

Caitríona O'Reilly (*b.* 1973)

254 Octopus
255 Calculus
256 The Lure
257 Pandora's Box

Alice Oswald (*b.* 1966)

258 Field
259 A Greyhound in the Evening After a Long Day of Rain
260 Shamrock Café
261 Woods etc.

Katherine Pierpoint (*b.* 1961)

262 Waterbuffalo
263 Burning the door
264 Cats Are Otherwise
265 Plumbline

Clare Pollard (*b.* 1978)

267 Puppetry
268 Fears of a Hypochondriac Insomniac
270 The Panther

Jacob Polley (*b.* 1975)

271 The Bridge
271 Rain
272 The Crow
273 The North-South Divide
274 The Turn

Diana Pooley (*b.* 1941)

275 The Bird
276 Listen Amelio,
276 Inscriptions
277 Back at Pathungra
278 King

Richard Price (*b.* 1966)

279 *from* A Spelthorne Bird List
280 Wake up and sleep
281 Languor's whispers

Sally Read (*b.* 1971)

284 Fog
285 Mastectomy

286   Mafia Flowers
287   The Death-Bell
288   Instruction

Deryn Rees-Jones (*b.* 1968)
290   Trilobite
292   My Father's Hair
293   *from* Quiver:

Neil Rollinson (*b.* 1960)
294   Dreamtime
295   Constellations
296   Between Bradford and Pudsey
297   Long Exposure

Jacob Sam-la Rose (*b.* 1976)
298   The Beautiful
299   Blacktop Universe
299   A Life in Dreams
301   Plummeting

Anthony Rowland (*b.* 1970)
302   Lésvos
303   Damrak
304   Pie
305   Golem

James Sheard (*b.* 1962)
307   Four Mirrors
308   Cargo Cult
309   The Lost Testament of R. Catesby
310   Café Verdi

Zoë Skoulding (*b.* 1967)
311   Trappist Brewers
312   History
313   Preselis with Brussels Street Map
314   New Year
314   Docks

Catherine Smith (*b.* 1962)
315   The Set of Optics You Wouldn't Let Me Buy
       in Portobello Road Market, September 1984
316   Wonders
317   Picnic
317   The Fathers

Jean Sprackland (*b.* 1962)

319   The Way Down
320   Bracken
321   An Old Friend Comes to Stay
322   Hands

John Stammers (*b.* 1954)

323   Mary Brunton
324   A Younger Woman
324   Funeral
325   Testimony
327   Black Dog

Greta Stoddart (*b.* 1966)

328   Salvation Jane
329   The Crossing
330   Verfremdungseffekt
331   Greece
332   Object

Sandra Tappenden (*b.* 1956)

333   Promise
334   Bells
334   Waroirrs of the Whiled West
335   People who are drawn to take free stress tests

Tim Turnbull (*b.* 1960)

336   Sea Monsters
337   Lullaby for an Alcoholic
337   What was that?
338   Ode on a Grayson Perry Urn

Julian Turner (*b.* 1955)

340   Bert Haines' Yard
341   Penalty of Stroke and Distance
342   A Nightjar
342   At Walcott

Mark Waldron (*b.* 1960)

344   The Brand New Dark is Getting In,
345   He's Face Down in the Lake
346   The Well Dressed Street
346   The Very Slow Train,
347   Underneath the Gone Sky

Ahren Warner (*b.* 1986)

348   la brisure
349   Legare
349   Near Saint Mary Woolnoth, EC3
350   Léman

Tim Wells (*b.* 1966)

351   My Own Private Ida Lupino
352   The 1980s Are a Long Time Dead
352   Comin' a Dance
353   L.A. Rain

Matthew Welton (*b.* 1969)

355   Poppy
356   An ABC of American Suicide
358   The fundament of wonderment

David Wheatley (*b.* 1970)

359   Chemical Plant
360   A Fret
361   La Ultima Canción de César Peru

Sam Willetts (*b.* 1962)

364   Home
365   A Child at Their Party
366   Truanting
366   Fur-sorting
367   Detoxing in the French Quarter

Samantha Wynne-Rhydderch (*b.* 1966)

368   Stately Home
369   A Pair of Antlers
371   Indiscretions

Tamar Yoseloff (*b.* 1965)

372   Barnard's Star
373   The Angle of Error
374   The Venetian Mirror

376   *Acknowledgements*

Introduction: The Pluralist Now

Identity Parade is an anthology representing the new generation of poets who have emerged since the mid-1990s. All the poets have either published first collections within the past 15 years or make their debut within the next year. It is a book in a tradition of generational anthologies which stretches back for decades. The most recent of these is Hulse, Kennedy and Morley's *The New Poetry*, published by Bloodaxe in 1993. Previously, there had usually been a gap of a decade or so, going back to Penguin anthologies from Blake Morrison and Andrew Motion in the early 1980s and Edward Lucie-Smith in 1970, then to A. Alvarez's 1962 *The New Poetry* and back further to various, generally factional anthologies – *New Lines, New Signatures, The New Apocalypse* – which aimed to represent what was happening in British and Irish poetry at that time.

There have been changes in the poetry world since the early 1990s, and since anthologies are as likely to be read by those with limited knowledge of the world of poetry as by the connoisseurs and critics within it, it seems useful to look briefly at what some of these are. Technological advances have made printing easier and less expensive, and the internet has fostered poetry networks. Britain now has three major prizes for poetry collections: the Forward Prize, the T.S. Eliot Prize and the Costa (formerly Whitbread) Poetry Award.

The culture of readings, performances and festivals is thriving and widespread in a way it wasn't in previous decades. As well as London's long-established Poetry International and the Aldeburgh Poetry Festival (in its infancy back in the early 90s), we now have a number of annual festivals dedicated only to poetry, including those in Ledbury, St Andrews, Essex, Bristol, Dún Laoghaire and Cork, most of which began in the 1990s, and many other venues with year-round readings; and poetry is now thriving at music festivals such as Glastonbury and Latitude. Meanwhile, the study of creative writing at degree and postgraduate levels has boomed in Britain and Ireland. In recent years, the number of women poets published has caught up with and, some years, exceeded the number of men, a fact reflected in the selection here, the first time this kind of anthology has included more women than men. In the publishing world, the situation has toughened as bookshops are stocking less poetry, but online sales and sales at readings have kept figures buoyant, and the poetry business is faring far better than journalists would have us believe.

Oxford University Press's decision to axe its ailing poetry list was one factor in Picador's development of its then small poetry list, and also the spur for the new Oxford Carcanet list. Random House's Cape Poetry list was revived in the mid-1990s. While the two main independent poetry presses, Carcanet and Bloodaxe – and Gallery in Ireland – continued to thrive, two newer presses broadened and bloomed: Seren, formerly concentrating on Welsh writers, flourished by seeking poets from a wider arc; Cambridge-based Salt began as a publisher of innovative poetry then widened the scope of its list. Nearly half the poets included here are published as part of poetry lists which didn't exist at the beginning of the 1990s.

Given a choice of around a thousand poets, it was necessary to restrict the selection process. I include only poetry in English, by those who are actively still writing poetry. Agewise, there is no restriction on poets who first published after 2000; however, I decided that a number of poets over 50 who first published in the 1990s belonged to the previous generation. It stretches any definition to describe a 55-year old who published the first of several books 15 years ago as a 'new poet'. I include a few poets born abroad who have lived here for over a decade and who have only published here. Eighty-five poets may seem a large number, but three factors warrant this: the breadth of poetry showcased; a longer gap (17 years) than is usual between such books; and the increase in the number of first collections being published each year.

Despite the amount of media attention given to poetry (often concentrating on prizes and personalities, with review space diminishing), there is a sense of scaling back by the commercial publishers of poetry, with imprints such as Faber, Cape and Picador only publishing a handful of books of original poetry each year. Faber's concentration on its backlist means there are only three poets in this anthology who made their debut with them. The commercial lists rarely have more than around 20 poets in their stables and are all but full. Much of the risk involved in introducing new poets is taken by independent publishers.

The main purpose of a generational anthology, as I see it, is *not* to act as a canonical document of an era, but to spread the word, to educate, to recommend. I'd be surprised if there is a single reader who is familiar with the work of all the poets I have selected. I want readers to discover them and buy the books whose range and vigour are represented by the limited selections from the poets here. Many of them are indeed new, or are undersung, or work away from the areas or kinds of poetry promoted by larger publishers and the media.

British and Irish poets have, over the past century, employed an increasingly diverse sweep of practices and compositional processes. Within *Identity Parade*, the reader will find poems in both conventional and innovative styles and which take their influence from both traditions at once. There are writers here whose main drive is narrative, while others are more interested in the texture and sound of language, or in metrical form. A number of poets here started out on the live poetry scene; others are affiliated with various groupings of experimental writers. In the past, generational anthologies have tended to overlook such poets, from outside of what is reluctantly and ambiguously described as 'the mainstream'; indeed some anthologists appear to have pretended that such poetries did not exist, or to have employed tokenism in this regard. Morrison and Motion's *The Penguin Book of Contemporary British Poetry* featured just 20 poets, less a generation, more a supper party. Though some commentators have suggested that an inclusive anthology is a diluted one, I can't agree – an open-minded reader will find poetry here to challenge their supposed tastes.

Edward Lucie-Smith's 1970 *British Poetry Since 1945* anthology – which served as my own introduction to contemporary poetry – was a hybrid, mainly documenting the poets of the late 1950s and the 1960s, but casting an eye back to the previous generation. He wrote then that, 'The evidence seems to be in favour of the notion that British poetry is currently in a period of exploration, and that it is not in the thrall of any dominant figure, or even of any dominant literary or political idea. It is for this reason that I have cast my net so wide, and have chosen to represent so many writers.' Forty years later, after a period with a supposed dominant figure (Seamus Heaney, according to Morrison and Motion's anthology) and a period of supposed politicised aesthetics, we are at ease again in 'a period of exploration' which appears to be the self-exploration of individualism.

So do the poets in *Identity Parade* match their times? The predominant social and cultural phenomena of the 1990s and 2000s have been diversity and information overload. We no longer watch the same handful of television channels, hear the same limited news, listen to the same clutch of bands, visit predictable tourist destinations; in our trouser pockets, most of us carry the colossal almanac that is the internet. Perhaps this is a contributory factor in the essential individualism which I see in this generation: though critics and academics will seek – and find – traits and trends in the larger bodies of work represented here, this might well be the generation of poets least driven by movements, fashions, conceptual and stylistic sharing.

1993's *The New Poetry* featured poetry which had been largely written during the turbulent years of Thatcherism, and its editors presented that generation of poets as being those staging a fight-back against a seemingly less cultured society, an exaggerated truth. Overtly political poetry has been comparatively scarce since then, and much of it is ineffective, unconvincing. Even in the growth area of socially aware nature poetry, the most powerful work has been incidental, rather than that written pointedly. Poets from Northern Ireland still have to deal with a fraught political situation, but no longer seem to feel an onus to make it a dominant subject. In Britain, perhaps the brief optimism of a new government was too soon replaced with familiar distrust and despondency to raise a batch of poetic hasslers. Nonetheless this book does contain its share of protest, satire, social comment.

This anthology takes some of its inspiration from a comparable American anthology, *Legitimate Dangers: American Poets of the New Century* (ed. Michael Dumanis and Cate Marvin, Sarabande Books, 2006). A subject of comment on that book was the number of full-time academics included – especially those involved in teaching creative writing. Around a third of the poets in *Identity Parade* are academics – though this number divides into those who are career literary academics, those who teach other subjects, and those who have entered the teaching world later via their writing. Another third do work which is literature-related – they are publishers, promoters, school teachers, librarians or freelancers doing a mix of these and other things. The remainder do a variety of jobs – advertising copywriter, business adviser, technical writer, prison worker, musician, lawyer – or are students, retired or raising families.

A common temptation for earlier anthologists was the making of great claims for the generation. The foibles and excesses of the previous generation were chewed over and inaccurate predictions made about things to come. This book represents my own generation of British and Irish poets, and although poets are always ready to bicker, to promote their own aesthetic, it does seem a more harmonious one, more outward looking and, at last, less dominated by men and more representative of the country's ethnic mix in the case of Britain.

It is tempting to look for connections between the writings of those in a generation. I am more interested in engaging with the poems than looking for theories of literary zeitgeist, but it is the pluralism of contemporary British and Irish poetry which stands out in the pages of this book. Plural in its register – monologue, memoir, satire, comedy, complaint; plural in its regional and ethnic diversity; plural in its subject-matter and – moving from traditional metrics to fractured syntax, from dialect to diatribe, mirror poem to prose poem – satisfyingly plural in its form and style.

PATIENCE AGBABI

Patience Agbabi was born in 1965 and grew up in London, Sussex and North Wales. She studied English Language and Literature at Oxford University and Creative Writing, the Arts and Education at Sussex University. After a brief spell in publishing, she has been a freelance writer and performer since 1990. She has also taught creative writing in a range of educational establishments including Cardiff and Kent Universities and has worked abroad with the British Council. In 2004 she was nominated one of the UK's 'Next Generation Poets'. Her collections are *R.A.W.* (Gecko Press, 1995), *Transformatrix* (Canongate, 2000) and *Bloodshot Monochrome* (Canongate, 2008).

A leading performance poet, Agbabi's early work helped to feminise British rap, though she has a strong formal bent influenced by an engagement with poets from previous eras (her 'Wife of Bafa', one of many persona monologues, is based on Chaucer's Wife of Bath). The subjects of race, sexuality and, more recently, motherhood have been strong presences in her work, along with an embracing of popular culture motifs, often drawn from her passionate interest in music.

The Wife of Bafa

My name is Mrs Alice Ebi Bafa
I come from Nigeria.
I am very fine, isn't it.
My next birthday I'll be... twenty-nine.
I'm business woman.
Would you like to buy some cloth?
I have all the latest styles from Lagos,
Italian shoe and handbag to match,
lace, linen and Dutch wax.
I only buy the best
and I travel first class.
　　Some say I have blood on my hands
'cause I like to paint my nails red
but others call me femme fatale.

My father had four wives
so I've had five husbands.
I cast a spell with my gap-tooth smile
and my bottom power.
Three were good and two were bad.
    The first three were old and rich
and I was young and fit.
They died of exhaustion.
The fourth one was ladies' man,
I could not count his women on one hand
but he'd rage if I looked at another man.
I was very wild when I was young.
They called me Miss Highlife,
I was not considered a good wife
but I always respected my husband.
He died when I returned from this London.
    The fifth one I married for love.
He was studying law at University of Ibadan.
He was not yet twenty-one,
wicked in bed and so handsome
but he liked pornographic magazine.
His favourite was *Playboy*.
One day I threw it on fire
to teach him a lesson.
He turned into wife batterer.
He was to regret his action.
I beat him till he begged for his ancestors.
Now we get on like house on fire.
    Some say I'm a witchcraft
'cause I did not bear them children.
They do not understand the Western medicine.
    You like my headtie.
It's the latest fashion.
They sell like hot cake on Victoria Island.
Fifty pounds.
I give you discount 'cause I like your smile.
The quality is very good.
If I take off more I will not make profit
and I travel to Lagos next week.
Make it my lucky day.
Please, I beg you.

Postmod:

a snapshot. Monochrome. A woman
in a '60s rayon suit. A knee-length pencil
skirt and jacket with three-quarter sleeves.
Hot aqua and a mod original.
That shade translates to stylish grey. It's me.
And on the back, someone's scrawled in pencil
Brighton Beach, 1963

for fun because I wasn't even thought of
in 1963. Imagine Rhyl,
'82, where the image was conceived
by someone with good taste, bad handwriting
and lack of a camera. Yet that negative,
in our heads only, was as sharp and real
as the suit so out of fashion it was in.

The London Eye

Through my gold-tinted Gucci sunglasses,
the sightseers. Big Ben's quarter chime
strikes the convoy of number 12 buses
that bleeds into the city's monochrome.

Through somebody's zoom lens, me shouting
to you, *Hello!...on...bridge...'minster!*
The aerial view postcard, the man writing
squat words like black cabs in rush hour.

The South Bank buzzes with a rising treble.
You kiss my cheek, formal as a blind date.
We enter Cupid's capsule, a thought bubble
where I think, 'Space age!' you think, 'She was late.'

Big Ben strikes six. My SKIN .Beat™ blinks, replies
18·02. We're moving anticlockwise.

Josephine Baker Finds Herself

She picked me up
like a slow-burning fuse. I was down
that girls' club used to run in Brixton,
on acid for fuel. Lipstick lesbians,
techno so hardcore it's spewing out Audis.
She samples my heartbeat and mixes it with
vodka on the rocks. I'm her light-skinned, negative,
twenty-something, short black wavy-bobbed diva.
She purrs *La Garçonne, fancy a drink?* I say
Yes. She's crossing the Star Bar like it's a catwalk. So sleek!
A string of pearls, her flapper dress
studded with low-cut diamonds
through my skin, straight to my heart.
Twenties chic! She works
me up and down. I worship
the way she looks.

The way she looks
me up and down. I worship
twenties chic. She works
through my skin, straight to my heart
studded with low-cut diamonds.
A string of pearls her flapper dress.
Yes! She's crossing the Star Bar like it's a catwalk so sleek
she purrs, la garçonne! *Fancy a drink?* I say.
Twenty-something, short, Black, wavy-bobbed diva:
vodka on the rocks, I'm her light-skinned negative.
She samples my heartbeat and mixes it with
techno so hardcore it's spewing out Audis
on acid for fuel. *Lipstick Lesbians,*
that girls' club used to run in Brixton
like a slow-burning fuse. I was down.
She picked me up.

JONATHAN ASSER

Jonathan Asser has published one full-length collection of poetry, *Outside the All Stars* (Arc Publications, 2003), and a chapbook, *The Switch* (Donut Press, 2002). His first screenplay, *Parker Knoll*, was a winner of the 2006 I-blink International Scriptwriting Competition. He is the originator of Shame/Violence Intervention (SVI), an award-winning therapeutic programme that works with violently enacting prisoners to help them reduce their levels of prison violence.

Asser started writing in his 30s, and first appeared on the London live poetry circuit in the 1990s with his sinister poems flavoured with dark humour. An interest in form, particularly the driving force of trisyllabic metre, led to a shift in his work, which tends to alternate between brief, crisp narratives, often informed by his prison work, and longer more musically directed pieces (such as 'No Mercy') where a wry narrator observes the piquant characters and minor calamities of London life.

Interlude

Terrified customers creep to The Snack Bar
scouting for liver, tomato and cheese.
They breathe on the glass and rehearse their requests,
before entering quietly, eyeing Constablesque
prints with hayricks that are covering wall contours
sculpted by a man with a dual-track passion
for swirls and for Scarlet from Oxfam, who's sleeping
with Connie – The Snack Bar's proprietor. Connie's
ex-boyfriend, no fan of interiors, stands there –
kebab knife erect as he dilates his nostrils:
this thinker with teardrop tattoos, fresh from Pentonville,
feeling the street when he's not shaving meat
or defrosting a chicken. The jukebox falls silent
and somebody, chancing it, mumbles an order.
The thinker looks through them, past bollards and plane trees,
at what we don't know and it isn't important.

What matters is Rufus – the dog in the corner,
whose dreams are intact – and the waitress called Tina,
who's smoking her ninth B&H of the last
eighty minutes, in spite of the fact that the world
has not ended and nor is it likely to, now,
here in Camden, or elsewhere, in Acton, or Shoreditch,
where HP Sauce, ketchup and mustard sit tight
and sugar dispensers continue to flow.

Something To Do

To lick each cobble in the mews, to feel
the individual curve against his tongue:
at night, when slugs are making love in compost,
foxes sifting air that's floating off
the Camden Road, before they veer and trot
underneath rows of postal vans corralled
between divergent streams of railway tracks,
whose points are wishbones bathed in moonbeams.
Peace. The pylons have it, gravel heaps and tunnels
have it, stagnant pools, mountains of tyres.

Spaced-out cars, untroubled by the shove
of congestion, glide everywhere on routes
of air. As if for practice, signals flit
from green to red and back again, observed
by flaking bark from plane trees, blackbirds thinking
through the small hours, chicken-flavoured cardboard
jamming storm drains. A student – salivating
on a biro – lit by Anglepoise,
awake on coffee laced with Pro Plus, stares
beyond Nirvana posters at the licker.

Turned-down rest-home televisions fizzle
over OAPs who've finally
dropped off. A leopard, currently a star
in nude revue on Wardour Street, is flipping
dustbins. Baby's mobile, dangling cartoon
heads above her cot, is still – a Disney

hippo looks at Daddy out the window,
crouching in his partner's nightie, licking
like there's no tomorrow, past the skip,
approaching 'Pets 4 Life' and '3X Vid'.

The Birdbath's Saying *Dive*

Saturday evening, I'm on my roof.
Brick exhales the day's quota of sunshine.
My Camel cigarette outglows a moon
that's harvest orange, edging a high-rise.

Textured bitumen dimples my butt.
Ants patrol a Russian vine's tips.
Ambulances wang in counterpoint
to traffic-light bleepers. Bach drifts up.

Dave, armed robber turned facilitator,
who does SVI work with me part-time
for Camden probation said I must learn
to understand the Little Jo inside.

A person opposite strips off, does tai chi.
Garlic wafts from someone's veg stir-fry.
Moths buffet sensor lights bursting
on to prickles of in-house cacti.

Dave stole a nanny goat when he was ten
and coaxed it on a train for Marylebone.
Policemen put the goat in a riot van.
Dave torched a batch of self-build mobile homes.

I stand and traverse coping towards air.
Skylights each side slope away in gloom.
I reach the end, flex crêpe-soled suede footwear
over the edge, experience a spasm.

Snails I can't make out three floors below
attack their thirst in two inches of birdbath.
Testicular frissons play the banjo.
I grip another Camel in my teeth.

No Mercy

He was tracked by his cleaner for days, through the bowels
of Camden, Kings Cross, Isle of Dogs, Barking Creek
Barrier and the Rotherhithe Tunnel. She sniffed
at his crushed stubs, the rim of his latte abandoned
in haste as she rounded the bend. She was good,
no denying it: raised in the Andes and taught
by her uncles the ways of the puma and coypu,
and how to outwit them on foot with no water
and only a catapult fashioned from twigs.
Pushing seventy now, overweight and arthritic,
her breathing was steady in spite of the asthma
and several packs of long menthols a day:
she'd been living off yoghurt enhanced with royal jelly
and sprouted alfalfa; for months she'd been pumping
in secret on Nautilus gear in the basement
he'd long since stopped using – a present from Bernice,
the one before Ailsa and just after Zoe.
His cleaner had pissed off them all in her manic
defence of the fixtures and fittings, her focus
on hairs in the plug curling clockwise instead
of the other way round. Like a fool, he'd ignored
all the signs: mesmerised by that skill with the iron
and spray starch, her deft divination of expiring
light bulbs, the lore of Domestos, her subtle
deployment of cubes – Mountain Pine to Wild Meadow.
But now he would pay for it, big time, despite
his disguise as a second-hand-dishwasher salesman
from Sutton in search of spare parts. There she was,
coming out of the newsagent, leafing the adult fun
personals, blanking some market stall socks
trying to pass for Argyll. Like a film in slow motion
with Clint, canyons, extras who barely speak English,
she lunged in her coat for a re-bored revolver
she'd nicked off her grandson. Then striding in front
of a cyclist, she leapt for the pavement and laughed
with such hate that a party of Austrians, craving
directions, turned back on itself like a shoal
of spooked mackerel. The bullet, meanwhile, was on course –
as if trying to prove that to halve all the distances
meant that the target could never be reached.

TIFFANY ATKINSON

Tiffany Atkinson was born in Berlin into an army family and has lived in Wales for many years. She is a lecturer in English and Creative Writing at Aberystwyth University. She won the Cardiff Academi International Poetry Competition in 2001. Her first collection, *Kink and Particle* (Seren, 2006), was a Poetry Book Society Recommendation and won the the Jerwood Aldeburgh First Collection Prize. Her second, *Catulla*, is due from Bloodaxe in 2011.

Atkinson's work is cleverly edgy and intimate, balancing the casual and the complex. The closeness and eroticism of love is explored and the quotidian imbued with layers of possible, plausible folklore. Its particular styles derive their effect from seeming familiar but winding round the reader their nagging difference.

Portrait of the Husband as Farmers' Market

The husband is a mud-on-the-boots philosophy
in old jeans, loving nothing so much as slow growth.

His thoughts are distinctively British cooperatives,
jovial stall-holders subbing each other loose change.

His chest is a trestle laid with rare meats, smelling
of the smokehouse, his belly a seed-loaf, knotted

and oddly exotic. The sex of the husband's a plump
trout, a one-off, lolling silverside-up in its shine

for a wife with the eye of a magpie. His heart,
apparently a leafy crop, is a loom of many rhizomes

reaching furlongs – who knows how far? The husband
is mineral-rich, irregular, leaving scraps of himself

all over the street for starlings to pocket. Is a crowd
of bright skins in a bushel, wheels of feral cheese,

impossible brews from the ditches. Is the season's
measure, taking the weather however it turns out.

Autobiography without pronouns

Driving back in the slipstream
of the windfarm, each arc of white-
through-blue reaping ohms from clean
air. The sky would be priceless but
for a hairline crack on its far curve:
everything in slo-mo, the sea
for miles on the passenger side
like the hiss of Super-8. Feathers by
the roadside. Breaking home for twilight
where the traveller selling quartz hearts
on the seafront prophesies a wild affair
and a light rain, though in no particular
order. The small girl rounding the corner
on a scarlet tricycle has just created
pigeons; an astonishment of beat and wing.
Mother's death was nothing unexpected
but Ricardo's came brutally. Pan through
sky to sea to road to quartz to pigeons
as the last train westward klaxons in. All
change. And love insists, like gravity.

In this one

he comes from the garden wearing
nothing but an armful of Swiss chard.
His hair curls to the collarbone, and he
has earrings in, for something with each
movement quips back light. And not

a slight man, no. A planetary type. His
skin has sun in its unconscious, not like
mine. He's whistling, bright and abstract.
I am certain he is not from hereabouts.

Of course, I have no garden. Still,
a vase of lilies streaks the air with scent
like spilt milk. And he's all for conversation.
Though my tongue's a husband in a dress-
shop, he does not mind. I could like him,
as it goes. And he could mix a margarita
blindfold. Once he asks, what were you up
to, when I found you here that morning?
I was only writing. Look. A likely story.

Philology

First, you write how heat
is like another body on your back:
you're losing *years* each day by way of minerals.
They teach you to drink Coke with salt in
for the sweating.
                    Certain things seem close to home –
there's always someone on the hunt for something new
to say about the moon, and everyone keeps chickens,
but you can't get butter, never mind a European paper,
and the language is a minefield.
                                    Sixteen nouns
to hold the shapes explosion makes of civic space:
all derived from ancient artists' names. An Institute
which manages the rhetoric of pain. Its scholars
are exempt from service but (dear god)
they're thin. To reach its top floor you must climb
from brute hurt, through the drab, split-
levelled middle-management of trauma,
to the triple-glazed panopticon where dons
plot points of suffering so fine they're whistled
through closed lips. To hear that language
is to lean so closely in a man might kiss
or cut your throat.

You find no word for *coast*,
for all that you smell salt at nightfall. And
you've lost your ID in a skirmish at the archives
so you'll have to trek inland. The letter
handed round for nineteen days says, underlined,
how [untranslatable] you miss the bloody seagulls,
strutting round *sans papiers*. And starling-storms,
above the pier in safe, safe Aberystwyth.

Rain –

It started unremarkably,
like many regimes. We sat like children
making quiet things indoors. The rivers

burst their staves and soaked the folds mid-
country; they were schlepping people out in pedalos,
and punting through cathedrals saving cats. One lad

clearing out his granddad's drain was still caught
when the waters lapped the record set in 1692.
Imagine. News-teams donned their somberer cagoules.

The house had more floors than we knew. In twenty years
we'd never spent so much time in one room. I'd no idea
you had a morbid fear of orange pips, or found French novelists

oppressive. On the seventh day, completely hoarse,
we took to drawing on the walls and staging tableaux.
In delirium all actions feel like role-play –

protein-strands against the ooze, the animals we made –
and rain, a steady broadcast on all wavelengths,
taught us everything we know about the tango. Only

when we grew too thin for metaphors was rain just rain.
We thought about the drowned boy, how he watched
the lid of water seal him in, for all his bright modernity.

Was it a Monday morning when the garden was returned,
tender with slugs, astonished at itself? Our joined hands
were the last toads in the ark. We walked, we needed news.

SIMON BARRACLOUGH

Simon Barraclough is originally from Huddersfield in West Yorkshire but has lived in London since 1996. He won the poetry section of the London Writers' Prize in 2000 and his 2008 debut *Los Alamos Mon Amour* (Salt Publishing) was shortlisted for Best First Collection in the Forward Prizes. He works as a freelance writer, specialising in technical writing, and in recent years has contributed pieces to BBC Radio 3 and 4 on a regular basis. His other writing interests include memoir, non-fiction and radio drama.

Barraclough is a witty and engaging live reader of his poetry and as a writer is fascinated by cinema, architecture and the poetic possibilities of physics and astronomy. Often formal, his poems have a touch of Northern ruggedness, but are informed and influenced by American poetry of the past half century. New York City and Italy are two places he has visited often and they turn up in his work, as passions or backdrops. The emotional journeys of relationships often feature in his poems also.

Frigidaire

There was plenty of danger at home
but we sought more in the bowels
of textile mills, reservoirs,
rubbish tips. Swings over dams
turned gallows or put us in traction.
Unleashed Alsatians coursed us from
building yards where we bathed in silos
of multi-coloured sands, sliced ankles
nimbling over Slinkies of razor wire.

'I dare you.' I watch his muddy calves
shuffle into the maw of the derelict
fridge. His shoes catch its rubber lip
and sneer it back. I grab the chrome handle
and whump it shut. It takes hours
for the rocking to stop, the chilling appeals
to peter out. Who'd have thought the tattered
seal would give such suck? Now it's dark, and there's
Battenberg and *Sing Something Simple* for tea.

The Open Road

What if colour film came first
and all these searing sunsets, curly copper mops,
pink-fringed parasols and gaudy frocks
were so much *blah* to an eye that thirsts

to watch an ashen rose unfurl,
see the charcoal sheen of a peacock's tail,
a seascape rolling in drab grayscale,
dun smudges on the cheeks of girls;

dancing flames of heatless brume,
rockets spraying asterisks of chalk,
greybells blooming on pallid stalks,
the world's flags starred and striped with gloom?

We wouldn't dress our hearts in motley threads
and fix the world in greens and reds,
projecting all the loves we said
we'd never leave but left for dead,

and might not glimpse the widening seam
between the separating reds and greens
of everything we'd thought we'd seen
on our memory's monitor or silver screen.

Desert Orchid

So much abduction, obituary and ossuary
that this long-jaw eye-roll flank-twitch
resignation gives me pause;
makes me long to lie amid the gamey straw
of a blameless life smoked out of nostrils flared
and into the paddock where souls strut,
on-the-muscle, unjockeyed, colourless.

Los Alamos Mon Amour

The second before and the eternity after
the smile that split the horizon from ear to ear,
the kiss that scorched the desert dunes to glass
and sealed the sun in its frozen amber.

Eyelids are gone, along with memories
of times when the without could be withheld
from the within; when atoms kept their sanctity
and matter meant. Should I have ducked and covered?

Instead of watching oases leap into steam,
matchwood ranches blown out like flames,
and listening to livestock scream and char
in test pens on the rim of the blast.

I might have painted myself white, or built a fallout room
full of cans and bottled water but it's clear
you'd have passed between cracks, under doors,
through keyholes and down the steps to my cellar

to set me wrapping and tagging my dead.
So I must be happy your cells have been flung through mine
and your fingers are plaiting my DNA;
my chromosomes whisper *you're here to stay*.

PAUL BATCHELOR

Paul Batchelor was born in Northumberland in 1977. He won an Eric Gregory Award in 2003 and his pamphlet *To Photograph a Snow Crystal* appeared in 2005 from Smith Doorstop. *The Sinking Road* (Bloodaxe Books, 2008) was shortlisted for the Jerwood Aldeburgh Best First Collection Prize and the Glen Dimplex Prize for Best First Collection. He teaches for the Poetry School, reviews poetry and literary fiction for the *Times* and formerly worked in the Northern Poetry Library in Morpeth. He is editing a collection of critical essays on Barry MacSweeney, to be published by Newcastle University and Bloodaxe.

Batchelor is concerned with of sound and rhythm and how they can resonate with the patterns of our lives: moods and memories and dreams. His poems explore history – what is recorded and what is left out – and how it shapes the present. He is interested in translation, and in the way cultures arrive at and depart from common motifs and images. His first collection is effective in its diversity, the styles often at odds with the work of many of his peers.

Keening

The quality of keening is not narrow.
It ranges freely: back roads, low roads,
a violin heard from a window at night,
a silken rubbing, a tune you can't place,
a fellside lapwing signalling in slate grey rain:
all these betoken keening. It travels incognito
as lyric, or as perfume from a dress;
passes customs unfazed; is taken as currency
everywhere, ache bearing witness to ache.
Keening puts words in hungry mouths,
gives tongue without language, longing without hope.
With keening no man's hand is strong,
no heart true. It mars the wild
and we who were not wild enough are marred

equally. Truly your riches are worthless;
your poverty yet shall be rendered more bitter
with keening, who has no tears. Let blood be drawn
and let the dog be driven far from the hearth
before keening shares tears: beholden to no one
it suffers all woes that none may evade it.

To a Halver

And the little screaming fact that sounds through all history...
JOHN STEINBECK

O halver, O haffa, O half-brick: your battened-down
century of faithful service in a pit village terrace
forgotten now you've broken loose; now you're at large
on CCTV, flackering out of kilter till you bounce
like far-flung hail rebounding off the riot squad –
or kissing the away support a fond goodbye –
or anyhow let fly, as fifty years ago
somcone aimed you at my father's skull
while he was being shepherded down Rutherglen Road
when it was raining bottles, when it was raining hammers & nails
after an Old Firm fixture – the decider: I exist
because you missed and broke his collarbone –
I weigh you now against the good you've done.
St George's Hill, when Cromwell's cavalry advance
we find you, or your country cousins, apt & good,
versatile in the hands of the True Levellers;
now Banksy has a laugh replacing you with flowers;
and what about your bit-part in that dockyard stand-off?
The gates swing-to, the scabs clock on –
as to the nitty-gritty of whose side you're on,
you stay, as they say, ahead of the curve.
But you were there at Peterloo & you were there
at Brixton. You were all the rage in Meadow Well.
Your ancestors were with us in the cave
before the wheel before the fire & ever since
we've never been without you: all our grand designs
can be reduced to you. You stand for stunted hope
grown wild among the backyard odds & sods
where the snubbed toaster and the jilted BMX

jockey for position with the unacknowledged honesty.
O root & seed of boxed-in lives! O token of dissent!
How often have I seen you in the thick of it
and raised my arm against you? On pitted tarmac,
by the gutted community centres of besieged estates –
borne as a gift or hurled down like a prophecy –
I've seen you taken up & even in the playground,
hidden in a snowball, you followed hard upon.
You've come a long way from the clay-pit, worked out & abandoned;
a long way from the vanished kilns of Langley & Eldon –
here: let me launch you on another posthumous career,
earthbound comet, stub of destiny, throwback. I have a
soft spot for you, so go on: make something happen,
O clod, O totem of the unaccommodated, O halver –
history's ellipsis point, sign to which we must attend –
when words fail may you always be at hand.

Secret Papers

Something has splayed
the oak trunk in a dozen knotted tongues.

Nobody heard
the sound it made: would its song,

pure air and fire,
have split the ear?

Or might a tree
slip from its bark

quietly
as a girl steps from her clothes

to stand, stripped to the skin,
secret papers burnt?

Everything conspired.
A singling-out occurred.

Triage

Assuming *noblesse oblige*.
Assuming responsibility. Assuming
disciplined dissent to desperate
measures, to boulevards of broken bones.
Laying your watch face down the way
an angler waits for silly fish to wash
your hands each time the phone
rings in the empty room to which
a rucksack opens like a mouth
that tells the concierge to get
some sleep. A landmine waiting.
A child: maimed, sent out begging.
A briefcase closing like a wound.
r u ok
Laying down the receiver as
you would a tired child & when
the room swims with the smell of soap & fine
Egyptian cotton closing your eyes. Not crying.
Hearing a train scrape home on time to ask
if soldiers joke about a smell
like rosewater. Allowing
laundered sheets to swaddle you. Allowing
the barber to sweep about your feet & slip
the conversation into neutral till
the world stands by to watch
a child play dead/ roll over/ lift
her paw. Only so much you can do.
Death comes in colours, who
can name them? Helicopters waltzing
heartbeats that provide us with
important information. After the massacre, easing
their consciences with smaller deaths.
Looking like rain. Laughing.

KATE BINGHAM

Kate Bingham was born in London in 1971 and has mostly lived and worked there ever since. In 1996 she received an Eric Gregory Award, and her first collection, *Cohabitation* (Seren), and first novel, *Mummy's Legs*, came out the following year (a second novel, *Slipstream*, followed in 2000). Her second book of poems, *Quicksand Beach*, was shortlisted for the Forward Prize in 2006.

Bingham started out as one of an increasing number of poet-novelists, but has moved away from prose fiction in the last decade, producing poems that have been described as 'profoundly English: understated, almost self-deprecating, but subtly rewarding'. *Cohabitation* explored the twenty-something world, with its foibles and ephemera, in narrative styles which ranged from the innocent to the erotic to the sinister (see the chilling 'De Beers'). The second collection is more concerned with place and with childhood, her own and that of her young children, as in the charming and original baby poem sequence 'The Mouths of Babes'. She has worked as a filmmaker and written for the screen.

The Island-designing Competition

starts with two blank sheets and a box of pencils
sharpened by Dad with a carving-knife.
We hunch at the table, squiggling headlands,
inlets, estuaries, then filling in the ground between
with swamps and volcanoes, rainforest, glaciers, a ski-resort.
It has to be imaginative and plausible,
needs water, for instance, dungeons and schools
and villages with names like Hiccupbottom, Lurch,
Thornton-le-Spam. By lunch, my brother
has moved on to climate: his palm trees lean north,
his capital springs shanties in the aftermath
of last year's hurricane, and every bus stop

harbours a scarlet dhow – for when there are floods,
his key explains. *Any excuse to draw a boat*,
I mutter, snatching the red for my stick men,
each to represent one hundred votes.
They stand in public squares demanding a recount
as the President mouths his acceptance speech
and such is the confusion no one sees
my brother's auxiliary fleet
tack past the mustard and salt and strawberry jam
and on through international waters,
gathering, now, in battle formation
half a league south of Quicksand Beach.

The Mouths of Babes

1 *Sucking*

Inside, your mouth is the shape
of a single perfectly accomplished gulp

but nothing can quench for long
the hour-before-breakfast saliva taste of well chewed gum

when bi-planes have the high blue hemisphere to themselves
and postmen crunch on broken emeralds.

2 *Tasting*

In a previous existence this tongue
was the tongue of Columbus,
five times coarser,
sticky with Italian and Portuguese,
as silver and elastic as a hooked fish
pleading for ocean.

Saliva, its element, sealed each farewell
as he set sail
imagining the first tomato

crushed and bleeding like a sunset
week after week no closer,
swallowing his mouth's horizon.

Mariners wept on deck
and salt from the beard of the great adventurer
fell like hail,
a scatter of crystals
in the savage glittering Atlantic calm.

3 *Speaking*

Harmonica and mumble
through the finger flavour of a weekday afternoon
accompanied by rain at the window
and the slosh of washing machine on bass,
your lichened buds wet babygrows
polishing the drum, so clotted with stodge
I taste like a voice on the phone
and the louder you hum the further off I seem –

you stretch like Wiener schnitzel,
wishing for the mouth of an anteater or frog.

Dalby Bush Farm

Acres of water-logged, half-frozen furrow tinged with winter wheat.
Ewes in the beet field. Mice in the wardrobes. Flies in the mice.
Leftover motorway biscuits for tea with Lapsang Souchong
by a leaky dimplex. Located, my cot in the stable beyond repair.

At dusk we shivered into boots determined to have what we came for
and walked together, pigeon-stepping through the clogged earth,
showing you hedge-rows, ditches and rusty gates,
the branches of trees we love.
                              It was the hour for deer.
Drenched heads shuddering at the edge of the pine plantation
watched our white umbrella ghost through the downpour.

De Beers

At first it's microscopic. A bubble in a bubble
in a stoppered bottle of champagne, it incubates.

It carries on a wind of violins, hooks into her finger like a thorn,
a wart seed chewing through layer after layer of skin.

Steadily it works itself to the very bone and grows
as fat and white as a blister, harder than a stone.

It ladders her tights and gets infected, snagging hair and coats
as she brushes up against them on the tube, in restaurants.

She keeps her fist in her pocket, learns to shop with gloves.
She gets verruca acid on prescription and a packet of elastoplast

which curls in the bath and peels off soggy polos of dead flesh
to give the parasite a more pronounced appearance.

Steadily she grows accustomed to its face. She cleans it
with a cotton-wool bud dipped in liquid nitrogen.

It starts to gleam. And now she looks at it all the time,
twisting her hand this way and that in the sunlight like a fiancee.

JULIA BIRD

Julia Bird grew up in Gloucestershire and now lives in south London. She studied English Language & Literature at Reading University and has an MA in Creative Writing & Education from the University of Sussex. She works as an arts administrator and literature promoter, both within organisations and as a freelancer. Her work has been published in various print and online magazines as well as in fresco form on the walls of the Arts Council's London office. *Hannah and the Monk*, her first collection, was published by Salt Publishing in 2008.

Bird's work is warm and witty, her poems often built upon clever conceits and strung with adroit metaphors. Some of her work is akin to modern fable; other pieces employ tableaux of everyday things made curious again or tales of night-time happenings. She is keen on voices and her characters are more credulous than devious. At a time when successful humorous poetry is scarce, her work is welcome.

Five Years Trying to Win the Flower Show Vegetable Animal Class

Highly Commended: a large baking potato –
     its shape already reminiscent of the humpback whale –
     set on a plate, surrounded by cabbage
     shredded from the centre of the head
     where its waves are tightest.
     Eyes for a blowhole, and also for eyes.

Highly Commended: a crocodile
     in cucumber, sliced out wedge
     for a gaping mouth, radish teeth and feet,
     and winding down its curving spine,
     a double crest of battlements, contrived
     from cocktail sticks and arrowheads of swede.

Highly Commended: a glossy purple eggplant
    as the body of a bird of paradise,
    wings from tiers of rocket, mint and carrot tops,
    comb from sprouting mustard seed and dill.
    Beak a nutshell, tongue a nut,
    side-dish of summer fruits, its song.

Third Place: the coconut gorilla.
    A corn dolly armature whose stooky thighs
    and sloping head are covered
    in the cracked-off shells of coconuts,
    the pile of the coconut fibres
    precisely matching the nap of gorilla pelt.

Highly Commended: an aquarium of fish.
    Goldfish, guppies and angelfish whittled
    from melons, peaches and artichokes.
    Highly skilled engraving suggests drift and flurry,
    fins and scales. A year's work wasted on the system
    to blow bubbles fat as berries from their mouths.

Your Grandfather Would Have Wanted You to Have This

So raise a glass of the whisky that was sunk
that this bottled boat could draw a schoonerful
of model sea, to the man who modelled it:
who teased each wave from putty and oil paint
through the keyhole of the bottleneck, who spent
all winter in the dry-dock of the dining room
ship-building a spillikin keel with hair-pin ribs,
who flocked the bottle's concave glass
with flake-of-salt-sized gulls, whose fingers
were made delicate by the tweezers and the button-hooks
it took to tat the rigging, gather-stitch the sails.

No champagne smashed at this ship's launch
but in the cross-trees of its mizzen mast
see, aloft, the balsa wood Ship's Boy

with his minute jeroboam? In that bottle,
your grandpa said, the smallest tot of sea.
On that sea, a fleet.

Breathing Pattern

That window has shifted in the night.
And dark blue daylight borders the blind

but dawn must be on hold:
it took the clock an hour to flick from four

to four oh nine, its winking figures
marking time where no time passes.

Who moved the window? Who made this bed
whose bedclothes fit like they were tailored?

The untucked covers match the dress
I modelled for a short three-hour stretch,

an evening dress whose cinched-in waist
and strapless top made even mirrors stare.

At this hour, no one stirs. I'm not sure *who*
or, woolly-headed, *where*, but know

I fell here like a feather would –
freely, no fear of the ground –

and touching down, am made secure:
a feather with a flight path in its curve.

The homespun logic of the half-asleep
has tomorrow holding to this new-found shape

if, drifting off, I make my breathing pattern fit
the zip / slow unzipping of his.

PATRICK BRANDON

Patrick Brandon was born in London in 1965. He studied painting at Norwich School of Art, and has exhibited regularly in the Royal Academy Summer Exhibition. In 2003 he was shortlisted for the Jerwood Drawing Prize. A recipient of a New Writing Ventures bursary in 2006, he won the Essex Poetry Prize in 2005 and received commendations in the Wigtown Poetry Prize 2005 and in the National Poetry Competition 2007. *A Republic of Linen* (Bloodaxe, 2009) is his first book of poems. Until recently he worked as a technician for the Tate galleries in London, and now lives in Bristol with his partner and two young children.

Brandon's observational, narrative poems are strangely confident and confidently strange. They appear to act as a mediation between tension and compassion, between the unease of real places and the nagging familiarity of invented ones. Quotidian subjects – cameras, canals, campsites – emerge scrambled and refocussed in his taut and energetic work.

Mountain Man

Hot-wired bears have foregone the berry,
ripping car doors off at night, prankster jocks
crashing through the brake on a candy high.

They pace their dens to a tight sugar clock,
and lie all day in the tall grass,
scratching at their dusty coats, idly tracking

long threads of milkweed butterflies.
Here and there he points out evidence
of ursine peaks and troughs.

He sets to showing me how to coax
a rag of flame from a nest
of shredded juniper bark... *Pay attention!*

But the forest scent, its list of bitters,
recalls me to the seam of moss pinched tight
between the paving slabs back home:

the velvet folds where Little-Boy-Green
has caught his princely britches,
fleeing to the underworld.

Dolphin

Alone with the secret stuff in the parts store, I heard a noise
like the grub of a bullet being dropped into a kidney bowl.

I held my eye to a cold strip of air, watched as you slid in
like a credit card through a lock, the bone glow

of your lab coat moving past the tables, swelling behind
the bell jars and demijohns. Any second the dozing lab might

come to with a flutter of strip lights. A room dreaming of itself.
A mix of cutting-edge and Victoriana: oak panel and tiled ceramic,

centrifuge and waxy parquet, fume cupboards and terminals,
the glass faced cabinets full of specimens whitening in liquor.

You made for the slab where the dolphin lay, black rubber
in the bad light, its smile reminiscent of... is it Gary Sinise?

Someone who is, perhaps, not taking you seriously?
I've seen that smile on so many faces. A wry line scored

with a thumbnail. You stood in front of it for a long time,
arms folded, considering the signature wave of the dorsal fin,

the body fat as a radio valve. Then five rapid punches,
the breaths between each hit tight as a prizefighter's.

My eye was weeping from the draught, my nose tightening
around the stink of formalin. I couldn't make you out.

In the morning they will find the five indents still there,
clustered to the side of the babyish forehead, the necrotised

skin and blubber holding the shape of your knuckles
like a mould; the smile evolved into that of a martyr.

Higgs Bison

Most of what has been attached to my name should not have been
JAMES HIGGS

It treks the stilled pulse of sap,
the tangled cabling under a lawn
where the root has outstayed the tree.

It sneaks across the faded denim of a lung,
picks apart the marrow, is couriered
by kidney and liver from bar to bar.

I've caught scent of it in the alkaline bite
of circuitry that hangs in the air
long after the blown moment has passed,

felt its shape within the heart's baste of threads
that tightens with each beat,
its longing in my hands, jaywalking

from collarbone to breast, the tripped-
over morse of boundaries long gone.

Grand Union

After a night of lasers, and one
outsized glitterball
scattering its hoard of coins,
what else to expect
but this muffled aftershock
and the canal lying like a pulled ribbon
beside the industrial park.
A questionable gift.
We jockey its leaden pulse
at a moonish pace,
the ground upholstered beneath
our exhausted legs.
The morning sets out its collection
of long, withdrawing shadows.
The xylophonic echo
of bicycle wheels over loose flags
plays somewhere ahead.
It's when we hit the backs of houses
that we find our first angler,
hooked up to his silent telegraph,
dreaming of lips rising to light.

A Sloping Pitch

Was it butane or propane, Gaz
or Triangia? I can never remember
that kind of detail. I do recall
the air heat-wavering like water
above the stove, the ring
of neat blue petals splaying so
compliantly beneath the kettle
and how it had been an uphill struggle
to sleep: someone tearing long strips
from the dark with their snoring,
cars returning late, and the sloping pitch,
the yaw of the ground rolling us together
as if all night rounding a corner at speed.

DAVID BRIGGS

David Briggs was born in 1972 and grew up in the New Forest. He lives in Bristol, where he is Head of English at the Grammar School. He received an Eric Gregory Award in 2002, and a commendation in the National Poetry Competition in 2007. His poems have appeared widely in magazines and in the anthology *Reactions 5*, edited by Clare Pollard (2005). His first collection is *The Method Men* (Salt, 2010).

Briggs began writing poetry in his late 20s, having first been a singer-songwriter and releasing an album *Landscape and Liability* in 1999. An interest in the forms and the musicality of lyric verse remains a strong feature of his writing, as does the inscrutable relationship between landscape and the mind. Although generally traditional in style, there are subtle influences from more experimental work, such as the poetry of John Ashbery and his near namesake John Ash. Briggs' personal narratives are imbued with ludic conceits, often played out in quirkily historical settings.

Asking the Difficult Questions

just as he might break into the deserted house,
sidle crabwise the sag-sad doorframe,
retract a steadying hand from its splintered lintel;

as he might scuff up dust and dead spiders,
the browned, thinly-strewn newsprint;
bat the bare bulb, set it swinging like Tyburn;

he might pause in the silence, count the Deathwatch
tick-tock from doomed joists and rafters;
might risk gingerly the febrile staircase,

tread the pepper-shot landing, shoulder a door,
jemmy the wardrobe, set coat-hangers jangling,
run a finger through dust on the dresser;

collapse on mouldering bedclothes, sigh
from his stomach, sleep through the sirens – far-off,
somewhere other; and hunker there gladly: his head

a deserted house, into which no one has broken.

Self-portrait in a Rear-view Mirror

The road home cuts through a floodplain
pocked with pylons, like those we climbed
when children, fleeing the suburb
in expedition to the river.

Myth warned of leeches
snicking piss-warm shallows;
of the kid who peeled wet trunks
to find one bristling on his bell-end;

of pike teeth snagging foreskins
like barbed-wire. We waded in
timidly, until a silt-ooze
between toes made us hazard

our bodies against currents.
A dense silage-musk seemed to bend
willow boughs low over cold water –
hopeful parabolas we dived

under skies too pure to conceive
drowning, too lucid to believe
the cautionary tales beloved
of adults. Distant tractor engines.

Lowing of milk-glutted cattle.
Marsh bird cackle. Sudden wing-flap
from green rushes. Barely one mile
from the industrial estate,

the motorway, the power plant
(though too far by half
we found in an emergency).
Now, the river is widening

as I drive into the city,
and the pylons retreat behind
my furrowed brow in the rear-view mirror:
the fresh-ploughed thoughts of the child.

Twenty Below Zero

After reaching the peninsula
we received a silver bullet,
edges flecked with powder, as a gift.

Steam from Turkish coffee
syrupped through our window
in the marbled night.

Wrapped in bear-pelts we huddled
on the stone floor, turning it over
in our hands, memorising duels

we had fought on our way to the sea.

Winter Music

In the cold earth, the fat turf, ravens claw
fretboards of stubble and potato root.

Washboard hands, scrubbed raw in Arctic air,
keep time to the wing-beat of wasteland ravens.

This is all there is, save granite outcrops
black with mizzle and quarrying:

what will they make of the song-thrush
when the hurdy-gurdy of January

churns out across sky? As wind cracks snow
from crags, tugs at loose roof-thatch,

the villagers sing vigil, from the rough-hewn
harbour of heresy, for those still at sea.

ANDY BROWN

Andy Brown's most recent books of poems are *Goose Music* (with John Burnside), *Fall of the Rebel Angels: Poems 1996-2006* (both Salt Publishing) and *The Storm Berm* (tall-lighthouse). He is the editor of *Binary Myths Vols. 1 & 2: correspondences with poets and poet-editors*, and *The Allotment: new lyric poets* (both from Stride Books). A new collection of poems, *Off the Back Roads*, is due in 2010. Brown is Director of Creative Writing at the University of Exeter, where he runs the undergraduate, postgraduate and public creative writing programmes. He originally studied Ecology, a discipline that informs both his poetry and his critical writings. He also tutors for the Poetry School and the Arvon Foundation and was previously an Arvon Centre Director at Totleigh Barton in Devon. He has been a recording musician with several bands and also writes and publishes short stories.

A prolific writer, Brown's innovative earlier work was clearly driven by modernist influences. More recent poetry has been less busy, more reflective and more concerned with family, ecology and mapping the landscapes of the South West.

The Last Geese

Partway there the tarmac vanishes, doubling back
in a blend of bayberry and heath; fringed dunes
where sparse grass forms a false horizon
between the pond-pocked leas. You have to proceed
from here on foot, parking by the haunting shapes
of padlocked beach huts skulking by the harbour.
Above, on phone wires, starlings string like beads,
while down below a fisherman trawls a line
clutching at the magnetised muscles of fish –
single mullet, flounder, bass – flipping them
finally into his bucket before he hacks off a head,
tossing the guts to a rabble of gulls on the wind.

Then a new sound – geese the size of the wind
taxiing over the crests and lifting their heads
above the port wall, a whistling tail wind pushing them
into the open bay, over the empty depths of fish,
the fishermen's buoys laid out in hopeful lines
marking crab and lobster creels like precious beads.
Their wings shadow the cradle of the harbour
as they follow the spring migration north, their shapes
lacing the downward shafts of light as they proceed
through the pink keyhole of the horizon.
You launch a shrill honk onto the air from the dunes.
The parting geese reply; the unseen echoing back.

A Poem of Gifts

'*Por el amor, que nos deja ver a los otros como los ve la divinidad*'

'*For love, which lets us see others as the godhead sees them*'
JORGE LUIS BORGES, 'Another Poem of Gifts'

I want to give thanks for the garden
        already in bloom this March
        as I sit here with you, curled
        like an aleph in your papoose;
for the balsam of your chatter
        echoic and fluid,
        like an elver in the wash;
for the flexion of your tongue
        throwing muscular vowels
        into the fuzz of sun & dew
        like the musical chimes of a gamelan;
for the brouhaha of the blackbird
        as it picks at a red berry
        or last winter's lingering
        hips & haws;
for the synod of starlings
        gathered in the oak;
for the peony's growth
        we can almost hear
        surging through the soil;

for my dibber pushing through the clod
  to sow the seed that promises blue
  borage at the bottom of the plot;
for the bubble of the acorn
  exploding underground;
for the dewlaps on cattle
  chewing cud in the fields beyond,
  their calves impatient
  at their udders;
for the kazoo of insects
  busy at the nectaries
  of cowslips & daffodils;
for the fresco of morning;
for the whole gamut & hex of Spring;
for your mother
  in her workshop
  unloading the kiln;
for the hubbub & jabber
of her radio;
for the hoop of love
that rolls on
with no beginning
and no end;
for the unknowable nuances
of change;
for the nub of pleasures
which elude me;
for the koan of 'Why?';
for the ingots of your eyes;
for the honey of your dribble;
for your *tabula rasa*.

As the tide sucks out at daybreak

the plash and waft of washed-up kelp
reveals black rocks that fling slant edges high.

From our rug beside a radiant gorse
we hear the grating cackles of the shag roost,

great fulmars and tussock birds squabbling
on ledges, while pipits unwind their songs.

Through spray-haze the combers arrive,
over the rotten timbers of the vessel –

her engines failed, her punctured hull sunk –
in search of the treasures that hang like grapes

bunched in blue on her sand-banked flanks:
the thrill of finding; the mystery of prizing open;

everybody focused, underneath the spell,
locked into the morning hunt for mussels.

Samhain

All leaf-fall week we let the pumpkin rest
on the courtyard's mossy steps. You carved
a *Janus* out of him – one face a cry,
the other smiling. Naked in its pot
the pinnate maple stretched its arms
to shelter him from tumbling red gum leaves.
Quinces, rosehips, autumn's roses; the slug
infested shells of rotting passion fruit –
these were all that clung on from the summer,
as I cling on to feeling this is how
I'll always come back home to you, shaping
pumpkins with the children and, when they've grown,
some other kind of love and, when they fly,
that grace turned face to face, to its own source.

JUDY BROWN

Judy Brown was born in Cheshire in 1962 and grew up in Northumberland and Cumbria. She lived in Hong Kong for four years in the 1990s and now lives between London and Derbyshire. Her pamphlet *Pillars of Salt* was published in 2006 as one of the winners of Templar Poetry's pamphlet competition. She won the Poetry Society's Hamish Canham Poetry Prize in 2005, and in 2007 was one of eight poets selected to attend the Jerwood Aldeburgh First Collection Seminar. Her first collection is due from Seren in 2011.

The strongest aspect of Brown's poetry is probably her subject-matter. She has the ability to find subjects which perhaps no one seems to have touched on before – some of them familiar yet unexplored, some brilliant in their curiosity: a woman who longs to mature into cheese, a religion based on things found on bus shelter roofs. These narratives mix conventional story-telling with less conventional diction and ambiguities. Another strand of her work examines dislocation and place and how that affects relationships, informed by her time in Hong Kong and her current situation of living between a large city and a small town.

The End of the Rainbow
(*or*, What I Learned at the House of Colour)

I was a Sultry Winter, said the lady in charge
having festooned me with swatches, tested
my skin for its base of yellow or blue.
The other girls took her side, buying the look,
that snow-queen palette: sorbet, purple and pine.
I felt like a postulant held in the chair
or someone in China being struggled
on the wheel of colour. *Can you see it?*
she said, with a touch of impatience.
With my dyed-red hair hidden like a nurse's
by a sort of white coif, I found a woman
bleach-faced, pale-mouthed, staring bemused

among monochromes, burgundy, grey.
The transition can be painful, they told me.
Border country this, my naked face shining
and visionary above the broken habit of orange,
above the sombre Dutch interior colours,
the black, the white, of hundreds of years of nuns.
The muddy-skinned girls go out blazing
with colour, drunk with it, loving their buffed
new faces, swigging pure hues straight
from the tube. But I can feel the weight
of the Holy Book under my fingers.
Go on without me, I say, catching my breath.

Peckham Poem(s)

1

Three empty buses cook to scarlet
in the stands. I split a sandwich for my son.
Its cut hypotenuse leaks mayonnaise

like something sick. I never have a headache,
almost never dream. All afternoon
I watch the bloom across men's backs,

wet roses blurring down their spines.
Or dark and blotted wings – I've always
known that scent of musk and flight.

The old man unveils his skin today.
Damp and shirtless, smooth as white Greek cheese,
he trades his week-old bread to dance

in this skirt of pigeons, his Aztec dress.
Towards evening even the palest girls
will show him the fragile gold of their shoulders.

2

At dusk I'll sit by the open window
in a slip that isn't silk, count my lovers
and (far fewer) my loves, smoke Marlboro Lights

to the drumming of the trains
on the viaduct, the power chords
of police helicopters, summer fireworks

popping and bursting like burned corn.
I want to wake, naked and cold
under the pilled poly-cotton sheet

to the riffling sound of rain. To learn
that, in the night, the four perfect tomatoes
have burst on the counter, the milk

in the old fridge has soured, bent
into butter when the weather broke.
And in the sluice of backed-up time

I find the boy has grown and gone –
left his razor still plugged in, a spill
of black dots, first dust from his new beard.

The New Neighbours

Through the party wall of yellow brick
I hear them rev and swing the roaring sander,
grind forty years of spinster's dust to dust.

Cats' piss sunk for decades in the grouting
of the black-and-white tiled hall rises
like a crowd of revenants beneath the bleach.

At last it smells almost like their house –
old pine pared back to paleness, both Dysons
choked with fur and epidermal stuff.

Under the hired tools their hot hands sting.
All night they leave the old lady's aluminium
windows slanted open. The angle follows

that of the foundations, which have sledded
out from under, on the London clay.
From one day to the next these houses move.

The girl coughs at dawn. When I'm old
I'll notice that. Will watch my bookshelves
grow this familiar pelt, werewolfing slowly

from dirt and time – as my house beautiful
heads back to beast. After I'm done,
another shiny couple will sweat

to rub my traces off the walls. And cough.
By then my neighbour may be glad to hear
a newly-minted girl unlock her throat.

Unfamiliar Festivals

They know someone's moved in,
my neighbour says, and there's talk
at the bedehouses. Plus
the Saturday kids keep an eye.
I buy bread full of local air,
flinch when the assistant says
There's better weather in London
than here. I crochet under the gaze
of people passing my window
on the churchyard path.
When I enter the transept
a volunteer asks: *It feels homely*
doesn't it? And so it should.
I live under its bristly skirts,
watch at its well-dressings,
their skies a tessellated fabric
of blue petals, feathered
and overlapped like a bird's
immaculate breast. At the carnival
I buy a strip of raffle tickets,
the prize a pair of stripy socks.
Are you a local girl, the man asks.
Yes, I am, I say, hoping to prove it
with my pound coin, which he palms,
his eyes already travelling on.

COLETTE BRYCE

Born in Derry in 1970, **Colette Bryce** spent her 20s in London before moving to Scotland in 2002 and then to North-East England in 2005. She worked in bookselling and editing before holding literary fellowships at the universities of Dundee and Newcastle. In 2009, she became poetry editor at *Poetry London*. Her three collections are published by Picador: *The Heel of Bernadette* (2000), winner of the Aldeburgh Prize; *The Full Indian Rope Trick* (2004), the title-poem of which won the National Poetry Competition; and *Self-Portrait in the Dark* (2008), shortlisted for the *Irish Times* Poetry Now Award. She lives in Newcastle.

Often praised for its lyricism, carefully articulated craft, and for its lively musicality when read aloud, Bryce's poetry scrutinises love, personal faith and the difficulties of growing up in a divided Northern Ireland. With the pamphlet *The Observations of Aleksandr Svetlov* (Donut Press, 2007), she added a new dimension to her work by exploring a different culture through a persona. Though short lyric poems are her speciality, spare descriptive pieces and longer poems offer ample variation.

The Smoke

The soul of the house was the one back room
to which his life had since retreated.

The soul of the room was the TV screen
that cast its blue and yellow light

that seemed when viewed from out in the night
like something close to flame.

My father sat alone, pipe
propped at an angle to inhale:

when smoke expelled – a dragon smile,
its scent of turf or heather fires,

the room about him stretched for miles.
It was slow dismantled, tipped and spilled

and tapped to empty, thumbed bowl full,
attended to by small soul-tools:

a blade, a spike, wires for the stem,
a tamping weight, a dipping flame.

Line,

you were drawn in the voice of my mother;
not past Breslin's, don't step over.
Saturday border, breach in the slabs,
creep to the right, Line,
sidelong, crab,

cut up the tarmac, sunder the flowers,
drop like an anchor,
land in The Moor as a stringball
ravelling under the traffic,
up, you're the guttering scaling McCafferty's,

maze through the slating,
dive from sight and down into history, Line,
take flight in the chase of the fences,
leap the streets
where lines will meet you, race you, lead

you into the criss-crossed heart of the city
of lines for the glory, lines for the pity.

Nevers

Passions never spoken,
never broken but preserved,
never layered under marriages
or burnt to dust by fast affairs
are saints to us,

the sacred ones,
bodily enshrined
to lie in state like Bernadette
at Nevers of the mind;
amazing, garlanded and fair.

Older, at the inkling
of an accent or a smile,
we travel there.

Self-Portrait in a Broken Wing-mirror

The lens has popped from its case,
minutely cracked and yet intact, tilted
where it stopped against a rock on the tarmac.
And this could be Selkirk, washed up on a beach,
in prone position surveying the sweep
of his future sanctuary, or prison.

But no, that's me, a cubist depiction: my ear,
its swirl and ridge of pearly cartilage,
peachy lobe and indent of a piercing
not jewelled for years. I punctured that
with a nerve of steel at fifteen in a bolted
room. It was Hallowe'en. I had no fear.

The ear is parted neatly from the head
by breaks in the glass, a weird mosaic
or logic puzzle for the brain to fix.
The eyebrow, stepped in sections, stops
then starts again, recognisably mine.
The nose, at an intersection of cracks,

is all but lost except for the small sculpted
cave of a shadowy nostril. The eye
is locked on itself, the never-easy gaze
of the portraitist, the hood half open,
the hub of the pupil encircled with green
and a ring of flame. I have make-up on,

a smudging of pencil, brushed black lashes.
I'd swear the face looks younger than before,
the skin sheer, the fine wires of laughter
disappeared without the animation.
The lips are slack, pink, segmented;
a slight gravitational pull towards the earth

gives the upper one a sort of Elvis curl.
The same effect has made the cheek more full.
I have never been so still. A beautiful day
and not another car for what seems like hours.
Also in the glass, bisected, out of focus,
a streamer of road and a third of sky.

Presently, I will attempt to move,
attempt to arise in a shower of diamonds,
but first I must finish this childish contest
where one must stare the other out, not look
away, like a painting in a gallery, where
only the blink of an eye might restart time.

from The Observations of Aleksandr Svetlov

In Defence of Old Men Dozing in Bookshops

There are days I drop in on Mikhail at the shop
when time will diminish like flour tap-tapped
through a sieve. I position myself at the window
and open a volume, selected at random
but normally fiction (for the window seat
is very well placed for the longest lies).
Having polished my glasses, I then proceed
to read and absorb the opening sentence.
For example: *During a small-bow contest*
one of the archers coughs. Isn't that odd?
I turn it over, open again, and feast my eyes

on the termination: *'It is premature*
to speak of Autumn', she replied,
'yet I feel myself ascending
nine times towards you in the night'.
Now what would you make of that?
Indeed. So consider that old 'has-been'
who seems to be dozing in a spot of sun;
he may be, in truth, in the act of applying
the logic derived from a lifetime of dying
to the problem of what could have possibly happened
in between.

MATTHEW CALEY

Born in Nottingham in 1959, **Matthew Caley** has lived in Newcastle upon Tyne, where he was a record-sleeve and poster designer and, since 1986, in London. During the 1990s he collaborated with artists and musicians in a series of exhibitions both here and abroad and he now works as a lecturer in Art & Design. He is also co-editor of *Pop Fiction: The Song in Cinema.* Caley's full debut, *Thirst* (Slow Dancer, 1999), was shortlisted for the Forward Prize for Best First Collection. He has been poet-in-residence at The Poetry Society's café and has been commended and placed third and second in recent National Poetry Competitions. His second collection was *The Scene of My Former Triumph* (Wrecking Ball, 2005), followed by *Apparently* (Bloodaxe Books, 2010). *Professor Glass* is forthcoming from Donut Press.

He is renowned as an engaging performer of his work. Equally influenced by the extravagance of the New York School and the linguistic and conceptual playfulness of Paul Muldoon, Caley's textured work is lush, humorous and intriguing, hopping with allusions, often using long lines and inventive sonic effects.

Acupuncture

Waking, needle-sharp and aching in the clearing,
naked beneath the pines
they began to recover the bits of themselves they had lost

making love the previous evening
when their loud moans and the pine-moans
melded and their veins ran with pine-sap and pine-zest.

Now that the low-level cloud is dispersing
and a held raindrop is tense as a xylophone
or wind-chime waiting for sound, they simultaneously sense the
          start of a quest.

They suddenly know that Theremin of the mind – a high wind
        singing
through pines. They know the pine-cone's
intricate complications. They even know that 'bon-san' might mean
        'priest'.

They know about the impurities of idle living
and the sixteen zones
of being. They recommend their therapist to go see a therapist

– a therapist of pines. There are fumaroles and geysers and the inkling
of a ground-tremor in their bones.
Pine-bark and pine-gum are sweet and sharp to their taste.

They know that the sky is the absolute blue of a painting
by Yves Klein,
that is, *Yves Klein Blue No 2*, against which their white bodies
        recently wrest-

led. They know that the taste of each other is the tang
of pine-resin and that a low föhn, supine,
is moving in around the bare knees of their pine forest.

They know all this without thinking,
pricked into life, pricked into being, emblazoned,
their backs stinging with hundreds of tiny needles shoaling east.

King Size Rizlas

Apparently, the high-caste dandy, arm enlivened by an octoroon
plots to take a taper to Arcady.
Her black-purple nipples are medallions
struck by the spell of a Petrus Borel or a Philothee O'Neddy.

His elegant verse sees nothing perverse in *Les Lesbiennes*.
He lives in 'The Painter's Studio' by Courbet.
A milk-swirl of syphilis-spirochetes are searing his mien.
His taste astringent as a lemon sorbet.

He observes the dirt on his shirt-cuffs
with as much care as he fashions the turn of a sonnet.
Miss Lemur or Miss Prosper plucks a sheaf

from the slush-pile of *Les Fleurs du Mal* to light up a spliff.
Her ankle rests on a cushion painted by Manet.
Her mind on the coa-coa palms and the roiling surf.

Big Sur

Instantaneously, the sound of a blood-orange being peeled came
       to my ear,
then the sound of its scent releasing. Henry Miller playing a nude
       at ping pong. Hieronymus Bosch.
The death rattle of sleek stones in the wave-wash.
A paperback splayed like a seabird. I've never been there.

The Argument

Apparently, contrary to popular belief,
it's land that makes advances on the ocean,
time and time again, the brink of a bluff
speckled with wet bayberry, juniper, split larch
sallies forth as the tide retreats, possessive only of stone,
and yet again, stone. As its back begins to arch,
troubled at the root, the Spit advance-
s, high with spate, with föhn,
and waits, as land waits, buoyed up by subsidence
building beneath. It's the ocean will always rescind
flounces, laces, forget-me-knots and favours, its backbone
of gilded spray at the least caprice of wind.

One night-star as referee,
and even then, alone,
averse to risk, the thinnest air seeming airy
in such company. The stand-off absolute. Only then does the ocean
      return
with its girdles of kelp, its sloughed-off shoulders of foam
to lap and lick the minerals, make moan
until the bluff is less a bluff
and more a quarry, the quarry less a quarry than a slum,
the slam of advancing land and inward ocean, their continuous rift
like Olson's *theory of continental drift*
wherein the Shenandoah once ran through County Durham,
the Belgian Congo through Angel, Islington,
the Ohio through a Carshalton Beeches car park, the sinuous Elbe
      along the M21,
the Lusatian Neisse through the palisades of Peckham,
the Niff through nowhere, the Yangtze through Hither Green,
the Susquehanna through the watercourses of Camden;
and the source of the Nile is Plato Road, Brixton,
contrary to popular belief.

For Howard Devoto

Apparently, the sound of a glacial stream or the great flows.
The trace a glacier leaves behind like a flaw.
No face since Isidore Ducasse
has calcified to such a carapace
or summoned what the curled-up fossil knows;
that is, everything time has been through. We can't suppose,
what with the world turning, that a stalagmite under the Northern
      Pole
isn't a stalactite under the Southern. So, no matter how we extol

the arctic tern, when a glacier moves, grit in its wake,
no one hears. No one hears the popping of bladderwrack
in the pebbled gulley. No one hears a glacier toil.

Not the passing fleet with their silos of whale-oil
run low. Not that scuppered hull. What time has lost
we summon as we skirt the permafrost.

SIOBHÁN CAMPBELL

Siobhán Campbell was born in Dublin in 1962. She spent a number of years in New York and San Francisco and worked as Director of Wolfhound Press before joining the Faculty at Kingston University, London as MFA Course Director, Creative Writing. Her third collection is *Cross-Talk* (Seren, 2009) which follows *Darwin among the Machines* (Rack Press) and two books from Blackstaff Press, *The Permanent Wave* (1996) and *The Cold that Burns* (2000).

Campbell brings the lyric close to the conflicts that spur passions, both personal and political. She is interested in archetypal patterns and often takes a dialectic approach, at times employing rhythmic narratives which can act as an antidote to stark subject matter. S.J. Litherland comments that the implications in the title *Cross-Talk* are 'carried on in the work, savvy to all sorts of undercurrents, not only the North-South divide but in the poet's own person, and even in her name. Her special skill is to expand an idea through a series of images, which are like stepping stones for the abstract argument.'

Almost in Sight

That was the summer of the early bees,
    of the big heat,
steam in the tamed street. We'd go up north,
It's always cooler by a few degrees,
take off, leave a smell of diesel on the tar,
glad that we would suck our stomachs in
at customs, braced for the questions,
Where are you going, where have you been?
spotting those braves, helmets branched in green,
out on manoeuvres on their knees.

71

All morning, we fight over the window,
        practice I spy,
put piggy in the middle
until the Cavan watchtower with one eye
comes into view, its high up door benign.
It ducks, begins a peek-a-boo,
tucks in tight behind the hill. We pace
the road that's blasted through the drumlin,
knowing our tower is shifting side,
will pop right up as soon as we say *zero*.

We're told that summer inches over ground.
        No bees here yet,
but midges that gather in the dusk.
Trees slow to leaf have not quite hid
the sign, 'sniper at work'. Light fades
just as we'll leave, afraid our southern car
could lead to something more
than cousins spending time as planned.
Even the bread is different, comes in rounds,
farls quartered with a steady hand.

Away on roads so good it could be Mars,
        we'll look for change,
white street signs and painted kerbs,
places where they trade in fair exchange,
gluts of kids who stand around on bikes
with haircuts we have seen in magazines.
We'll stop to get some sweets we haven't tried,
new bars to keep for after lunch at Gran's,
when we have lost the maze in willow plates
and go to visit graves with names like ours.

But look, we missed the cross; meant for the lark
        to ask the guard,
how many feet, how many inches from the posts,
if there's a line that lets you know your place,
and if they ever feel like slipping out and jumping
through at night, to say *I was in Ireland once*.
No matter, there's always next month's trip,
the day that Granny gets her pensions in,
she hands us pounds, clean and strange and crisp,
we grin at her majesty, check the watermark.

Massy Wood

I see you sitting beside a lamp made of leaves,
its base a lily, petalled flutes its globes,
in each a bulb. A greeny light
with a tinge of orange falls on the blank book
as you write in intermittent days,
sometimes recording a bird or a tree,
the way a hoarfrost remains
under a weak winter sun before the year turns.

When I show you that painting of the girl in red
through the leafless wood, your recognition
runs my spine. I can feel us slide
to a sadness and a warmth that is myself,
who today I may have met in that wood
where light through trees shows us
the aura of themselves and us walking
as if we were some of the belonged.

Miner

Once I used to dread the dark, the hardness,
how it could catch me watching my own smallness
or listening for fear (my second heartbeat),
always listening for the quiet crack of an opening
or the low rumble of stone.

We believed that we lived on the brink of the terrible,
toughened with the strength of overcoming fear,
and every month brought gories from South Africa –
of parallel collapse, of poorly slatted shafts,
of glory for our brothers underground.

Then we would go threading women in the town,
travel for hours in the hot jittering dust
to find that women only want a drunkard
or a clown and soon I began to stay behind.

They hate to call me miner as I have no miner's wife
and mothers fear to leave me with their sons,
but I go below where I can tell the light
that fades a lady blondly from my eye and where I know
a pure one when she draws me through the deep.

Sometimes I have been down so long
I yearn to sink inside her and be gone.
I know some morning I may be found out.
They will come upon me where I lie –
prostrate, naked, my fingers in her mouth.

VAHNI CAPILDEO

Vahni Capildeo was born in Trinidad in 1973. She read English at Christ Church, Oxford and completed a doctorate in Old Norse literature in 2001. Since holding a Research Fellowship at Girton College, Cambridge, she has worked at the Oxford English Dictionary and is a Contributing Editor to the *Caribbean Review of Books*. She currently holds a Teaching Fellowship in Creative Writing at the University of Leeds. Capildeo's main collections are *No Traveller Returns* (Salt Publishing, 2003), *The Undraining Sea* (Egg Box, 2009) and *Dark & Unaccustomed Words* (Egg Box, 2010). Her poetry has been anthologised in *The Oxford Book of Caribbean Verse* and *In the Telling*.

A prolific poet, Capildeo's work is disparate, straddles genres and is by turn lyrical, comic, experimental. Her training in music and as a medievalist make her especially attentive to the aural qualities of poetry. Bernard O'Donoghue has commented that her 'profoundly intelligent poems are original in a very unusual way. They are modern, but composed without fear of traditional subjects or language. Every topic springs to life, in a way that is both disturbing and beautiful.'

Lilies

The room heaves with scent before you see them.
A humming smell, thicker than polished church.
Vaginal cyprine. Gelled and sweetened ashes.
Between your fissured teeth, a crush of cloves.

A pallor which does not go through phases.
Extravagance is all, couture white.
A claw-shape of undersea dictation.
Albino buds unclose crustaceous birth.

Haunting, hunted. Exquisite. They require
Another lexicon than I possess.
A toxic bouquet of hitchcock-women
Compelled to a longstemmed waterglass death.

You tell me their pollen stains are serious.
A different tropical from what I know –
A burning continent – they look glorious.
I cannot gauge their habits by my own.

They will stand: lovely, oppressive, alien
To my traditions as your cult of Eve,
Brought to my house as a gift from someone,
To be arranged in absence of belief.

White as Jasmine

They say, in the family,
usually the women,
though not in whispers,
they say, At this time –
or, At that time –
the same day, the day before,
months or years after someone
died –
a sweet smell.
Visiting?
Not a blessing, not a warning.
It is no mystery.
The sweet smell visits the living
in their living place,
inhabits the dying room.

Why then, in the coach station –
rank oil, ranked taxis,
plastic toys, plastic money,
packed sweat, packed lunches –

Why, then, the smell of jasmine
two days before I
fly home?
Lord white as jasmine,
has died?
Life is
long in me, lives long before
long after me.
The senses
are too violent
to bear evidence, in this sun
this afternoon,
yet jasmine visits,
strong like evening.

Is it a country has died
within me? Is it
I have died to it, to the past or future
that is my own strange land?

Memory is a professional whisperer:
I smelled a sweet smell.
Who has died?

from Winter to Winter

August: North

The sun has been revised. So the cold fades
about bewilderment upon the wing.
The track from Arctic to Antarctic glides
into this estuary. They'll stay too long:
the migrant tern, on fire for ice, can't rate
this air they clap and suffer – for such heat
belongs to earliness, heat can't belong –
they cope as if they had not been caught out,
defend the stalling of their powerful young.
And flight becomes a lingering estate.

Take back that sky. There's something you forgot.
You left your looks behind, or threw them out:
those settler-invader lights that lock
a pulsar in each centred mine, no heart
and not sapphire. You were for the dark,
dark through and through, not to be found until
abandoned. Light casts milk on seas that numb,
I'd call it perfect, still – how Iceland's hills
act like your eye-bones. Here your cover's gone.
For night is you playing invisible.

I saw you running softly, swept with rain,
and dipped my neck. That is the proudest place.
When dogs first suffer human touch, the nape
retains its wildness longest, drops at last.
The owners don't know how much they have won.
Rain offers softness, seen through panes like these,
a fight of shadow sticks, a fleece embrace.
I thought I could go out. We would not meet.
At once my running feet begin to sink in place,
their shoes' thin canvas soaked, words misconceived as grass.

Nine thousand memories, one for every mile
and back again, and the same over, race
to summon to these eyes a double Nile
in pressure under leisure, snub that face,
the soft copy of a crocodile.
That's distance sounding like a present. I've
false intervals of time, to like you less –
time taken off my hands, given as if
I lived routinely by your foreignness:
nine thousand guesses that come true as love.

You love them all: the strangers, and the dead:
yours to come home to, in the night, alone.
Work said this nowhere. You know saying stayed
between the I and air: heat sheathed in cold:
a sunset fell of courtesy: no saying fades…
You…give the time to claim forbidden words,
the ones marked SAFEST WRITTEN, LOVE, and DEATH.
Speak, our times fuse, make these the usual words.
We have no sure address for happiness.
What then? Just this: now, here, glad. You. That sheerness holds.

Vacant Possession

Now see them moving in: the couple, double-glazed,
refitted, lit up through slow markets, low seasons,
efficiently...except by lamplight, by lamplight
allowed only on holidays in old houses
where old fuels burn and, daubed with claw and feather,
slaughterboards, scrubbed, brought down from bloodshine to beechgrain,
stack unsplitting beside the steel racks and cleaver,
the invoices (ultimately at the hosts' cost)
that after all say Christmas... Well spent, the year turns.
The couple take this house unto themselves. To own...
And to be owned? Is it in the fixtures list?
How in the long room shadows linger; the cold spot;
the skirting-board's release of one knitting needle
downstairs, when the damp was being done. Victorian,
two previous owners, so much almost untouched, some
rediscoverable. With vacant possession...
A silent donkey brays in his stone pen, coal hole,
child's jail, the inevitable garden shed.
The sale is completed. Cardboard, rain-torn, reused,
the couple's faces pucker. Vacant. Possessed.

What Is Your Guy Really Like?

Mr Performance is not too happy.
Another survey has been done on him.
He saw it onscreen in his wife's study
Before she quickly clicked and minimised.
He glimpsed it obliquely in the mirror
She keeps next to her. During long downloads
She plucks her eyebrows and attacks her hair.
Her mystery is that she seems to have none.
She also does not hide the pot of wax
Destined for stripping from her burning legs.
But she hid the survey. He saw her click.
He is even more hurt than by her friends.

Mr Performance is distracted.
He eats a pot of chocolate elbow cream.
Mr Performance denies he bought
Venison sausages, or organic
Hot dog rolls; Mr P. denies he thought
Of doing a course in Thai massage; Mist'
Perf. denies liking real country music;
Mr Performance is taken aback
(Not to say sexually challenged) by his
Own name. Doubts his existence. Poor record
With ice cube trays. He called his wife VENUS.
Now she has transformed him into a quiz.

Does the answer really lie in fleece blankets?
This was the tragedy of Mr Performance. Oh, man.

MELANIE CHALLENGER

Melanie Challenger's book *Galatea* (Salt Publishing, 2006) was shortlisted for the Forward Prize for Best First Collection. An Eric Gregory Award winner, she is Creative Fellow at the Centre for the Evolution of Cultural Diversity at University College London, for which she is completing a prose book, *Extinction*. She was Arts Council International Fellow for the British Antarctic Survey and spent 2007-08 summer season researching in Antarctica. *Stolen Voices* (Viking Penguin, 2006), co-authored with Bosnian writer Zlata Filipovic, was translated into many languages and adapted by Amnesty USA as their curriculum guide on human rights. She has also worked as a librettist.

Her forthcoming second collection *The Vulgar Tongue* is a poetic history, influenced by an interest in the relationship between language and ecology. Challenger's work is elaborate and unreservedly poetic, embellished with the mythic and the erotic. The eminent critic Harold Bloom commented: 'I have not seen poetry of the eminence of *Galatea* brought forth by anyone so young...no poetry in English since D.H. Lawrence's matches Challenger's controlled exuberance...'

Sleeping Beauty

*Inspired by seeing 'Sleeping Beauty with Floating
Roses', a memorial photograph taken in 1910.*

What is the part of me to become this girl? Her outline
An iceberg in the death-world persevering fragilely as passion.
What might she have done to devour
The world's prospects? Bare possibility weighed by
The logic of rotten fruit on the garden floor.

Now the ultraviolet womb's sunk under her,
Closing ranks on the grail of another,
And her body little cherishes the disco-purple of her sex
Like a handbag's soft clasp – instead the same generous

Tulips of flesh expire as if her body of chance
Always envied what she'd thought ugly, the carcass
Delighting in the diet of her inheritance:

The Sodom of her bruised heart, atrophied fruit of Eden.
O that I might love my unbeautying.

Blue Whale

In the dark of the museum's unhallowed arcs,
They've hitched high the lazuli coma of her fin,
Lashing the bearded pannier of her craw.
Mortified, bellying the air – Ocean Boudicca –
Gliding as a jumbo-jet, the ocean her night-terror.

The philosophic smile brooks all agonies,
    willing sacrifice,
And the afterthought eye, like a portrait's intimate study,
Plays shadows from the mind's den –
An apocalypse of all that's undergone,
Earnestly with flesh as the decoy.

Her gargantuan heart is the holy ark, a fleshy jeroboam
Whose brew is the *Weltliebe* where the infinite
Possibilities of human love find glittering passage;
Or a subsidiary brain in whose glistening sanctum
Man's *Sturm und Drang* silts like tealeaves in porcelain.

Subdued to so much meat, she's heavy
In the air, drowning beneath her fathoms,
The mighty eloquence of her breast-stroke, attuned
To the echoes of waves, leadens to extinction,
Blood's alchemy conjuring the glorious jeroboam
    into a tomb.

Everyman has recurring dreams in which he swims
Through her veins, intending to his profoundest depths,
Sifting for perfection as her magnitude commands.
In the dark, all eyes askance, the memories
Of her monolithic ego begin to heave.

Stac Pollaidh or *Regret*

(Anglicised as Stack Polly)

Virile in the snowlight, she drifts by soft opening,
The softer rhymes of her name a lowly gift – and my love,
His curls gone white over the moonless insult of a single night,
Trades his dim root to these tenses of darkness.
Each spouseless storked end of his body
Consummates the sting of a moment lost. Yet the more
Perfect and terminal sign of the hoar stays rich
Below the point of love's vein, and the coming on
Of soft hail falls like the jewels of nameless fingers
Bedrocked again to unnaturally bright infancy.
My love made silvery first fruits of his beauty,
Grizzled as a newborn child lying in my arms
At the uncreated heart of the mountain-top.
Pretty heart-shaped stack, scar of hours on the land,
By each footfall ingraining springtimes that weren't mine
But part of another's stroke and echo –
Now there's little time left for our delight, and the bleached
Eggs into which we bite against these pricks of snow
Unclose their gold and sterile hearths.

Pygmalion

I

In sculpture exercis'd his happy skill,
And carv'd in iv'ry such a maid; so fair
As Nature could not with his art compare,
Were she to work.

My hands are pacific tonight, the silent minds
Drumming in their directionless tips, limed
As if, an hour before, they'd daubed day to night,
Carrying off the taint of daylight,
Or as memory ghosts at the close of activity,
The burning loss of her inner thigh
Still acting on my fingers. Why can't flesh give the lie
To immunity? As a plaster saint – she'd be

The chasteness of gypsum, the planchette
Of her sternum inscribed with the working habit
Of how I – and all men as me – notion
To sleep, lovelock and ambition.

II

his hand on her hard bosom lays:
Hard it was, beginning to relent,
It seem'd, the breast beneath his fingers bent;
He felt again, his fingers made a print;
'Twas flesh, but flesh so firm, it rose against the dint.

He yearns for the stroke of genius
In every carving of the purple crocus.
He designs me to the scales of infinity,
Rams each marble cell with infinitesimal versions of me of me
        of me.
But my blood still sings in its rich maze,
Of the secret hieroglyphs that characterise
All our motions to death. Sire, no touch is
The reciprocal of your fingers. Of this fathomless
Flesh, you must give way to casket and ruin
All this quarried consummation.

KATE CLANCHY

Kate Clanchy was born in 1965 and grew up in Glasgow and Edinburgh before going to university in Oxford. She lives in Oxford with her husband and three children. She has worked as a teacher, broadcaster and journalist and is currently Creative Writing Fellow at Oxford Brookes University. She has had seven radio plays broadcast and adapted *The Monkey's Mask* by Dorothy Porter for Radio 4. Her first collection, *Slattern* (Chatto & Windus, 1995), won the Forward Prize for Best First Collection and a Somerset Maugham Award. *Samarkand* (Picador, 1999) and *Newborn* (Picador, 2004) were shortlisted for the Forward Prize. Her memoir *What Is She Doing Here?* (Picador) won The Writer's Guild Award for Best Book in 2008 and was adapted for Radio 4, and her story 'The Not-Dead and the Saved' won the 2009 BBC National Short Story Award.

Clanchy started writing poetry in her mid 20s and quickly published her debut, a formal and personal book of great charm. Although narrative poems about men, women and family life are prevalent in her work, she has also written on wider subjects such as education, travel and identity. Her impressive third collection *Newborn* relates the story of her pregnancy and the birth of her first child in short, moving lyric poems.

Patagonia

I said *perhaps Patagonia*, and pictured
a peninsula, wide enough
for a couple of ladderback chairs
to wobble on at high tide. I thought

of us in breathless cold, facing
a horizon round as a coin, looped
in a cat's cradle strung by gulls
from sea to sun. I planned to wait

till the waves had bored themselves
to sleep, till the last clinging barnacles,
growing worried in the hush, had
paddled off in tiny coracles, till

those restless birds, your actor's hands,
had dropped slack into your lap,
until you'd turned, at last, to me.
When I spoke of Patagonia, I meant

skies all empty aching blue. I meant
years. I meant all of them with you.

Poem for a Man with No Sense of Smell

This is simply to inform you:

that the thickest line in the kink of my hand
smells like the feel of an old school desk,
the deep carved names worn sleek with sweat;

that beneath the spray of my expensive scent
my armpits sound a bass note strong
as the boom of a palm on a kettle drum;

that the wet flush of my fear is sharp
as the taste of an iron pipe, midwinter,
on a child's hot tongue; and that sometimes,

in a breeze, the delicate hairs on the nape
of my neck, just where you might bend
your head, might hesitate and brush your lips,

hold a scent frail and precise as a fleet
of tiny origami ships, just setting out to sea.

The Bridge Over the Border

Here, I should surely think of home –
my country and the neat steep town
where I grew up: its banks of cloud,
the winds and changing, stagey light,
its bouts of surly, freezing rain, or failing that,

the time the train stuck here half an hour.
It was hot, for once. The engine seemed
to grunt and breathe with us,
and in the hush, the busker at the back
plucked out *Scotland the Brave*. There was

a filmic, golden light and the man opposite
was struck, he said, with love.
He saw a country in my eyes.
But he was from Los Angeles,
and I was thinking of another bridge.

It was October. I was running to meet a man
with whom things were not quite settled,
were not, in fact, to ever settle, and I stopped
halfway to gaze at birds – swallows
in their distant thousands, drawn

to Africa, or heat, or home, not knowing
which, but certain how. Shifting on the paper sky,
they were crosses on stock-market graphs,
they were sand in a hoop shaken sideways,
and I stared, as if panning for gold.

Love

I hadn't met his kind before.
His misericord face – really
like a joke on his father – blurred
as if from years of polish;
his hands like curled dry leaves;

the profligate heat he gave
out, gave out, his shallow,
careful breaths: I thought
his filaments would blow,
I thought he was an emperor,

dying on silk cushions.
I didn't know how to keep
him wrapped, I didn't know
how to give him suck, I had
no idea about him. At night

I tried to remember the feel
of his head on my neck, the skull
small as a cat's, the soft spot hot
as a smelted coin,
and the hair, the down, fine

as the innermost, vellum layer
of some rare snowcreature's
aureole of fur, if you could meet
such a beast, if you could
get so near. I started there.

Dark, Dark

He is calling down the night,
the way he calls out
next door's dog and sees
the word grow ears
and eyes, emerge on heavy
loping legs, a furry
manifest of name.

The dark will have
a lion's neck. He'll ride
its muscled back all night.

Scan

They showed me on the screen
some star lit hills, a lucky sky,
then, resting among haar-filled fields,

a settlement round the outlet
of a phosphorescent river, all low windows
flickering with early electricity.

And they pointed out with a line of light
a hub like the start of a knotting city,
like a storm in a weather front, coalescing.

POLLY CLARK

Polly Clark was born in Toronto in 1968 and brought up in Lancashire, Cumbria and the Borders of Scotland. She has worked variously as a zookeeper, a teacher of English in Hungary and in publishing at Oxford University Press. Her first collection, *Kiss*, was a Poetry Book Society Recommendation; her second, *Take Me With You*, a Poetry Book Society Choice and shortlisted for the T.S. Eliot Prize. *Farewell My Lovely*, her third book, was published in 2009 by Bloodaxe. In 1997 she won an Eric Gregory Award and she has also published short stories. Clark now lives on the West Coast of Scotland, and runs the Fielding Programme for new writers at Cove Park.

Her work has been described by Sean O'Brien as 'a kind of poetic cubism' and by W.N. Herbert as having 'mastered the necessary art of saying two things at once'. She approaches autobiographical subjects from an often surreal perspective and conversely adapts unexpected subjects – often animals – to explore familiar themes of love, identity and loss.

Women

I sail into the world of women,
in a magnificent ship that does not interest them.

I imagine this is what loving them is:
adding up the piecework of them,

the pale neck, the sudden crow's feet,
the expensive lips saying *of course of course.*

I have learned their language, I can say
what do you think? like a native,

but they detect an accent in spite of me.
Their eyes rest on me over the wine.

Their secrets are palpable as money.
We trade, and I grow rich. I feel free.

We compare songs, the cuts on our wrists.
Sometimes I think I have found my home.

When I hold them, I hear their bones crying.
Their costly hair drifts and shines.

South Uist

In the morning the track paled
to fit only two feet pressing down
to the proud wreckage at the sea's breast.

All the long night I lay in your damp bed,
felt how the sheets that wrapped you
loved me less, breaking the hours

with sips of peat-treacled water.
I dreamed of you as dawn
flooded over the dry stone walls.

I never spoke of it. I broke instead
the bull's skull from its armoury of shells,
dragged it home, to bleach away its shadows.

Nibbling

Devastated cobwebs
cling to her lashes. She's

a crazed dictator, disappearing
whole families of scorching pink.

The pin faces of forget-me-nots
giggle as she opens wide.

She rips the hearts out of dandelions
and snaps the backs of mint in two.

In dreams I take her with me,
tightly in my arms,

and I set her gently down
wherever lawns have lost their mind.

Dog Opera

...tracking between
rigidity and delight,
never resolving,

so I thought of him as music,
but he was simply waiting
for the moment

that would reveal him,
and one afternoon
she emerged –

her speckled belly
set him moaning:
he fixed on her heels,

his body a god
unfolding in black.
His tongue begged

for a taste of her
as the trees parted,
the mud applauding,

calling them back
and back again
to reveal the finale:

a spotlit clearing,
a dog bowing,
flowers everywhere.

Thank You

It was the kind of light
that rocks bend to drink,
and the man in the cowboy hat
with the swans at his feet
braced himself against the gleam.
All the sadness of the hills
was on fire. The swan-galleons
sct sail across the grey.
And I ran the length of the loch
to press into your hand this –
for the shining silver of my life.

JULIA COPUS

Julia Copus was born in London in 1969, grew up in Hampshire and now lives in Somerset. Her first collection, *The Shuttered Eye* (Bloodaxe, 1995), was shortlisted for the Forward Prize for Best First Collection; it was also a Poetry Book Society Recommendation, as was her second collection, *In Defence of Adultery* (Bloodaxe, 2003). In 2003 she won First Prize in the National Poetry Competition with the poem 'Breaking the Rule'. She has also written drama for radio. She tutors regularly for the Arvon Foundation and The Poetry School and is an Advisory Fellow for the Royal Literary Fund and an Honorary Fellow at the University of Exeter.

Many of Copus' poems have a metaphysical bent, sometimes using science as a metaphor for an aspect of human nature. Her first collection contains a number of poems about her parents' divorce and she remains fascinated by the complexity and difficulties of relationships. She is a clause-building poet, deploying intricate grammatical structure, which has helped her develop her influential 'specular poems' (see 'Raymond, at 60'), where the top half is mirrored by the lower half.

Love, Like Water

Tumbling from some far-flung cloud
into your bathroom alone, to sleeve
a toe, five toes, a metatarsal arch,
it does its best to feign indifference
to the body, but will go on creeping
up to the neck till it's reading the skin
like braille, though you're certain it sees
under the surface of things and knows
the routes your nerves take as they branch
from the mind, which lately has been curling

in on itself like the spine of a dog
as it circles a patch of ground to sleep.
Now through the dappled window,
propped open slightly for the heat,
a light rain is composing
the lake it falls into, the way a lover's hand
composes the body it touches – Love,
like water! How it gives and gives,
wearing the deepest of grooves in our sides
and filling them up again, ever so gently
wounding us, making us whole.

In Defence of Adultery

We don't fall in love: it rises through us
the way that certain music does –
whether a symphony or ballad –
and it is sepia-coloured,
like spilt tea that inches up
the tiny tube-like gaps inside
a cube of sugar lying by a cup.
Yes, love's like that: just when we least
needed or expected it
a part of us dips into it
by chance or mishap and it seeps
through our capillaries, it clings
inside the chambers of the heart.
We're victims, we say: mere vessels,
drinking the vanilla scent
of this one's skin, the lustre
of another's eyes so skilfully
darkened with bistre. And whatever
damage might result we're not
to blame for it: love is an autocrat
and won't be disobeyed.
Sometimes we manage
to convince ourselves of that.

Raymond, at 60

The 185 from Catford Bridge, the 68 from Euston –
those same buses climbing the hill long into the evening.
This is what stays with him best now, this and watching,
in the ward where Mother had finally died,
the way the rain had fallen on the window –
a soft rain sifting down like iron filings.
The whole of that evening he'd kept his eyes fixed on the rain,
out there in the O of the buses' steel-rimmed headlamps.
Now I am I, he thought, his two dark eyes ablaze – as if he'd found God
the very moment she'd left him. He took off his hat,
and he put his dry lips to her cheek and kissed her,
unsettled by her warmth, the scent of her skin
so unexpected he found himself suddenly
back on Bondway, crushed to her breast, in a gesture
that meant, he knew now, *You are loved*. There he was with her
pulling his bobble-hat over his ears in that finicky way she had.
What was he? Eleven? Twelve? Too old, in any case, for her to be
holding his hand the entire short walk from the house
that first time she'd taken him down to watch the buses.

That first time she'd taken him down to watch the buses,
holding his hand the entire short walk from the house,
what was he? Eleven? Twelve? Too old, in any case, for her to be
pulling his bobble-hat over his ears in that finicky way she had
that meant (he knew now) *You are loved*. There he was with her
back on Bondway, crushed to her breast, in a gesture
so unexpected he found himself suddenly
unsettled by her warmth, the scent of her skin,
and he put his dry lips to her cheek and kissed her.
The very moment she'd left him, he took off his hat.
Now I am I, he thought, his two dark eyes ablaze – as if he'd found God
out there in the O of the buses' steel-rimmed headlamps.
The whole of that evening he'd kept his eyes fixed on the rain,
a soft rain sifting down like iron filings,
the way the rain had fallen on the window
in the ward where Mother had finally died.
This is what stays with him best now, this and watching
those same buses climbing the hill long into the evening:
the 185 from Catford Bridge, the 68 from Euston...

Topsell's Beasts

Who can say for certain that such creatures
don't exist – sea-wolves and unicorns,
and lamias with their *exemptile eyes*
which they can lever out and lay aside
for rest after a kill? Why can't we believe,
as people like us used to believe,
that lemmings graze in clouds,
that apes are terrified of snails,
that elephants grow meek and timid when they see
a lovely girl, that mice may be spontaneously
ingendered in the earth, weasels give birth
through tunnels in their ears, or reindeer
when they walk make noises like
the sound of cracking nuts? So much
of what we know we take on trust.
Trust, then, that though you find me 'hard to handle',
on long late days full to the lintel
with love like this, I may be calm and gentle –
pliant, even, like the camelopardal
with his fifteen-foot long neck diversely coloured
and *so easie to be handled that a child
may lead him with a line of cord, homeward.*

A Soft-edged Reed of Light

That was the house where you asked me to remain
on the eve of my planned departure. Do you remember?
The house remembers it – the deal table
with the late September sun stretched on its back.
As long as you like, you said, and the chairs, the clock,
the diamond leaded lights in the pine-clad alcove
of that 1960s breakfast-room were our witnesses.
I had only meant to stay for a week
but you reached out a hand, the soft white cuff of your shirt
open at the wrist, and out in the yard,

the walls of the house considered themselves
in the murk of the lily-pond, and it was done.

Done. Whatever gods had bent to us then to whisper,
Here is your remedy – take it – here, your future,
either they lied or we misheard.
How changed we are now, how superior
after the end of it – the unborn children,
the mornings that came with a soft-edged reed of light
over and over, the empty rooms we woke to.
And yet if that same dark-haired boy
were to lean towards me now, with one shy hand
bathed in September sun, as if to say,
All things are possible – then why not this?
I'd take it still, praying it might be so.

SARAH CORBETT

Sarah Corbett was born in Chester and grew up in rural North Wales. She has published three collections with Seren: *The Red Wardrobe* (1998) was shortlisted for the Forward First Collection and T.S. Eliot Prizes; *The Witch Bag* was published in 2002 and *Other Beasts* followed in 2008. She received an Eric Gregory Award in 1997 and Arts Council Awards in 2000 and 2006. She is a graduate of the writing MA at University of East Anglia and is currently writing a verse novel as part of a PhD at Manchester University.

Corbett's poetry mainly uses autobiography as subject matter and is notable for its intimate and sometimes disturbing portrayal of childhood and family relations. Her poetry is concerned with body, dream and the erotic, where the figures of animals, especially horses, take on mystical or shamanistic roles. Corbett's third collection fulfils the strong promise of her earlier books and though not generally a formalist poet, her occasional more formal work (such as 'The Dog's Kiss') shows she is a writer of great craft as well as imagination.

Taking the Night Train

All night the train followed the Rhine.
I watched the river, and opened seam,
bend to the sway of the track,
the forest a hackle raised along its back.

Every now and then we'd leave it and enter
deep wood, a sort of muffled trap descending
like an outlaw's hand on the muzzle of a horse,
until a new turn returned us to the water's course.

Above the haar, raised and lit in staged intervals,
hung the crenellated turrets of castles,
like cut-outs you might paste to a book
and light with tissue paper in windows.

I slept in fits, caught glimpses between naps
from the snapped up screen, the rocking berth
waking me, a sea-sickness or rolling dream.
I knew the Alps were close, felt the unseen

bodies of mountains press out the dawn,
a whole village a rare night bloom
blue as first milk, hung like a lantern
in some unnamed crevice of the hills.

Shame

I have turned the tide from the shore,
watched the blue whale drown,
singing as he drifts to the sea bed.

I have listened a thousand times
to the pig, his throat's red shout
spilling an ambush of stars in the yard,

and I have seen the hanged woman,
swinging musically on her rope,
her hands, folded to a paper hat,

big jointed and thin as cuttlefish;
the scent memory of place
that lingers and will not show itself.

I know the exact angle of her face
in the dark, the butterfly wings of her shadow
flitting against the wall,

how she gave me a handful of shells
to pass the game of time with,
the ruined clicks of my heart.

Kisses

They are a kiss just in the way they stand.
He leans softly in to her; they have that look.
He holds his first decade in his hands
like his awareness of her, her small heat.

In the next frame they have turned to kiss,
the boy's black hair a scruff in her fist
as she holds him to her. There in intimation
of tongues, of give, and something fiercer.

There is innocence in this, an untaught wisdom,
a curdled-down riff in the pit of it,
a beetle brilliance that catches us once in its heat
as children taking our first kiss.

In the alley by your grandmother's house
he held you to the wall; his mouth, open-lipped
on yours, tongued the gaps. You recall
the pressing heat of his breast, a faint tinge

of urine on his breath, the kissing
of legs as he lifted your yellow dress.

The Dog's Kiss

It's an old memory, the one
I have of the girl, her father
and their dog – a white English Bull
with a blue eye

pink-rimmed, a pirate's patch, paper
hats for ears. It lay on its back
on the kitchen table, eight black
studs for nipples

and a stitched seam for its navel,
its tongue the flat end of a flecked
purple tie in the father's hand,
whose bald head bent

101

to the domed chest. For a moment
he looked to be strangling it,
then his hand moved and covered
the slug black muzzle

as you might a small, stunned creature –
with gentle hand – not mortal fight,
but, his mouth stretched over the dog's
mouth, mortal kiss.

Minutes earlier, it had hung –
a fish lifted from a river,
a plumb at the end of its line
on the yard door.

It had leapt for a fox that stuck
its snout under the crack to where
the dog slept on its short rope,
left its freedom.

Swinging then, its body softened
into the fall, its paws up-curled –
like being born, like being rubbed –
was how he found it,

turning back on his outward path
for his wallet and smokes.
He'd taken up that dumb weight
just as his own weight,

the weight of his heart, left his mouth.
The dog lay, weighted with his grief.
Wet glistened on his cheeks, his eyes
falls of cut glass

as he drew back, looked up, and spat
a long finger of saliva
on the floor. Only us two, just
at the door, saw

the dog leap and aerial twist –
like its nemesis the cat – and
righting itself in mid-air, land
square, on all fours.

CLAIRE CROWTHER

Claire Crowther grew up in Solihull and has worked as a social worker, journalist and editor. She won the George Gissing Prize and the Shakespeare Prize while at Manchester University and has an MPhil from Glamorgan and a PhD from Kingston in Creative Writing. Her first collection from Shearsman, *Stretch of Closures* (2007), was shortlisted for the Jerwood Aldeburgh Best First Collection Prize. A second collection, *The Clockwork Gift*, followed in 2009. Crowther has lived in a number of English suburban landscapes, providing a major site of enquiry for her poems, which often work on a number of levels and can appear elliptical, even cryptic, until rereading offers up possibilities and illumination. She is a classic cusp poet, her work engaged with both experimental and traditional methods of composition. The concept of family, especially its female members, is explored in many of her poems, as is the sense of unease and fracture of a narrator out of her own environment.

Investigating the Easter Issue

A featured fish leaps in the air, its frail
snow-white flesh encased in a monument
of salt then resurrected. The picture editor
described the cookery shoot: how trains shook

the assembled towers of lights behind Waterloo.
But I was interested in the serious section,
Trad Stuff, especially that box where the subs list
reader-martyrs who have died for the Word

(whatever it happened to say). A double-page spread
full-bleed picture of gorgeous Roman streets
showed the ancient marble kerbs worn
into dips. Perhaps by wagons of animals

going to circuses? We start you thinking,
the editor beamed. Flora, Lucy, Felicity.
Did they run home for orechietti first,
little pasta ears, rehearsing the final

no to sacrificed meat? Were those flashes
of exquisite clothing, the miraculous
makeovers of martyrdom, a living
sign of faith in hand-painted words?

Lost Child

Scrape the ditch that fits Hob's Moat
to Hatchford Brook. Look through oak roots,

the horse field, uphill to Elmdon.
Is she hiding behind that sky-blue Lexus?

Shout toward the airport. Planes rise
and fall as if ground were a shaking blanket.

Up there, the air-hostesses smile.
Inflate your own life-jacket first.

The small, original airport building stands
apart, a mother at a school gate.

Pearl was playing quietly alone.
My ear is like a shell the wind swept.

Summerhouse

It stalked me in its brochures, Majestic, Alpine.
At last I found the factory, grown-over
down a lane. Nobody there? A fifties'
sign in the forecourt: *Sound Your Hooter.*

There was a sediment of geranium pots
on the balcony of the showhouse.
I talked to the manager in purest Wilton,
which he'd used to carpet Rome.

But I could see the future: torn wallpaper,
swathes of web, buckled boards, damp,
and under a raddled Cedar Red porch,
the visits and revisits of a vixen.

Next Door Moon

The boat man is throwing *Claire de Lune*
in the bin. Tiny jackets of sound
hang on the curl of his next door moon.

Black nails. Her hair ripples like sand
when the sea has packed its big blue bag
and run. Driving home, we startled an owl.

It rushed across the motorway, ruffed up
and tabby. *The bridge of your nose will break
if you sniff at moonlight through the wall.*

Open Plan

They took the walls away without warning.
The roof floated, a miraculous over of shelter.
We were caught out. We cooled quickly. A sty?

My hands paws? My lover stamped in the open.
Who took the decision? Editorials argued
about iconoclasm. We'd had a tradition

of opening the inside but obscuring doors.
But doorlessness isn't just trailing ivy
over a letterbox or bricking the front

to look like the side. Our family walls were all sides.
The trick was to show passers-by a gleam of room.
One of our walls had had an exquisite *trompe l'œil*

library. No stranger could find a way in
and on one knew how we had done it, which book
the idea came from. Every unwalled home

can't be called a ruin. I missed the rally.
Thousands met in a park – that seems so ironic.
Were they protesting about their gazebos?

My bed is a perfect copy of straw, comfortable.
I hold you as close as when we were walled in,
though nearer the pavement, though clearer to them.

TIM CUMMING

Tim Cumming was born in 1963 in a children's home and brought up in the West Country. He has lived in London since 1982. The pamphlet *The Miniature Estate* was published by Smith Doorstop in 1991. Stride published his collections *Apocalypso* (1999) and *The Rumour* (2004), and Wrecking Ball Press brought out the book-length cinematic poem *Contact Print* in 2002. He writes regularly on music and the arts and has made a film for the BBC about the rock band Hawkwind. The late Ken Smith described Cumming's work as 'poems that read like a Thesaurus of brilliant one-liners held together in a tentative and unstable world'. Although Cumming's poetry is relatively direct and narrative based, it has its share of influences from non-mainstream writing and has often drawn praise from innovative-leaning critics. Cumming is a protean poet – his writing can be sharp and streetwise, driven by collage and chance, or tender and lyrical.

Snow

It is the nineteenth century, and it is snowing.
You're wearing a long overcoat and heavy black shoes
and ahead of you the future's a white sheet
over antique furniture before an auction
of all your effects, including even
your posture, temper and appetite
and what you're thinking of is food,
steaming plates of everything in a room
you've built with postcards of the view
from the best years of your life
but you're late and your past is catching up with you.
There's a report of thunder
but remember this is before electricity
and the downloadable bodycount.
The new diseases are knitting their clothes in the cellar
and everyone ahead of you's asleep or hanging curtains.

The gas light in the stairwell is a great fall of snow,
and from this you press and peel off the imprint
of families living five to a room
at thousands of different points in history,
the effects of interior light.
It is morning. You are late. Somebody has spilled the milk.
Concorde and the noise bomb are busy being invented
and the bus lane is just around the corner
behind the gasometer. Camps of all kinds
are establishing themselves on the horizon,
on television. You can see their fires, spill their beans,
walk their moonwalk. The air smells of burning fat,
but this is progress and you are late. You can't stop.
The future's behind you, and ahead of you the past.

Days

In those days there were days that seemed
to last for days, that climbed up into high places
and wouldn't come down again.
Days that resembled the back of a clock
or a man smoking cigarettes with a milky eye,
a man with a heartbeat like a traditional harvest dance.
The insect life of some of those days.
Endless summer days with killer soundtracks
and acts of kindness, tears of joy lifted straight
from the original, from the heart, and who knows
what's real any more, where do you put the full stop,
and who gets to drive the fast car out of here
into eternity? Days that had nothing to prove,
days that fell out of their best underwear
and spent their nights in the back of a taxi
playing a saxophone with no shoes and what
does that tell us? That days were numbered
for tone and brilliance and some of them
came at the same time, red letter days
that flew like fugitives over the top
of a hill, the kind of hill a child would draw.
Away days, salad days, pay days.

108

Days that glowed like the end of a cigarette,
that hung like a favourite jacket
across your shoulders, down your arms.
Days that just wouldn't fit in the door,
like the colours of the spectrum
and who felt young any more,
where would it end?
You counted the days.

Foreign News

They sink the posts in, flatten aggregate
under temporary shelter, god borne by slow degrees
from the big hill down to where we are
and peace be upon us, blackbirds in the pie,
wrecks in the river; a train pulls in, pulls away,
tobacco and perfume in the ticket hall.
The first directions fall into place, the rungs
on the ladder, the boxes of evidence, spots
in the mirror, days moving at wingtip speed,
speech slurred, mouths wreathed in blue smoke,
foreign news jumping in the needle,
local boys nightfishing with the fireflies
and river police, small boats slipping silently upstream
as snow settles on open ground, the city harmonics
a cavalcade of feathers and guitars, the mathematics
of the pocket knife. Which port of call?
The distant thud of the production line,
bunker busting bombs and clouds of hair and steam.
Bugs Bunny runs out of the mist in a gas mask,
face bloated in the official record, leaping to
the drum and bass of aerial bombardment.
The king is in his counting house and laughter
in the dock. It was him getting his bearings,
smoke pouring from the holes in his face
as the line snaps from far flung quarters,
suspicions among the gold merchants,
streets of mirrors and wild electricity,
the president and the national executive

laughing at the podium, drunken sumos
wrestling on ice, spots on the mirrors,
trucks and cyclists filling the boulevards,
blue neon and sharp faces like trump cards,
trumpets sounding from the old town.
The old herbalist draws the screens down.
Anonymous messages, and spots before your eyes,
coins in the meter, the last hours of electricity
ticking in the hallway, members of the board
standing in the street sharing the one cigarette,
illegible birdsong in the telephone wires, the drumming
in the belly as the line snaps, the coin falls,
spots in the obsidian mirror, bodies on the sheet,
great schools of fish turning in the Gulf Stream,
tongues twisting at the plane with no surface,
slabs of masonry falling from the tower, sheets of foreign news,
spots before his eyes, hands sinking through
distant sands, the old moon burning between stars,
the old moon falling into the young moon's arms.

Danebury Ring
(for John Cumming)

Old Man's Beard and wild barley
flourish on chalk banks draped
in sunlight, mushrooms among
the rare grasses, the late season
flight of a bee, timekeeper
of the old kingdom. If time
was honey...
The sickle
moon's adjunct to Jupiter
like tobacco is to whisky,
air the amber of remembrance,
the evening's early renaissance
when the sun falls across the Roman
Road and spreads itself with all
the lustre of a temple dancer.

Late Picasso

It was the morning after the house party.
Everyone had gone to work and she was rooting
through her handbag for cigarettes
and pills. I raised my head from a book
of Impressionist art I'd used for a pillow
and nudged a blister pack in her direction.
She bent down low and let me see her breasts
swing loose in her boyfriend's work shirt.
'Impressionism,' she said, 'The most
boring art movement in history.'
She was into abstract expressionism,
artists with a hairy back. She took a pill
and gave me a look. Chaka Khan was singing
in the kitchen and that's how the day started,
falling open like a loose gown or prophetic book.
I pushed the book away, sat up and watched
her walk across the room on bare feet
and drop onto the sofa under the window,
legs falling open like the women in late Picasso,
the line of their haunches jerking
like a cardiograph, a catch on the line,
scribbled shapes bulging like tubers from the mind,
mouths agog, pulling her rosy mouth
to mine, lovers knotting through
the exhibition catalogue.

Following the Bloom

One tree bare in a row of three,
the barrels emptied from that life,
leaves the colour of burnt sugars on
Boston Common, swollen polar melt
on the banks of the Charles River.
A single canoeist counts down the bridges
to open sea and court music
of the old world, Elysium projections

111

onto wilderness, mixed messages
as the fleet settles under a bowlful of stars,
the crew breaking casts, astrological
portents as big as the silver screen.
Can you see the vines creeping towards
the polar caps, voyages ahead spinning
into snowmelt and silver wind?
The past was filled with thickets
of sex scenes, limbs uncoupling, mouths
popping like bubble wrap, hour-long
explosions under the ice, the ice opaque
with the cloud and stars of constant lovers,
the weight of rivers, fathoms of sleep
wound round itself and spooling up the spine
as the swarm flies south, following the bloom,
the seasons trailing inky jets from the underworld.
Fruits the heart opens in a sweet mouth,
the world her mouth envelops with a kiss.

AILBHE DARCY

Ailbhe Darcy was born in Dublin in 1981. She currently lives in South Bend, Indiana, where she is doing a PhD in English Literature at the University of Notre Dame. She has written critically for a range of publications and co-edits an online magazine of new art and poetry called *Moloch*. She has a BA in English and French (and studied in Paris for a year), an MA in Publishing and an MSc in Development Studies, which included research work in Zambia. Her work featured in the Bloodaxe anthology *Voice Recognition: 21 poets for the 21st Century*, edited by James Byrne and Clare Pollard (2009). A pamphlet, *A Fictional Dress*, was published in the tall-lighthouse Pilot series in 2009, and her first full collection is forthcoming from Bloodaxe. Darcy is an engaging reader, whose readings, complete with charming asides and linkings, feel more like cohesive performances. Places turn up a lot in her work. Time spent in Romania, Africa and the US has been rewarded with poems. Her work is full of semantic leaps and juxtapositions, sometimes graceful, sometimes intriguingly choppy.

Crossing

The border between Hungary and Romania,
travelling and destination, outside and in,
was a sword swallowing act.
He was a small man on a tall stool
with feathered wings tattooed on his back.
He crowed a spiel about putting money in his hat,
shocking the children in the audience:
if a man can swallow the whole blade of a sword,
should we not fête him, pay all his bills?

First you must overcome the gag reflex.
You must learn to breathe in without breathing out.
Line up the muscles of your gut,
make your mouth a gin trap.

The thing slides in slowly,
take it to the hilt.
Your throat becomes the rut for the runners of a sleigh,
your tonsils lean to lick at it,
the metal of your fillings sings,
your tongue tastes the cold, a long, cold drink.
Fillings singing like blades in a drawer, the train entering a tunnel,
things that go where they belong, belong where they are,
a carp's scale in a shepherd's purse,
the sword is gone.

Children wonder at the trick.
They wonder that an adult hasn't clapped hands
over their eyes, sent them to bed.
They wonder at the man passing round a hat,
what it will take to make their lives heroic.
The border police came and went.
The train was like the Orient Express
and we shared our compartment with a Romanian
coming home from a student union meeting in Prague.

The Art of Losing

It's all, then, a slow accumulation:
a rock thickening with trilobites, a doll

acquiring layers of paint, the weight gained
with age. I travel lightly, but I stow

my treasure hoard somewhere. Wallpaper peels
to reveal pattern: my skin peels from skin:

I graze my skin and the pain is disproportionate.
Roald Dahl's talisman, mica on his desk,

was a ball of silver wrappers added
to each other over years, and I have seen

the same done with rubber bands for no
other reason than accumulation. What's less

plain is why, with all I gather to me, I dwell
so often on the things I've shed. I could

sooner list my losses, the denim
jackets, watches, dignity, perfectly

affable friends, than all the curiosities
I've collected, troved finely on shelves.

The mornings you turn into a grub

it begins with the heart.
You lie listening to thunder
of binmen hoisting garbage larvae
from outside every house. Your housemate
showers, bangs things, jangles keys, moves away at a trot.

You feel your blood thickening; slurring;
think of Henry Sugar, able to self-diagnose. Warn the ceiling,
'I think I'm having a heart attack.' Your chest
seems to swell or contract. You wonder if you have woken
as a fat, middle-aged man,
instead of beside one.

You feel all sclerotic. No, you feel soft.
You feel like a scrambled egg omelette,
having once read the recipe in a Sunday supplement:
Edward de Bono's Jolly Good Eggs.
'Most omelette fillings,' wrote Ed,
'are boring and detract from the eggs.'

For this recipe you make the omelette as usual,
but before you fold it in two,
you fill up its belly with scrambled eggs.

The result is an omelette with an omelette taste
but a soft and runny interior. The taste
is pure egg all the way through. You are pure egg,
all the way through,
the mornings you turn into a grub.

115

Swan Song

In the dark times
Will there also be singing?
Yes, there will also be singing.
About the dark times.
                         BERTOLT BRECHT

1

When I used to span and busk my sails
I was a rare pen, black as a bassoon,
Blacker than basalt, a black ampersand,
Symphony in black minor.

But now she seems to float toward me:
An Aisling, light as a bird swing.

She leans to hand me the white feather:
I'm swan-upped, whoops, into the pot.

2

You crashed me to earth, ransacked me,
Shuddered the god in my gooseflesh.
My blank look, your red letter,
A complete and elegant theft.

Now I'm white as the whale, a folded crane,
Your mute bird, a paper moon,

Salty lees, a bathful of ashes,
The ghost of a signifier.

3

I brood, yellow-peppered
In my own chawd-wine, sheepish, out
Of my element. Happed in you, my feathers
Scales, wings fins, maw brackish.

You try to speak in pica, your claws kerns:
We lay a blotched ligature.

You have bitten off more than you can mew:
I've lined your throat with feathers.

116

PETER DAVIDSON

Peter Davidson was born in Scotland in 1957 and brought up in Scotland and Spain. He has taught at the Universities of Leiden and Warwick. He is currently Professor of Renaissance Studies at the University of Aberdeen where he is also Scholar Keeper of the University's collections, which date back five hundred years. His prose book *The Idea of North* was published in 2005 and his first poetry collection, *The Palace of Oblivion*, was published by Carcanet in 2008.

In research and writing, his main interest is in the dissident cultures of Britain, especially Recusant Catholics and Jacobites and the remote areas where they flourished. His versification is indebted to Latin metric and its subject-matter and style to Spanish poetry from Góngora to Lorca. Davidson's poetry deploys a singular style – baroque and delightedly wordy – which mirrors the often historical settings of his poems and sequences. *The Palace of Oblivion* moves from an intriguing, spring-like 17th century to a more wintry, northern and elegiac present.

The Englishman's Catechism
(for Alan Powers)

And what does the mirror show you?
Pale self, tweed coat, half-light, stillicide.

Where does the mirror hang?
Contrejour, tall windows, between dark and waking.

Beyond the windows?
Grass walks, ice house, yew henge, frost pavilion.

What lights your travels?
Gas lamp, oil light, headlamps, silence.

Describe your ideal divisional officer.
Midwinter, insomniac, baroque, time-bomb.

Permitted colours of dress on duty?
Ploughland, saltmarsh, tidewrack, claret.

Your sacred plants?
Wallflower, potato, leek, sweet william.

Correlatives of innocence?
Rag rug, auricula, brick path, cold frame.

Materiality of Paradise?
Millstone grit, ashlar, cobble, brick.

Safe houses?
Lock cottage, railway cottage, terrace house, hill farm.

Showings-forth. One example only.
Dog days, saltmarsh, drifting boat, garlanded.

Consider qualities of air.
Flint, turning, softening, stasis.

Speak to qualities of water.
Canal, fenmist, fall plume, lake glass.

Minute operations of the rain.
Wet stone, wood drip, sea blur, bright lane.

Your theology?
Expiation, unfashionable things, passing things, caducity.

The cost?
Sorrow, loneliness, hurt in devotion, this dying island.

Your passport for the Gates?
No. Hush. Caution. Echoland.

And how might you envisage your own death?
Far provinces, small rain, October dusk, last love.

Of Death, Fame and Immortality

And so she died, her crystal rosary wreathed about hands white as
      though they were marble already,
Pale, rain-glimmering briars wound about columns of snow.
Her husband looked forth into violet and silver of twilight,
We are breath on cold glass, we are wind-blown smoke, we are nothing.

It was far into Cumberland, beyond the mountains, late in the autumn,
The swans had long since passed over through cloud-wrack of shadow
      and sable, harried on gales out of Ireland.

So the question arose how to mourn one who had been so much loved,
How her household might give voice to their loss and devotion;
For strictures from distant London prohibited customary rituals, the
      words of old comfort,
And all that remained was for each to make verse of their grief.

They ordered a canopy of carpenter's work to be raised where she lay
      in the stone hall,
Which ardent chapel was also their castle of sorrow.
A winter's worth of wax tapers blazed there on high for one evening,
The papers of verses being fastened below to the columns,
When the carriages came after nightfall in crackle of frost over gravel.

Some knelt and their hands dropped pearls and gold for a moment,
Others stood, heads bowed, then read the wonderful verses –
The parterres of her virtues, orchards of her charity –
A rose from the hand of Aurora, cast down, overborne amongst snows.
When the last had departed, they laid her in the bare chancel in silence.

It was a shadowed time, an unpropitious time, remote, in a place of no
      consequence,
A manor lost beyond drowned furrows and sodden impassible roads.

Her daughter, forty winters after, in the convent parlour at Antwerp,
Burnt the papers of verses to ashes – cold light in the brick streets
      outside, the cranes crying over the rooftops.
She was old and at peace and had done with the things of this world.

Roses fall, summers go over. Nothing can ever recover them.
Their strew of mourning verses is lost as last rain-spattered August,
Whose ardours and beauties would have been wonders of Europe.

Concerning Stillness and Distance
(to Robert Macfarlane)

This is the evening Scotland dreamed in exile:
October clouds, hill shadows, lucid smoke
Moving on slopes below. Sanguine and grey
The mountains and the sunlight hold the west:
The Cairngorms, with Torridon beyond.

I think you make such distances your own,
Your far dispatches bring remoteness near:
Climbing to silence, the loud scree beneath,
And stillness of the granite tops beyond;
Keeping the temporalities of snow
On silent margins of the frozen tarns.

Your quiet reports of summer progresses:
Fathoming gulfs of leaves in western shires,
The elder overhanging the green water,
Verdure redoubled, liquid depths of light.

This autumn you have travelled further still –
Parting with summer, wintering out the year,
So it takes maps and atlases to trace
Your far asperities of wastes and ranges,
And on you travel whilst I barely stir.
Head-down, below the snowline, keep the house,
Setting my mind to correspondences.

Letters grow almost voices at this season,
These words compose a fragment of our long
Conversation in the rooms of autumn –
Remoteness, woodsmoke, stillness, distances.

The sun's gone in: leaves litter the pathways,
The broken ash-frails drift on the upland wind,
Fret in our gravel alleys, pass and fall
To overlay the symmetries of gardens.

NICK DRAKE

Nick Drake lives and works in London. *The Man in the White Suit* (Bloodaxe 1999) won the Forward Prize for Best First Collection and was a Poetry Book Society Recommendation. He was chosen for the Poetry Book Society's Next Generation promotion in 2004. *From the Word Go* (Bloodaxe) appeared in 2007. He also writes for film and stage. *Romulus, My Father* won Best Film at the Australian Film Awards. He has adapted *To Reach for the Clouds*, Philippe Petit's account of his high wire walk between the twin towers in 1974, and Anna Funder's *Stasiland* for the stage. He has also published two historical crime novels. Drake has an interest in Central Europe which informs his work and he has written about Romania, his Czech grandmother and the poet Ivan Blatny who was exiled in England. He has also written several poems on gay themes and some effective political poetry. He is an elegist, a poet of the minor scales: his first book contains moving poems about the premature deaths of friends and his second has a lengthy sonnet sequence about his father's illness and subsequent death.

Eureka

Displacing exactly and only yourself
You glissade into the bath;
From one angle you look
Sunk in a paperweight of crystal and quicksilver,
Your severed head humming and chatting;
From another your submerged limbs are lensed,
Refracted, swimming, shoaling
In your own star-sign element's
Negotiated buoyancy, until you arise,
Mr Venus in your birthday suit
Of Saturday morning sunlight.

They say water has no memory,
Rebalances inevitably
To equilibrium; but what if
When you pull the plug
This volume diminishes like a dying mirror
Twisting away down the gargoyle's thirsty throat
To the banshee rattle and bang of these old pipes –
And elsewhere – from a source,
A long-lost stream, a scrambling wave – is raised
Exactly and only your displaced ghost-body, naked,
Crying *Eureka!* in the falling rain?

Babylon

These nights the summer's slowly burning down;
Under the moon's arc-light, the acetylene
Showers of traffic and the Perseids,
The shadow city stacks itself like cards.

Closer than for sixty centuries,
Mars blinks on and off in the spoiled haze,
Between the celestial holding patterns
Of planes and stars. Live on the late news

Baghdad's white phosphorus moon blazes
On fallen apartment blocks, the river's cracked
Ancient pavement, and the fused trees' leaves
That fray, not in golds and reds, but khaki.

A sparkler of static, and the screen goes black.
The TV's stand-by is a small red eye.

Sea Change

Under the balanced ball of the white sun
He's flat on his back, abandoned by the tide,
Flippers shrugged to his corpulent belly –

A comedian having the last laugh, mouth ajar
Yellow canines like the razor-clam castellation
Of a sandcastle's eroded keep.
                                    The sea's
Withdrawn now, stood down, bored after the storm's
Jaw-jaw of repetitious khaki waves
Conceding drifting suds, and this grey creature,
Not the emperor from a Chinese opera
Surrounded by his faithful concubines;
More a dead soldier in his combat jacket
On a bier of detritus, webbed in wreathes
Of sea-grass, frayed rope, plastic junk and sand,
Rendered from sea change to the Promised Land;

A sandpiper makes enquiries of the breeze
Like a war reporter, urgent, for the sea
Reminds him of the meaning of his story.

The Hunt By Night (1990)

The coast of Bohemia was every lake,
Inland seas on summer maps of wheat;
And the citizens, freed from history
By the winter's Velvet Revolution,
Abandoned works and cities to the heat
As if these were the first days of the world.

Crossing the open border from the West
New Mercedes ran the country like a film
On ironic chrome and polished bodywork;
Out on the lakes, guest-worker families
From Vietnam picnicked in pleasure boats,
An idyll from the old ideology.

At night we sang on benches in the dust;
We all live in a Yellow Submarine,
Each drinker's roaring face half-shadowed
By the single naked bulb of a sausage van;
Passing cars caught out the revellers
Mid-anthem, as their headlights searched the trees.

A Slovak home from Austria declared
His boot was stowed with language books to sell;
A smuggler of English, he would talk
His way into the future, speak the truth,
Learn superior words for sex; he slammed his beer
And proffered me a gherkin from his jar.

And then the hunt by night, sounding our horns
Down blind paths through the woods to a lost park
Where sleepers lay, dropped bundles in the dew;
We rode the roundabouts, danced naked, plunged
Our bodies, un-political and free,
Into the starry carp lake, under a full moon.

The Ghost Train

(i.m. Ivan Blatný, b. Brno, Czechoslovakia, 1919, d. Colchester, 1990)

Along the esplanade the season's last
Empty deckchairs fret with winter spooks
Braving the North Sea's bitter apparitions.

The donkeys leave their circle in the sand;
The fortune-teller closes up her shrine;
The floral clock withers to its sticks.

Patience and pebbles, tealeaves and cigarettes;
Between the windows and mirrors, time steams.
Rain taps its homeless fingers at the pane

Where Mr Blatný drafts his poetry
In code-words, every day of the lost years
Marked page by page since he was cast away

On this asylum island; where he deduced
The enigma of the sands, drank tea from urns,
And rode the ghost train round and round and round...

SASHA DUGDALE

Sasha Dugdale studied German and Russian at Queen's College, Oxford. She worked in Russia for five years, managing the British Council's cultural programme and setting up writing ventures between the UK and Russia. On her return, she became a freelance theatre and poetry translator. She has translated over thirty plays for theatre and radio and has worked with the Royal Court and RSC as an advisor on Russian theatre. Her translations of the poet Elena Shvarts' *Birdsong on the Seabed* were published by Bloodaxe (2008). She received an Eric Gregory Award in 2003 and her two Carcanet/Oxford Poets collections are *Notebook* (2003) and *The Estate* (2007).

Her work has been praised for its originality – although seemingly conventional, there are unexpected syntactical shifts and twists. Fiona Sampson suggested that, 'resolutely displaying its own unfashionable delicacy, her verse offers us a portrait of a sensibility' while Sean O'Brien added, 'Dugdale is doing one of the hardest things for a poet, staking out an individual terrain…she seems to prefer an unadorned language which requires her to be truthful to rich and contradictory areas of feeling.'

Ten Moons

And then came the ten moons
Full in the sun's glare, and the seraphim,
And it was light all night in the orchards
And on the plains and even in the towns
And mankind rejoiced, because it was now the case
That the wrecking and equivocating could carry on
The pale night long. Mankind rejoiced
And went forth to those places twelve hours of light
Had not made it worth the while to despoil
And gambolled collectively on the cliff tops
And regarded the night-broiling of the sea
Hitherto forbidden, but now opened in festival.

Half the world's time unpeeled and exposed
So fruit might ripen faster and tree flourish higher
And forced photosynthesis green all the land.
Then night ramblers, night-sun-worshippers,
Night-motorists fanned out and made the most
Of spectral light, which bleached out stars and even
The cosy old moon herself, who had
Once held a sickle broadside to the sun, and now
Was a hollow daytime shadow.
Only a few old-believers slept
Hand in hand, shoulder to breast,
As if their lives depended on it, knowing yet
That the morning would bring nothing
Because the day knew no beginning
And had no end.

Carnation, Bible

Flower of your mother's eye
When you first took flowers from him:
Little bespectacled man who bowed
And offered violets to your simpering
And his hand to your hand. Temptation
And the flower was a dry carnation
Folded in a Bible and it snapped
From its pale stalk as you tripped
Through the factory one last time, oh Eve,
He said, oh submissive one, walk with me
In my worker's paradise, in your heeled shoes
And smartest coat, let me lead you
To the door of my heart, peer round it, Eve
All flour to the elbows, aproned, unsleeved,
Beckon me in for pie and love
And slap and tickle. And the children we have
We will instruct in Bible ways and temple,
And temperance and temper, temper.
And the flower dries flat between leaves of the Bible
And the serpent weeps, but goes unheeded
In the terrible mornings, the stuck-pig-screaming
Of the littlest ones, her Cain and Abel.

Maldon

And there on the coast like a Chinese lantern hung the sun.
Whatever you do, you should not let them pour off the half-island
To mix with the birds and the silts, said the wise woman.
For there they will become us – body of our body
Blood of our blood. And theirs and our flesh will hang
On bushes, like the undershirt of Midas. Dead throats
Will shirk in the sedge like spiderwebs, whispering
Of how the victors took pliers to teeth and chopped charms out.
No one left to remember the women, but they were deer
Fleet and hunted, springing sideways, stunned by a fist.
And when the sun rises, it will seem to our ancestors, that a new
      race
Has come up out of the sea, dripping with gold, crueller than the
      last.

Moor

And for days it seemed she was climbing
Knees bloodied – as quick as she knew how
So that one said to another: hey Phil
Did you see how fast that girl was walking?
But as she herself could see nothing, she could not tell
It was just an endless effort of heather and fern
As rancid as closed windows and pencil shavings
And the red water tippling from flush to ocean
So slowly fast her walking was but nothing
To its coronation dance. She had heard of men
Who married this place with its hares
And lay their heads on stones and begot
With water making utterance of its sifting
And shifting and spouting –
And after that chasing quivering throatful
All the women in the world were no more than
Spoons of cough medicine
How well she knew her limits
Although she had jumped the golden trickling

127

Just like a boy, was as stupid as any man.
When he comes, she said, and takes the water
Over me, then what shall I be?
Faster and faster she goes, plaiting the fibres of grasses
Hoping the sky will take pity on her
Make a rapid stream of me that he might love me deeper
Put finger and thumb in me, and nape of neck
And break the lip of me with startled face
And we will be quite apart, and yet
Down in that city, shivering and shining with rain
He will long for the red halo, climbing his forehead
Clinging in drops to his shoulder, lifted in his hands
For certain downfall.

from The Red House

Imagine this: there is a room in the red house,
Infernal clutter, brocades and periodicals, and a mirror full of
          gloaming
And when the place is empty, she takes a basin of apples
Into this room and sits on the bed. There she is, in the mirror.
The room is not fresh. Everything here was bought in another time
By the long-spent, oft-bereaved who own fruit knives
And sugar tongs and no memory of the provenance of anything –
Except the hard little apples, which fall so close to the tree.
So she escapes from childhood and taking refuge
In the red house inhales the historical sweat
The ancient hair-grease of its inhabitants
Who have sloughed off desperate times
And left their wearied skins
Folded breast-up like night shirts on the pillow.

Stolen

It always seemed to me that the half
Dropped shawl, the skirt hitched high
And the careless open shirt
Are beauty itself. It is the clothing
Veiling flesh and not the flesh alone,
I felt: peeling down a stocking from the top,
Or kicking off a boot so it collapses, spreading –
Or merely the voltage of clinging nylon around
The breasts. Stolen glimpses are cherished longer.

And it is the act of transformation, I understood –
Not the clothed, nor the naked skin which thrills.
It holds the open promise, but issues from the past
Of unvoiced, unchannelled desire. Sudden paradox,
Before the eye is flooded with the full.

CHRIS EMERY

Chris Emery was born in Manchester in 1963 and studied painting and printmaking in Leeds before pursuing a career in publishing. He now works for Salt in Cambridge, England. A first full-length collection, *Dr Mephisto*, was published by Arc Publications in 2002, and his second collection is *Radio Nostalgia* (Arc Publications, 2006). He is also the author of a writer's guide *101 Ways to Make Poems Sell* (Salt Publishing, 2006) and editor of *Poets in View: A Visual Anthology of 50 Classic Poems*. He lives in Great Wilbraham near Cambridge with his wife and three children.

Like a number of poets, Emery moved over in his twenties from visual arts to the literary world, and subsequently publishing, drawn by the linguistic experiments of innovative writers. His early work is busy, buzzing and dystopian, though it was as likely to appear in mainstream magazines as modernist ones. Though equally socially charged, there was less grit and more lyric in *Radio Nostalgia* and occasional poems which were more linear and traditional. His welcome efforts as a publisher have broadened the British poetry scene and encouraged the current climate of pluralism.

The Lermontov

The cruise ship was
A weak heart grinding.
Weighing in cold presence
The grief.

The Lermontov fathoming
Industrial pine beside the tiered
Ice cliffs. In its wake
That month of bells

Our crew embraced Lenin.
He boiled on lapels,
His savage index and globe
Ardent, dilapidated thesis,

Yet no red life was made.
Ideas foiled the smashing
Waves and boiled under
The manoeuvre's wasting feature.

New negative horizons
Fused the common purpose.
The natal sea was antic. The lanes showed
Severe ash drop permanence

Making life its excavation.
Ancestors in leather
Jewelled fields and outcrops
Were just tattoos of earth.

Years sunk in black throats.
The ruined heads of bears starcd
From the intaglio of it.
3,000 miles below

The frozen heart
Still spins with abstraction.
We adhere to its iron crystal,
Faster, darker polyps,

Love's scouring creatures,
Electric weight unbedding
The banal arc
Of the salt path.

Carl's Job

'We need you to cope with all the *little* jobs,' smiled Carl.
'We want to make sure you target single losers, too.'
'*Sure*,' I laughed. '*I was very sad to hear about Verna.*'
'How the hell do you know about my wife?' asked Carl.

'*I was the one who ran over her that time,*' I replied.
'You mean that time at Hennessy's; the time she died?' said Carl.
'*Right*,' I said. '*The time she died; running off of the verge.
She kept her left leg twisting. It was a little strange.*' I smiled.

'What the hell do you want with me?' asked Carl.
'*I've come to apply.*' I said. '*I want to work with you now.*'
'You want to work with me? I'm speechless. What do
you want to do, kill me in a wreck, maybe?' said Carl.

'*I've no further plans on killing,*' I said. '*Those days are done.*'
'Let me tell you, Bud,' said Carl. 'Those days are sat here now.'
'*Your daughters are safe from me,*' I said. '*Your son, too.*'
'How do you know about my kids?' asked Carl. 'What is this?'

'*There's no risk here.*' I said. '*No risk at all. No graves or anything.*'
'Who mentioned graves?' said Carl. 'I don't know about no graves.'
'*This was part of my general assistance.*' I added, scraping a boot.
'Assistance?' said Carl. 'Get the hell out of here, you freak.'

'*I can't do that,*' I said. '*To my mind, things need traversing here.*'
'What kind of things are we talking about?' asked Carl.
'*Once a month,*' I said. '*I come and clean the place down. That's it.*'
'Just the lounge and shit? Nothing with the boys on the door?' asked Carl.

'*Just that.*' I said. '*Once a month. Though I want to bake, too.*' I said.
'What kind of baking are we speaking of here?' asked Carl.
'*I'll turn up with some gram flour and ghee, a little chicken,
some kalonji seeds and I'll cook up fresh pakora.*' I said. '*Every day.*'

'Forget it,' said Carl. 'We advertised this as a one-time loser's job.'
'*Yes,*' I agreed. '*I am right for this. No pressure here. No acid nights.*'
'Please,' said Carl. 'I can't take this from you. I lost my wife already.'
'*The pain'll cease,*' I said. '*Tomorrow I'll begin. Let's open up at five.*'

The Destroyer's Convention

All day the destroyers have arrived
handing in their burnt umbrellas to the coat check boy.
His acne shimmers above the escritoire.

He constantly derides the hotel's silver service
and the baked Alaska, the indolent chicken supreme.
Yet these ones pouring past him with abandon

squander menus like the Raj.
For hours inside the bar, their ideal urgency swarms
below a surfeit of monocles and moustaches.

They are ravening with the history of leather,
entire family kills, evenings of Domestos.
And then their bulbous taxis draw away

into hours of grey gas.
Alighting at the Gaumont, the vetches
of the establishment watch from the gold vestibule

as the audience is reeled in over velvet and gold
to stare at the screen's reservoirs of fuming water,
terraces and offices, top brass

where the candour of twill and brogues eats up
a life of hats, wholly whirring up.
Later they drink pink gins in fixed abysmal light

their whiskers rouged, they are simple dented dolls
discussing lime kilns on their circuit of
oblivion.

Is it all so pointless, loose in pit smoke?
The gabardine life catering for
bomb blasts and mice.

BERNARDINE EVARISTO

Bernardine Evaristo was born in London to an English mother and Nigerian father. She was raised in Woolwich, South London, and trained as an actress and worked in theatre. She is the author of two novels-in-verse: *Lara* (1997, with a new version from Bloodaxe, 2009) traces the roots of a mixed-race English-Nigerian-Brazilian-Irish family over 150 years, three continents and seven generations; *The Emperor's Babe* (2001) is the story of Zuleika, a girl of Sudanese parents, in Roman London. *Soul Tourists*, a novel-with-verse, appeared in 2005 and her latest novel is *Blonde Roots* (2008). She has written for theatre and radio and has undertaken international tours and fellowships, ranging from one-night readings to teaching residencies. She has been a Visiting Professor at Barnard College / Columbia University in New York, Writer-in-Residence at the University of the Western Cape, Cape Town and Writing Fellow at the University of East Anglia. Among the most successful writers in the verse novel genre, Evaristo has skilfully blended verse, prose and monologue in order to explore both personal and political aspects of history.

from Lara

FROM *Chapter 2*

Clerkenwell, 'Little Italy', London, 1911

PEGGY invested in the future, the past – a pit to fall down,
but sometimes memory was stronger than the mind

and there she was, sweet Margaret 'Peggy' Robbins,
whose long brown ringlets bounced down to her waist,

whose white cotton petticoats were always starched,
whose button-up boots were always hand-me-downs,

looking up as the strange Zeppelin bird glided overhead,
or the wonderful Corpus Christi procession paraded

before her in Little Italy where they lived, the dazzling
monstrance held up by the priest, golden rays shooting

out from The Host, older Italianate girls from church
wearing white veils and walking ceremoniously behind

a statue of Our Lady on a stretcher, scattering petals.
Or long-dead Gran appeared at No 31, Old Emma Robbins –

an apparition in front of the front parlour's coal fire,
come to pull Peggy back to a childhood where Gran

was a shapeless sack of black in front of the hearth:
black bonnet, rustling skirts, gnarled, brown-spotted

hands knitting blankets. Not talking to anyone – 'living',
muttering in a language only she could understand.

FROM *Chapter 12*

LARA'S SKIN oozed honey in late summer's oven,
lounging amid triffid grass where dandelions fainted.

Diseased apples were decimated by maggots, wasps
sucked the sugar of bleeding cherries. She languorously

gorged purple flesh, her lips stained Midnight Mauve.
Lara's sepia cheeks rouged with the heat of summer,

sunk into a ripped deck chair, she bathed, tired
of the school holidays, six weeks down, two to go.

What was the sea like? she wondered. 'All blue and grey,'
Peggy told her, 'but the beach makes your toes messy.'

Face full on to the sun, its strokes painted her a rusty brown
until sun-drunk, she stumbled inside. 'Look, I've a sun tan.'

'Don't be silly, dear,' Ellen mumbled, rolling thick pastry.
Three at a time she vaulted the stairs, passing Fabian.

'Jagger-lips!' he teased, sliding down the banister
out of her reach. 'Watusi-head!' she retaliated loudly,

reaching her attic bedroom and slamming the door.
She studied her lips in the mirror. They weren't too big,

not like her father's or that Nat King Cole man
whose boring *Mona Lisa* drifted up the stairs at night.

Still, she'd suck them in from now on, just in case.

from The Emperor's Babe

The Language of Love (II)

After you have emptied yourself
of all the wars you have fought;
after you have shuddered and roared
and collapsed on top of me, sobbing,
your snores do not reverberate on my spine,
nor do you offer me your back, cold.

Always you ask who I am.
'What do you dream, carissima?'
your head heavy upon my breast.
'To be with you,' I quietly reply.
'To leave a whisper of myself in the world,
my ghost, a magna opera of words.'

I feel the sweep of your lash on my skin,
for my boy slips inside himself again,
to return to his core, his composure,
and I am left rowing with his legions inside,
a galley on a barren horizon,
when the battle is finally over.

Vivat Zuleika

It is you I have found to wear, Zuleika,
lying in a panel of summer,
your golden couch moved into the atrium
to feed your skin for the last time.

I enter quietly from Watling Court,
the pounding bass and horns of the City's
square mile, suspended. Between
two columns, your couch faces a pool

fed by the aching stone mouth of Medusa.
A cloud chills you in its shadow
of passing – *Zuleika moritura est.*
Now is the time. I glide to where you lie,

look upon your pink robes, ruched,
décolleté, a mild stir with each tired breath,
pronounced mould of your face, obsidian
with light and sweat, so tranquila

in your moment of leaving. I slip
into your skin, our chest stills, drains
to charcoal. You have expired, Zuleika
and I will know you from the inside.

PAUL FARLEY

Paul Farley was born in Liverpool in 1965 and studied at Chelsea School of Art. His first collection, *The Boy from the Chemist Is Here to See You* (Picador), won him the Forward Prize for Best First Collection in 1998, as well as a Somerset Maugham Award and the *Sunday Times* Young Writer of the Year Award. His next book, *The Ice Age*, won the Whitbread Poetry Award in 2003, and a third collection, *Tramp in Flames*, made the International shortlist for the 2007 Griffin Prize. He edited a pocket-book of John Clare's work for Faber's Poet-to-Poet series, has published a collection of his BBC poems, *Field Recordings* (Donut Press, 2009), and received the 2009 E.M Forster Award from the American Academy of Arts & Letters.

Farley's work mobilises memory, often drawing on a pop-cultural iconography familiar to any post-war working class childhood, but he also seems attracted by the differences between city and countryside, and the imaginative region in-between. Seeing the world – through the various distorting lenses of our age, as well as first-hand – seems to be another abiding theme, perhaps rooted in his visual arts background and training.

Dead Fish

Remember how the made us play Dead Fish?
If it rained, the dinner-ladies kept us in
and we cleared the canteen of its chairs and tables.
Have you forgotten how we lay so still?
The smell of old varnish, salt on the parquet,
or how the first five minutes were the easiest?
You'd find an attitude that you were sure
could last until the bell. Foetal, recovery:
each had his favourite. I'd strike a simple
flat-on-back, arms-by-my-sides figure
and concentrate.
                              Some fell asleep,
easy after seconds of tapioca,
and this proved fatal. Sleep is seldom still.
Others could last as long as pins and needles

allowed, or until they couldn't frame
the energies of being six years old:
some thought would find its way into a limb
and give the game away. But you were good,
so good you always won, so never saw
this lunch-time slaughter of the innocents
from where we sat out on the bean-bagged margin.
Dead fish in uniform, oblivious
to dinner-ladies' sticks poking their ribs,
still wash up on my mind's floor when it rains
in school hours. Blink if you remember this.

Diary Moon

You are the plainest moon. Forget all others:
shivering in pools or spoken to when drunk,
that great Romantic gaze of youth; shed all
sonatas, harvests, Junes, and think instead
of how your phases turn here in a diary:
stripped of sunlight, surface noise and seas,
you move unnoticed through the months, a bare limn
achieving ink blackness, emptying again.

You who turned inside the week-to-view
my father carried round each year, past crosses
that symbolised pay-days, final demands;
in girlfriends', where red novae marked the dates
they were 'due on', and I shouldn't've been looking;
who even showed in weighty Filofaxes,
peeping through the clouds of missed appointments,
arrivals and departures, names and numbers.

On nights like these, which of us needs reminding
to set an eel-trap, open up the bomb doors,
or sail out of the harbour on a spring tide?
What sway do you hold over our affairs?
Although for some you're all that's there, printed
across the white weeks until New Year;
moving towards windows that will not frame us,
into the evenings of our sons and daughters.

Keith Chegwin as Fleance

The next rung up from extra and dogsbody
and all the clichés are true – days waiting for
enough light, learning card games, penny-ante,
while fog rolls off the sea, a camera
gets moisture in its gate, and Roman Polanski
curses the day he chose Snowdonia.

He picked you for your hair to play this role:
a look had reached Bootle from Altamont
that year. You wouldn't say you sold your soul
but learned your line inside a beating tent
by candlelight, the shingle dark as coal
behind each wave, and its slight restatement.

'A tale told by an idiot...' 'Not your turn,
but perhaps, with time and practice...', the Pole starts.
Who's to say, behind the accent and that grin,
what designs you had on playing a greater part?
The crew get ready while the stars go in.
You speak the words you'd written on your heart

just as the long-awaited sunrise fires
the sky a bluish pink. Who could have seen
this future in the late schedules, where I
can't sleep, and watch your flight from the big screen;
on the other side of drink and wondering why,
the zany, household-name years in between?

An Interior

They ask why I still bother coming back.
London must be great this time of year.
I'm not listening. My eyes have found
the draining-board, its dull mineral shine,
the spice rack, still exactly how I left it,
knives, a Vermeer vinyl table-mat.
How many hours did I spend watching

the woman pouring milk into a bowl
that never fills? I never tired of it.
Vision persists, doesn't admit the breaks
the artist must have taken, leg-stretching
alongside a canal twitching with sky
not unlike the leaden one outside;
or just leant on the door jamb, looking out
onto a courtyard, smoking a pipe
before going in, to sleep on his excitement.

Newts

The golf course pond where all ages collided.
The slime and larval casings of prehistory
but on hot days more a Rococo mirror

from the swing in the trees. The silvering had gone
but we could fish fragile Kingeys and Queenies
out of its dark using newsagent nets

and study their webs and crests, their fronds and finery,
the English language mating without touching
in the shade of a hedge where we shrank from used sponkies.

I looked into the element of newts:
Knorr spring vegetable cold packet soup.
The same indefinite days we must all pass through.

And then one day the pond drained and its bed
a shock: an Eden Project of lost golf balls,
and all that delicate kingdom dissolved.

North Atlantic Corridor

Halfway it's noisier than you'd expect.
A wind-up gramophone is playing Caruso
in a U-boat underneath a convoy lane,
whose crew can testify to whale-song,

and most have heard the eels and salmon pass
on moonlit nights, when the click of binary
cabling the ocean floor is deafening,
and the elements compete above the swell

where the tern's wave-top flight-path intersects
with ragtime from a glittering liner,
where woodworm in the Old World's darkwood hold
meets the tongues of RKO and MGM

and there's no peace, even at altitude:
halfway between London and New York
an in-flight movie can't make up its mind:
A Matter of Life and Death / Stairway to Heaven.

The Scarecrow Wears a Wire

The scarecrow wears a wire in the top field.
At sundown, the audiophilic farmer
who bugged his pasture unpicks the concealed
mics from its lapels. He's by the fire

later, listening back to the great day,
though to the untrained ear there's nothing much
doing: a booming breeze, a wasp or bee
trying its empty button-hole, a stitch

of wrensong now and then. But he listens late
and nods off to the creak of the spinal pole
and the rumble of his tractor pulling beets
in the bottom field, which cuts out. In a while

somebody will approach over ploughed earth
in caked Frankenstein boots. There'll be a noise
of tearing, and he'll flap awake by a hearth
grown cold, waking the house with broken cries.

LEONTIA FLYNN

Leontia Flynn was born in 1974 in Co. Down, Northern Ireland and now lives in Belfast. She won an Eric Gregory Award in 2000 and *These Days* (Cape Poetry) won the Forward Prize for Best First Collection in 2004. Her second collection, *Drives*, was published by Cape in 2008, when she also received the Rooney Prize for Irish Literature and a major individual artist award from the Northern Irish Arts Council. She has also written a PhD thesis on the poetry of Medbh McGuckian which she is adapting as a monograph. She is currently research fellow at the Seamus Heaney Centre for Poetry at Queen's University Belfast. Flynn's first collection consists mainly of short, crisp poems which wittily dissect the travails of twenty-something life. Her second book contains a number of potted poem histories of famous writers and details a number of trips abroad, exploring the twin dislocation and delight of foreign travel.

The Furthest Distances I've Travelled

Like many folk, when first I saddled a rucksack,
feeling its weight on my back –
the way my spine
curved under it like a meridian –

I thought: Yes. This is how
to live. On the beaten track, the sherpa pass, between Kraków
and Zagreb, or the Siberian white
cells of scattered airports,

it came clear as over a tannoy
that in restlessness, in anony
mity:
was some kind of destiny.

So whether it was the scare stories about Larium
– the threats of delirium
and baldness – that led me, not to a Western Union
wiring money with six words of Lithuanian,

but to this post office with a handful of bills
or a giro; and why, if I'm stuffing smalls
hastily into a holdall, I am less likely
to be catching a greyhound from Madison to Milwaukee

than to be doing some overdue laundry
is really beyond me.
However,
when, during routine evictions, I discover

alien pants, cinema stubs, the throwaway
comment – on a Post-it – or a tiny stowaway
pressed flower amid bottom drawers,
I know these are my souvenirs

and, from these crushed valentines, this unravelled
sports sock, that the furthest distances I've travelled
have been those between people. And what survives
of holidaying briefly in their lives.

Airports

Airports are their own peculiar weather.
Their lucid hallways ring like swimming pools.
From each sealed lounge, a pale nostalgic sky
burns up its gases over far-flung zones,
and the planes, like a child's mobile, hang at random.

Like hospitals, they are their own dominion.
We have tried their dishes with plastic knives.
We have packed our bags ourselves, no one has tampered with them,
and as we pass through the eye of the charged needle,
our keys and wallets drop from us like stones.

But now we are passing quicker, colder, clearer,
from East to West un-policed, a gate of light
which lengthens like some animal proboscis
or a hoop bowled along at speed beside the sun.
And when we return, the airports remain in us,
We rock, dry-eyed, and we are not at home.

By My Skin

Mr Bennet in *Pride and Prejudice – The Musical!*,
my father communicates with his family almost entirely through song.
From the orange linoleum and trumpet-sized wallpaper flowers
of the late 1970s, he steps with a roll of cotton,
a soft-shoe routine, and a pound of soft white paraffin.

He sings 'Oft in the Stilly Night' and 'Believe Me, If All Those
Endearing Young Charms'.
He sings 'Edelweiss' and 'Cheek to Cheek' from *Top Hat*.
Disney-animals are swaying along the formica sink-top
where he gets me into a lather. He greases behind my knees
and the folds of my elbows; he wraps me in swaddling clothes.

Then lifts me up with his famous high-shouldered shuffle
– 'Yes Sir, That's My Baby!' – to the candlewick bunk.
The air is bright with a billion exfoliate flitters
as he changes track – one for his changeling child:
'Hauld up your head my bonnie wee lass and dinnae look so shy.'

He sings 'Put your shoes on Lucy (Don't You Know You're in the City)'.
He sings 'Boolavogue' and 'Can't Help Loving That Man of Mine'
and 'Lily the Pink' and 'The Woods of Gortnamona'.
He sings   the lights are fading – 'Slievenamon'
and about the 'Boy Blue' (who awakens 'to angel song').

My father is Captain Von Trapp, Jean Valjean – Professor Henry
          Higgins –
gathering his repertoire, with the wheatgerm and cortisone,
like he's gathering up a dozen tribute roses.
Then, taking a bow, he lays these – just so – by my skin
which gets better and worse, and worse and better again.

Belfast

The sky is a washed out theatre backcloth
behind new façades on old baths and gasworks;
downtown, under the green sails of their scaffolding,
a dozen buildings' tops steer over the skyline.

Belfast is finished and Belfast is under construction.
What was mixed grills and whiskeys (cultureless, graceless, leisureless)
is now concerts and walking tours (Friendly! Dynamic! Various!);
A tourist pamphlet contains an artist's impression

of arcades, mock-colonnades, church-spires and tapas bars;
are these *harsh attempts at buyable beauty?*
There are 27 McDonalds, you tell me, in Northern Ireland
('but what are we supposed to *do* with this information?')

A match at Windsor Park has fallen in Gay Pride week.
At two A.M. the street erupts in noise.
I listen as 'We are the Billy Boys'
gets mixed up, four doors down, with 'Crazy' by Patsy Cline.

And gathering in the city's handful of bars,
not sunk in darkness or swathed in beige leatherette
men are talking of Walter Benjamin, and about 'Grand Narratives'
which they always seek to 'fracture' and 'interrogate'.

ANNIE FREUD

Annie Freud was born in London in 1948 and studied English and European Literature at Warwick University. A pamphlet, *A Voids Officer Adopts the Tree Pose* (Donut Press 2006), was followed by her first full collection from Picador, *The Best Man That Ever Was* (2007) which was a Poetry Book Society Recommendation and received the Glen Dimplex New Writers Award. She has taught the Advanced Poetry Writing Course at City University. Since 1975, she has worked intermittently as a tapestry artist and embroiderer, exhibiting work and undertaking commissions. She is the daughter of painter Lucian Freud, maternal granddaughter of sculptor Sir Jacob Epstein, and the great-granddaughter of Sigmund Freud. A late starter with poetry, Freud is renowned for her live performances. Her poems are vigorous and entertaining and are often character sketches or monologues, many containing a pair of characters, generally a man and a woman. Food and France make regular appearances in her work.

The Study of Disease

He knew her immediately for who she was;
and she, though aghast at his raincoat
and the almost sacerdotal manner of his greeting,
led him up Copenhagen Street
in blazing sunlight
and spoke of a recent dream she'd had
of pale blue missiles arcing in the sky
while her heart thudded like
a boot against her ribs.

In a bar they exchanged jokes, one each.
He talked about his work, the study of disease;
that pleased her, and she felt a shadow at last
get up and leave her to her own devices.

The badger snarling in the taxidermist's window,
the women at the bus stop with their shopping,
and the bus itself – all seemed suddenly benign.

She sat on his hand throughout the journey.
The conductress did not come to take their fares –
something her remarked on later
when he spread her out in several different ways.
In the lull they talked, drank wine and ate quails' eggs.
He watched her as she cracked hers on the wall above the bed.

The Symbolic Meaning of Things and Reasons for Not Dying

Fighting the habits of my filthy mood,
I stood at Centre Point, soaked to the skin,
when suddenly, in the street's ecstatic fugue,
I knew that it was you I had been thinking of
and with a book about Velázquez in my hands
open at *An Old Woman Cooking Eggs*,
I saw the shadow of her knife curve in her bowl
and the third egg that I will one day fry for you
ready in her hand – and just today I notice that she's blind.

I'll intimate the prospect of a small but steaming pie
on your return from some exploit on the field –
then, like two reptiles dressed as ordinary modern folk,
we'll grind down the nutmeg of speculative thought
and with our *double entendres*, split the air.

And if I should outlive you, would I, in the full
saturation of my grief, for ever breathe verses at your photo?
Or in the tradition of my race, rip my libidinous negligee to shreds
and stock the fridge with all your favourite snacks?
And will I, when I take my final breath,
remember when you asked me to uncross my legs?

Daube

Towards midnight, he shouted: carrots!
and the nurse put down her cup.
What's that, dear? Were you dreaming?
I was not dreaming... I was in Paris;

there was a place I used to go
and have a dish of melting beef
that always came with *Carottes Vichy*.
Is it still there? Does anyone know?

It must be possible to find someone
who knows the recipe for melting beef,
Juliette Greco sitting on my knee,
and *Carottes Vichy*. How was it done?

A Scotch Egg

After forty years spent in the novitiate of the abstract,
his predilection now was all for hands-on and bric-à-brac.
Hanging out, he said, was one of life's pleasures.
He loved the sense of entering the realm of the inanimate:
to riffle the flyleaves of old books made him think
of being nobbled for fivers by a wayward nephew,
and to see one's passing self in the blade of a fish-slice
was like hearing a familiar voice say *Ah, there you are at last*.
He could not forego the acquisition of a tiny cannonball,
nor the Pop-Up Book of Great Women in History,
nor a set of ocarinas painted with blue polka dots.
These things would find their place inside the flat
beside the family of Confucian china rabbits,
a bedspread stitched by soldiers wounded in the Boer War
and, carved in balsa, a bas-relief of trysting lovers on a stile.
When Amanda praised him for the pleasure that he gave her,
that set him thinking of a Scotch egg he'd bought from a stall –
delicious, the best he'd ever had: he'd remember it forever.

A Canaletto Orange

He remembers how she pulled him down with her laugh,
lips ghoulish with wine, kingfisher glitter on her eyelids.
'Ain't Nobody Here But Us Chickens' was playing
and when she tap-danced to it, the crowd stood agog
at such velleity and he was like a man in a blizzard.
Twenty years on, the kids grown up, the marriage gone,
it's a late lunch at *La Baracola* with the loquacious Marianne
(these days, he deploys women's names like well-bred swear words
or types of land-mass phenomena or famous makes of cars).
Her legs are stunning, but that's not really the point,
he reasons in the final seconds of his self-possession.
As he drags their Gewürztraminer from its silver bucket,
there she is, framed in an alcove, lips blocked in Canaletto orange,
one heel cocked for combat. *Christ, she's keener than I thought!*
he wheezes as she coils herself into her throne of cane.

ALAN GILLIS

Alan Gillis was born in Belfast in 1973 and was raised in nearby Newtownards before leaving there to live and study in Dublin for four years,. He now lives in Scotland, where he lectures at The University of Edinburgh. His first collection, *Somebody, Somewhere*, was published by the Gallery Press in 2004. It was shortlisted for the *Irish Times* Poetry Now Award 2005 and won the Rupert and Eithne Strong Award for best first collection in Ireland. His second book from Gallery, *Hawks and Doves*, was shortlisted for the T.S. Eliot Prize in 2008. As a critic, he is author of *Irish Poetry of the 1930s* (Oxford University Press, 2005). A third collection is due in 2010. One of the strongest writers in the reflourishing of Northern Irish poetry, Gillis' work shifts between flamboyant, colourful lyric poems and a more demotic and conversational style. A formally adept poet, another division in his poetry is between the personal lyric and social commentary.

The Ulster Way

This is not about burns or hedges.
There will be no gorse. You will not
notice the ceaseless photosynthesis
or the dead tree's thousand fingers,
the trunk's inhumanity writhing with texture,
as you will not be passing into farmland.
Nor will you be set upon by cattle,

ingleberried, haunching and haunting
with their eyes, their shocking opals,
graving you, hoovering and scooping you,
full of a whatness that sieves you through
the abattoir hillscape, the runnel's slabber
through darkgrass, sweating for the night
that will purple to a love-bitten bruise.

All this is in your head. If you walk,
don't walk away, in silence, under the stars'
ice-fires of violence, to the water's darkened strand.

For this is not about horizons, or their curving
limitations. This is not about the rhythm
of a songline. There are other paths to follow.
Everything is about you. Now listen.

Harvest

I

The two of them were forever banging
on about keeping your conscience spick and span
as a scoured kitchen surface and grafting
bone-hard in life's grim dockyard, each time giving
it everything. If a peeler took one through
the cummerbund outside the secret policeman's
dancehall, or Marks and Spencers blew
its windows one hundred and seventy-
five feet in the air to rain down arrows on the newly
disfigured, they'd be livid if I didn't wash my hands.

Maybe this is why I'm licking my chops
at the thought of microwaved trays
of pork bangers and bleached potato slops,
driving to Killymoon through hay fields and green
fields decked with pat-caked cows;
why my parents have turned into odd
truisms, viruses mutating through the thin streams
of my brain into screenplays of low-beamed
corners in dancehalls; why I'm wondering how
two free wills become two peas in a pod.

II

Half-baked under the spalding orange rays,
they birl and dunt their pitchforks in the fum.
A horse's scream of rain will soon come
and wash all this away, but now the women lay

the table with hot boxty bread. She sucks an orange finger.
His breeks are ripped to flitterjigs
as he snuffles his neb and spies the stoppled eaves
of her breasts, before gobbing a pure emerald yinger.

152

And he can't help but to think
of her in a bool of earth-swell, the hurt
weaver's kiss of her tights, raising her skirts
against the clay-baked orange-brown turf bink.

Now they trudge back along the oaten
shingle, a bunch of branny-faced boys in jouked
breeks by the reed-kissed bebble of a brook.
It's hard to judge when the sky will be opened.

III

Trigger-happy tomcats and hornets jet
into the sun, their motherloads dead set
on the clay-baked cities of Iraq, as I sit
back and order an overcooked frozen fillet
of salmon with hard potatoes and spoon-
mashed turnip with my parents at Killymoon's
nearest hotel, my newborn son on my breast
with my Ma insisting, despite my cloud-dark frown,
that a brandy-soaked sugar cube is best
for traumatic nights as the rain knuckles down.

Someday I might return, and tell him this
is near where they met, where they might have been
married, as the rain batters remorseless
on watchtowers, their camouflaged polytetrafluoroethylene,
as I lead him down the road of falling
hazels and vetch, finger to finger
until he lets go and leaves me by a reed-shushing
brook under the sky's orange plumes,
the fallout winds and elder
stealing kisses on the road to Killymoon.

Whiskey

Listen for the whist of unrippled wells
of water, still ponds, dead quiet lakes
you might walk to through wheatfields
and rolled fields of new-flowered flax
into an otherworld of woodland

where boys have stopped playing
soldiers and laid down broken branches
to finger caterpillars, where you might
first have opened lips to feel a tongue
alive in your mouth moons ago.

Lie still by such a low pond and catch
the thistled breeze and shallow flies,
insects twitching in the verbena
and firethorn, the tufted clouds'
degression, a distant Citroën engine.

Better still, go on a winter's night
when you might catch the chattered tink
of your own teeth, the buffets of a barn
owl's wings, shadows that flusker and flitch
over the silver pool's ice and secrets.

For the days are taken and poured
like whiskey into the well of a glass:
for a while we hold the sunset
in hard-worked hands, then drain the glass.
Look through the window on a winter's

night – some might possess your body
but none the hole vented through
that two-way glass, no more than hold
the snow, the lunatic, the vanishing child,
as you lose your reflection in the frost.

For we are swept up in the city's
cashflows and contusions, violet mouths
and japing eyes, until one night,
landlocked in our poverty, caught and cut
up by the glaze of cold eyes, we feel

a sliver of still water, a midnight pool,
and in that fleet stretch of time
before we empty our rusting spirits
into the well of a glass, deep within us,
broken cubes of moonlight tinkle and chime.

JANE GRIFFITHS

Jane Griffiths was born in Devon in 1970 but brought up in Holland. She has worked as a bookbinder, lexicographer and university lecturer in London, Norwich, Oxford, Edinburgh, and most recently in Bristol. As well as poetry, she has published extensively on the Tudor poet John Skelton. She won an Eric Gregory Award in 1996. Her most recent book *Another Country: New & Selected Poems* (Bloodaxe, 2008) was short-listed for the Forward Prize. It contains a new collection *Eclogue Over Merlin Street* and work from two earlier books from Bloodaxe, *A Grip on Thin Air* (2000) and *Icarus on Earth* (2005). Griffiths' work has been described as having 'a migrant's sense of estrangement'.

Her syntactically taut poems observe and record scenes, whether around the home or in foreign lands. Bernard O'Donoghue has noted the balance 'between the image and the idea. The images seem to have a verbal life of their own, generated by a dominating thought that the reader is hardly aware of. But then it dawns on you...'

Epitaph for X

who'd have focused less on the final choice of words than on the angle
of the chisel hand, the nick of time in the composite strokes, the depth
of the incision
                        and how after rain the serifed feet grow bulbous
as a cat's eye whose membrane glosses over the iris.
Who'd have doodled this as a cat neatly inhabiting its own skin
and watchful among the over-head-height iris and narcissi,
chin on its feet, seraphic and unblinking.
                                                    Immaculate.
Who hopelessly lacked a sense of perspective.
Who'd spend hours with an eye to the dark ground of her garden,
matching the green-black undersides of shadows, the sun
skeltered through the ivy, the washing-line's blade of white.
Who had antennae for the silence under the sound drift,

who called the sky articulate in its cat's cradle of cable
and aerial, its traffickings.
                           Who said this was all matter.
Who'd have counted thrips in August, who'd hear the air seal
behind a kite string, who couldn't think without a likeness
(the garden shadowing its own shadows: wing over leaf over trellis).
Who moved like a small grey cat at the bottom of her tall world,
who'd take an afternoon trying out the word *striation* on the rushes,
whistling sotto voce.
                     Who may be living still, but differently.

Valediction

Island-bound, the things I leave you with:
a coast road out of season, land down
to a bar of low pressure between sea

and ocean and the light mercury
stopping each boulevard. The spring
in the boardwalk, wire-wrapped roller

coaster track, and the striped awnings.
A want of interiors: wood drifts from
dormers, masts through windows shifting

in and out of alignment and the sky
jarred between boarding-house turrets.
All the spiralled escape routes,

the sidewalk barred, the finned
Cadillac we never hired, our amphibian
shadows. The boardwalk flexing

like bones in our hands' skin, a strong
undertow of desire. An abiding
distrust of countries without a coastline.

Clairvoyance

Spring, and the river is rising: klaxon
of geese, shrill of forsythia's five
stems forked in a glass jar,
and wavering. An oak sprouts waterfalls,

the house paw-talks in the roof at night,
there are toothmarks in the butter.
Industrious, bees batten on the carpet,
the upholstery, signing like mutes,

and rain nets me in. Your messages slip
through with arrowed wakes, migratory
in formation. You say there's snow,
you've banked an enormous fire,

have been out walking among the trees
I couldn't name, gauging their sextant angles
with the measured glance of a fisherman.
That you'll drive by another river, fetch

bread, jalapenos, liquor. Unpacking,
the brown paper bag spells contraband;
in your glass room the whisky glows
amber through a forest in silhouette

like fish bright among water-weed,
the current under ice. It will be late there.
Here tower bells tumble as turbines.
You'll be heaping up coals before sleeping.

I open all the windows. Early light
rimes the bees' carpet of fur.

Travelling Light

Like flotsam curtseying on the spot, things
are coming back to him. Honeysuckle. Lavender.
The weighty press and scent of blackcurrant
bushes as he walked out, and his mind edgy

as a cat testing the sun, all vertebrae.
A five-runged swimming-pool ladder hung
from a brick garden wall, but no pool.
How this (more than anything) irked him.

And the way the village High Street dead-ended
in *Danger Cliff Fall Road and Path Destroyed*
and someone had raised the red and white
barrier to an arch, and someone was growing roses.

How the last house that day was aerial –
yellow tin butterfly roof open to the sky,
marram grass coiled in chicken wire and a wall
of railway sleepers topped with blue and green

bottles like skittles, like a seismograph – and how
the breakwater below crissed and double-crossed
before coming up with a red flag with an air of
surprised finality. Why he took it for an omen,

so when the plane strummed over and its propeller
cut a corkscrew spiral like the final flourish in
a game of consequences or conclusive proof
that air is thicker than water he looked askance

at the barricade and for *Danger* read *Dance*
and brushed past the roses to step out in
its wake lightly as a cat with artful insouciance
ringing down the ladder onto the lawn.

On Liking Glass Houses:

the untidy ones, skewed down gardens like an accident
with a log pile, windows for hindsight, or wedged
anyhow in the angle between hedge and railway line.

The way their emptiness invites a pause,
the way a sinuous movement against the glass
resolves into a cat weaving through iris

as if spooled down a thread: the length of
its spine an updraft of single hairs fine enough
to paint themselves a perfect likeness.

                       Years ago

on the canal you passed a studio, an old man
lifting gold leaf on a comb of badger's hair,
holding his breath as the boat's wake ran

clopping gently along the wooden wall of the shed.
And you held your course past the ironworks
and the cemetery, through lock over lock

but thought back and gave a name to it: *illumination.*

You remember that now, out on the edge of town
where a woman has walked into the room holding

an almost spherical pot of jam: the ruby globe
of the word rolled on the tip of the tongue,
and the sense of likeness, of trying it out for size.

VONA GROARKE

Vona Groarke was born in the Irish midlands in 1964. Her poetry collections, published in Ireland by the Gallery Press and in the US by Wake Forest University Press, are: *Shale* (1994), *Other People's Houses* (1999), *Flight* (2002), which was shortlisted for the Forward Prize, *Juniper Street* (2006), and *Spindrift* (2009), a Poetry Book Society Recommendation. Her translation of the classic 18th-century Irish poem, *Lament for Art O'Leary*, was published in 2008. She has been Poet in Residence at Wake Forest University and currently teaches at the Centre for New Writing in the University of Manchester. Her awards include the Brendan Behan Memorial Award, the Hennessy Award and the Michael Hartnett Award.

Groarke is a lyric poet, often formal, who has been praised for the thoughtful qualities and relative quietness of her work. A poet of place (buildings and their constituent parts feature prominently) and family, she is fond of emblematic metaphors and her poems often build subtly towards dramatic revelations.

To Smithereens

You'll need a tiller's hand to steer this through
the backward drift that brings you to, as always,
one fine day, August 1979. A sunlit Spiddal beach.

Children ruffle the shoreline. Their nets are full
of a marvellous haul of foam and iridescent sand
and water that laughs at them as it wriggles free.

They hardly care: they are busy spilling buckets
of gold all over the afternoon. But further back,
something spreads over the beach like scarlet dye

on the white-hot voice of the radio. The mams
and aunts pinned onto Foxford rugs put down
their scandalous magazines and vast, plaid flasks

as a swell from over the rocks showers them
with words like *rowboat, fishing, smithereens.*
You hear it too, the news that falls in slanted beats

like metal shavings sprayed from a single,
incandescent point to dispel themselves
as the future tense of what they fall upon.

Let's say you are lifted clear of the high-tide line
into another order of silence. Exchange the year.
The cinema's almost empty. She has taken you

to *Gandhi* at the Ritz. You are only a modernist
western wall away from the Shannon and the slipknot
of darkness the river ties and unties in the scenes.

Her breath is caught up in it: she's nodding off.
Her head falls back on the crimson plush and then
her carriage bears her on and on, shunting towards

the very point where all the journeys terminate
with the slump and flutter of an outboard engine
reddening the water with its freight. It's here

that every single thing casts itself off, or is brightly cast,
into a flyblown, speckled plural that scatters tracks
in the heat and dust of the locked projection-room.

The railway bridge one up from ours shakes out
each of its iron rails in readiness, and she is woken
by words that spill over the confluence of the Ganges

and the Shannon at our backs. 'To smithereens?',
she says. 'I'm pretty sure it's Indian. It means
to open (like an Albertine); to flower.'

Ghosts

Not exactly. Something like breath on your cheek
or an aftertaste of summer, years ago; one,
two metallic notes with the cadence of a name;
silverfish throwing your reflection off a beat.
Or a peony petal blown onto your path.

I don't think so. The children know.
They breathe ghosts into January
that stand for the split second
it takes to take us in, and then they're off
as though released, like figments of the air.

Bodkin

A word from a dream, or several, spiked on it
like old receipts. Something akin to a clavicle's
bold airs; a measurement of antique land;
a keepsake brooch on a quilted silk bodice;
a firkin, filled to the brink with mead or milk;
a bobbin spinning like a back-road drunken bumpkin;
borrowed, half-baked prophecies in a foreign tongue;
a debunked uncle's thin bloodline; a Balkan
fairy-story, all broken bones poked inside out;
a bespoke book blacked in with Indian ink;
a bobolink in a buckeye or a bare-backed oak;
a barren spindle, choked ankle-high with lichen;
a fistful of ball-bearings dropped on a bodhrán.
Body skin. Kith and kin. Other buckled things.

The Return

The bricked-up door still comes as a surprise
though the new roof struts, like a punchline
to an old one about a slack gable and rain.
I know this house: I wrote our summer here
into words that closed over years ago, and still
I'm back to pick over the same grass as though
I've just come up from the lake with my hair all wet
and you are waiting for me on the porch.
Even your hand stops as I unhook the gate
and there it is, our young day, like the blue of your eyes,
a noticed, simple thing that leaves me dumbfounded
in a half-hearted ruin. My hand on the door admits me
to those months where our lives bedded down in layers
I could no more uncouple now than your wrist
could turn some key or other and have us both
walk out beyond this final door, into the glare
of our release, another headlong day.

JEN HADFIELD

Jen Hadfield was born in Cheshire in 1978 and studied English Language and Literature at the University of Edinburgh. She went on to earn an MLitt with distinction from the Universities of Glasgow and Strathclyde, tutored by Tom Leonard. She has dual citizenship with Canada and used an Eric Gregory Award in 2003 to explore that country. *Almanacs* was published by Bloodaxe in 2005. She returned to Shetland to live in 2006, where she has been working as a gallery assistant and teaching and writing. In 2008 she was presented with the T.S. Eliot Prize for her second book *Nigh-No-Place*, described by the judges as 'a revelation: jaunty, energetic, iconoclastic, even devil-may-care'.

Shetland landscape and language continue to influence her poetry and visual art. She is a member of Veer North, the most northerly artist's collective in the UK. In 2007 she received a Dewar Award to research Mexican devotional folk art. She often returns to the idea of the secular-sacred as it relates to landscape. Liturgical rhythms underpin many of her poems about place, home, ecology, space – an idiomatic mythology of the here-and-now.

Melodeon on the Road Home

I love your slut dog,
as silent with his three print spots
as a musical primer.
He sags like a melodeon
across my spread knees.
When I dig my fingers
into the butterfly hollows
in his chest, he pushes my breasts
apart with stiff legs.
Isn't it good
to forget you're anything but fat
and bone? I'm telling you
it's good to be hearing your dog's tune
on the broad curve out of town,
a poem starting,

pattering the breathless little keys.
To see more than me, I flick
the headlamps to high beam
and it's as if I pulled an organ stop –
black light wobbling
in the wrinkles of the road,
high angelus of trees.

Unfledging

*Hold the bird in the left hand, and commence to pull off the feathers
from under the wing. Having plucked one side, take the other wing
and proceed in the same manner, until all the feathers are removed.*
MRS BEETON'S HOUSEHOLD MANAGEMENT

I raise Paisley wounds,
spill yellow pollen of fat.
This is reversing time, like a vandal

who scores shellac blooms
from a soundbox, tightens to snapping
the strings of a lute.

As if I scraped a poem's lard
from vellum. As brattish
as kicking a cat.

In pale skin are magnolia buds:
the muscles that worked wings,
but I've undone the wings,

gripping each pinion
as if to slide home the marriage ring
and never dream of flying again;

I've plucked the eyed seed feathers,
the chicky down, the fine human hair
like first casing of mushroom spawn,

the long quills that striped across
the evening sun this week,
trembling in the rainstorm's target.

165

Hedgehog, Hamnavoe

Flinching in my hands
this soiled and studded but *good* heart,
which stippling my cupped palms, breathes –

a kidney flinching on a hot griddle,
or very small Hell's Angel, peeled from the verge
of a sweet, slurred morning.

Drunk, I coddle it like a crystal ball,
hellbent the realistic mysteries
should amount to more than guesswork

        and fleas.

Prenatal Polar Bear

He hangs in formaldehyde
like a softmint or astronaut
dreaming in his moonsuit –
a creased, white world.

His paws are opalescent
and dinted with seedclaws –
the flattened, unripe,
strawberries–of–the–snows.

Full Sheeptick Moon

Weedy drymouth Feb
       LES MURRAY,
       'Feb'

An hour at high-tide,
edgy patience with the fankle-line
of July, bail-arm jammed,
hooks gripped in the grind.

A ribbon teaseweed
to flutter my spinner,
greenly.

           *

Dimps of season July,
new dot to dot galaxies of freckle,
clear dabs of midge honey;

July, our sun
in wee wet bursts
that bless the heads of orchids'
ragatag magenta.

A raised red season
but nerveless as the quenched wineglasses.

Woke at four to their fingerprints
and pale mouths, a tremulous
cooling hour,

watching the lighthouse
smear the haar.

           *

Now summer is the season
of clingings-on, high dithering grasses,
this-an-that of mackerel.

Summer sky peeled from your soles
in grey crescents.

The swallows come, wings
black boomerang,
loaded with ticks
and pearly winter weathers.

Thrimilce – Isbister

> *The Anglo-Saxons called [May] thrimilce, because then cows*
> *can be milked three times a day.*
> BREWER'S PHRASE AND FABLE

Cheddared, the light sealed
in rind of dry road;
bloom and sheen of the ditches
I've been dreaming all this life;
the close-quilled irises
rooted dense and deep
as flight feathers.

Recognition rises –
cream in a tilted pitcher.

The Blokes and Beasties

I defy noctiphobia to watch the summer constellations rise, and
name for the first time the blokes and the beasties – Leo, the kite
of Libra, Virgo's long torso, the Huntsman Boötes, whose dot red
cock is named Arcturus. The blimp Ophiuchus is a cross between a
python and a manatee, Serpens Caput to Serpens Cauda. Satellites
score the sky as tiny bubbles crawl up a glass of cola. Had I reached
the wilderness I would see yet more shuddering stars, clinging to
the strapping constellations like greenfly. Kyoots or wolves are
shouting in the black flames of poplars. I am backed up against the
porch door with all the lights off, a torch just to find the handle.
I'm scared of seeing something Big; they say moose, wattled like
jigsaw pieces, emanate in the halflight. And yet I sleep on my belly,
under the bent knee and flexed bicep of the big man Hercules.

SOPHIE HANNAH

Sophie Hannah was born in Manchester in 1971. She has been Fellow Commoner in Creative Arts at Trinity College, Cambridge, as well as a Fellow of Wolfson College, Oxford. *The Hero and the Girl Next Door* was her debut from Carcanet in 1996. Her fifth and most recent collection, *Pessimism for Beginners*, was shortlisted for the 2007 T.S. Eliot Prize. In 2004 she won the Daphne Du Maurier Festival Prize for her suspense story and her first short story collection was shortlisted for the 2009 Spread the Word Award. She also writes bestselling psychological thrillers. She lives in West Yorkshire with her husband and two children.

She is a witty poet with popular appeal. Her poems tend to use traditional rhyme and metre, combined with contemporary subject-matter which is, in the main, psychological, social and emotional, focussing on people, relationships and human behaviour. *The Guardian* said of her, 'Sophie Hannah is among the best at comprehending in rhyming verse the indignity of having a body and the nobility of having a heart.'

Long for This World

I settle for less than snow,
try to go gracefully, as seasons go

which will regain their ground –
ditch, hill and field – when a new year comes round.

Now I know everything:
how winter leaves without resenting spring,

lives in a safe time-frame,
gives up so much but knows he can reclaim

all titles that are his,
fall out for months and still be what he is.

169

I settle for less than snow:
high only once, then no way up from low,

then to be swept from drives.
Ten words I throw into your changing lives

fly like ten snowballs hurled:
I hope to be, and will, long for this world.

The Bridging Line

If, as it now appears,
a second time can lean across the ditch,
retrieve, like a dropped stitch,
the first, long in arrears,
how badly I've misjudged the last five years,

potholes beside our past
I thought they were, when all the time they've been
linear, in between,
travelling (if not fast)
towards next time, back from next time to last.

Tonight's no precipice,
merely one station on the bridging line
where incidents combine,
kiss throws a rope to kiss,
last time connects to next, next time to this –

a better fairytale
than scattered breadcrumbs on the forest floor;
wind howls, rain starts to pour
and soon you've lost your trail.
The bridging line is like a polished rail

beneath our years of space
that I can almost rest my hand upon.
I clutch it now you're gone,
find it reflects your face,
find I believe the next five years will race

straightforwardly ahead
as five have raced straightforwardly behind.
The gaps are redefined.
I hold my breath and tread
the bridging line towards a waiting bed.

'No Ball Games etc'
sign outside a London block of flats

Honestly, do we have to spell it out?
No tents, space-hoppers, orgies, Brussels sprout
enthusiasts, no sponsored squirrel fights,
no Ayurvedic quacks, no woolly tights,

no weeping for the joy you think you're owed,
no winking at the house across the road,
dividing rainbows into seven strands
of single colour, no quick show of hands,

no pastry-cutting, origami, chess,
no taking pleasure in your own success,
no sand, no shark impressions, no culottes,
no Christmas pantomimes, no liver spots,

no lurking in the shadows by the shed,
no improvised salutes, no olive bread,
no weightless floating with an auctioneer
in the small pond. No ponds. Hope that's now clear.

TRACEY HERD

Tracey Herd was born in East Kilbride in 1968. She graduated from Dundee University with a degree in English and American Studies and has lived in Dundee ever since, working as a bookseller. From 1998 to 2001 she was Creative Writing Fellow at Dundee University. Her first collection, *No Hiding Place*, appeared from Bloodaxe in 1996 and was shortlisted for the Forward Prize for Best First Collection and her second book *Dead Redhead* (Bloodaxe, 2001) was a Poetry Book Society Recommendation. She participated in the Bloodaxe / British Council Russian Poetry Festival and has read her poems in the winners enclosure at Musselburgh racecourse.

Herd's work emerges from darkness, often disturbing and painful, and she both bears and relishes the tight squeezes of lives played out in adversity. For relief, there is the escapism of the worlds of fashion and of children's books. A "flood subject" for Herd is the horse, particularly the muscular beauty and nobility of the thoroughbred racehorse and she has written several of the best equine poems of recent decades.

Spring in the Valley of the Racehorse

In her well-tended garden,
March is always a revelation, a generous
parcelling-out of leaf
and feather, the branches
sieving dark green onto pale
and the small bird fluent.

An untried colt, he ran green,
tilting awkwardly at the windmills
of spring that swung the shadows
and the sun around
in dizzying beats
upon the firm ground.
Still, he ran out an easy winner,
unbothered by the coppery
heat of the afternoon.

172

She shines the window-glass;
her cloth, a starter's
old-fashioned flag. The breeze
is brisk, her pace easy.
She is well within herself.
The fine weather holds.
Any cloudbursts will be light
and temporary.

He tenses against the hot
metal of the starting-gate,
eyeballing the wide swatch
of flat green that vanishes
sweetly in the distance.
He's learned to ignore
the impure source of noise,
the sharp, irregular
flashes of the sun
on glass discs, to keep
his mind within
the miraging posts of white,
evenly spaced along the track.
He blows a little, not too hard,
focused as the noonday sun
that would blind a person
were they to look at it too long
and too hard.

Sir Ivor

Even those watching
the race repeated will swear every time
that he's beaten. He *must*
have sprouted wings between
the furlong pole and home. Press
your nose up against the screen
till the light blurs
on an imperceptible shifting
of gears, a heavenly guidance:

poor Connaught, only second
when you knew you'd won, your
big white face vanishing
like a ghost from the winner's enclosure
as Sir Ivor stepped through you.

Black Swan

An English garden, its lakes and lawns,
a corps de ballet of pale roses,
the drifting midwinter of swans.

She is lost in her shifting reflection.
The miniature bridge is stiffly arched
in its heavy slipper of stone.

Gone is the dark-haired, dark-eyed Russian
girl, bare-faced, black hair scraped back
from her aristocratic bones

who would sit mutely watching her swans.
Her breath tears at her throat
in a feverish spray of thorns.

In an empty theatre, the bouquets are strewn:
the elaborate costumes carefully hung
backstage in the many-mirrored room.

The sky darkens behind its stars.
The air is chilled. A frozen moon defines
the black swan rising from the lake.

Coronach

The skylark's melody is sealed in ice:
a coronach as blue as the winter
sky. The moon wobbles over the rock face,
throwing into high relief the climber
in a gully below the glittering maze.

He is a brilliant figure in this frieze.
His genius walked him into space
and left him to find a foothold there.
The moon is sheer ice or a cracked watch-face
that swings on its fragile chain of stars.

Night is falling at its own modest pace.

KEVIN HIGGINS

 Kevin Higgins was born in London in 1967 and grew up in Galway on Ireland's west coast where he still lives. For many years he was a political activist, a member of the Militant Tendency. He now earns his living as a writing workshop facilitator. He is co-organiser of Galway's Over The Edge literary events. His debut, *The Boy With No Face* (Salmon, 2005), was shortlisted for the Strong Award, and followed by two further collections from Salmon, *Time Gentlemen, Please* (2008) and *Frightening New Furniture* (2010). Higgins is interested in the intersection between the written and the performed word and won the 2003 Poetry Grand Slam at the Cúirt Festival. Many of Higgins's poems are character studies dealing with the difficulties of political engagement from his standpoint as a disappointed idealist and offer an absurdist take on the commonplace tragedies of everyday life. An appealing performer, and at heart a satirist, in his poetry, Higgins picks apart the human condition, its disappointments and indulgences, with vigour and acumen.

From the future, a postcard home

After the imagined ice-cream clouds
and warm blue rain, the frost bristling
picturesque grass, the parties
where the women were topless, the men
all wearing tuxedos; each day's

metallic tap-water taste. Outside
the chapped lips and tea-cosy hats
of a winter afternoon's typical trajectory.
In your head, these dissonant fingers
still plinking along with some mad monologue
banging its gong. Outside

the freezing fog bothering their nostrils.
In your head, the essential details
of an August evening: the angle
of her bra-strap as the books
came tumbling, the minus signs

massing at the border. Elsewhere
nothing now but the present
as the cat gives up sniffing your sad
cheeseless hands, and goes back
to catching the giant mice
of its dreams.

Almost Invisible

When winter's chill and pallid spectre
ripples across the horizon
to thrust itself once more
upon a gilded autumn's final fling,
and to roughly wrap dead hands around
the sultry traces of those lingering summer days,

     the rust-red leaves in swollen gardens,
     the buoyant banter of candent girls
     who pulsed the wild streets
     aggravating the symptoms,

then he will, again, venture from his shady hollow
to hang on the frigid corners of unfrequented lanes
thickly stained in the jet-black of dusk. Almost invisible.

Shapeless Days Shuffling

Constant as stopped clocks or money
under the mattress. Your weak tea,
discoloured secrets and voice like snow through
a sulk black afternoon. The shapeless days shuffling
your serviceable drawers once more down the hallway,
like a minor character in one of Jane Austen's
lesser known novels. Until with its high pitched laugh
the universe signals not last minute Valentines
in big red envelopes – some cut-price Napoleon
in the end maybe taking you to the gates of Moscow –

but coming cobweb hair and rumours of cat food:
the slow multiplication of all your small disappointments
into the bound volumes of broken promises
opening nightly now across the mahogany.

The Great Depression

Since love took its clown questions
and vomit-coloured clothes down
the fire escape that dusk, the woman
who once put the *quoi*
into Je ne sais quoi has gone
from the city of caffeine
and glittering websites
                     to wander late
the boulevards of Stalintown handing
out yellow-pack tuna fish to the poor, her face
like a ruined bank-holiday weekend, her talk
like LSD and downers in a country
where it's always Tuesday.

The Candidate

Who, without opening his mouth, tells you
that, for him, it was stay there forever
making up worlds that will never be
in a side-street with nothing to offer
but the monthly *Tea-dance and sing-along
for the over fifty-fives*, or grow up to be
Junior Minister for Counter-Terrorism;

that you can scowl all you want,
his suit will just keep beaming back, now
the miracle of modern dentistry has given the boy
with the shrieking red t-shirt
and mouthful of bombed-out teeth
this ice white New Labour smile;

that as you stand there,
looking suddenly old in the Post Office queue
used, by now, to the idea of not being played
by Jack Nicholson in the film of your life
that'll never be made;

he daydreams he's signing the order
that'll send you away across the courtyard
to have your head shaved
by the Anti-Everything Police.

The Couple Upstairs

Your husband's last set of golf-clubs
in their vest of cobwebs; and the chair
you've sat in since Jimmy Carter
often empty now, as you tumble away to a life
of medicine, mash and Sunday night
nephews. Moments though

when every sound upstairs
is sex: every rustle across a table-top
some ecstasy of underwear
whistling to the floor, every whisper
of a floorboard her once again, turning
her pale backside to the sky; times

when all he has to do is drop
his *Penguin Book of Poetry from
Britain and Ireland Since 1945*
and you shudder at the thought of them
about to commit an unnatural act
on a Tuesday afternoon. And your stick's

suddenly frantic against the ceiling,
or you're ringing the bell
to tell them to stop, till you settle
back to a big, black afterwards now
fractured only by this last lightning
across its sky.

MATTHEW HOLLIS

Born in 1971 in Norwich, **Matthew Hollis** studied at the universities of Edinburgh and York. He won an Eric Gregory Award in 1999. His first collection, *Ground Water* (Bloodaxe, 2004), was a Poetry Book Society Recommendation and was shortlisted for the Guardian First Book Award and the Whitbread Poetry Award. He edited *101 Poems Against War* (2003) with Paul Keegan, and *Strong Words: Modern Poets on Modern Poetry* (2000) with W.N. Herbert. He works as an editor at Faber and Faber and as a tutor for the Poetry School in London. In 2005-06, he was Poet-in-Residence at the Wordsworth Trust. His biography of Edward Thomas will be published in 2010.

Hollis's years in East Anglia are an abiding influence on his work. Jules Smith wrote of *Ground Water* that its 'poems of love and elegy are remarkable for their controlled emotion. Predominant are images of water in all its forms, especially as rain and flood, invariably prefiguring loss.'

Hedge Bird

You're almost home. You've been numb
a long time. You didn't see the daylight slip out,
nor the fieldfares raiding the windfalls;
you didn't notice the holly in fruit,
or the wind lift wild garlic and whin
to your nose. Dusk gloves the hill;
soon the woods will back into shadow.
You could lose your way, even still.

Something is calling from the thicket.
You know the song, it was with you
when you started. Try not to think
you can find it with your eyes, reach out
and you'll only silence it. Listen.
The world comes in by the ear,
nudging the spirit to here and there,
waking the heart-step, conjuring the air.

Turn into the lane, the house is in view.
She loves you. You will make it through.

The Sour House

Through the frost-hole of the passenger window
your tenant's house is ringed in winter.
He's turning the snow from the path

that lay in the night. He can far less
handle a spade than you, dipping the lug
as though the shovel itself was unbalanced.

And what you found inside you would not forget:
room on room of bottled milk, gagging
the stairwell, the hallway, bookshelves,

like a stumbled-on ice world, a sweep of winter.
For years he maintained the world his parents left,
taking in milk he never drank. Evenings spent out

in the yard, piecing apart the Ford his father drove –
sill-lines, cogwheels, dippers fanned round him,
working each burr to a touch.

For years I coloured your world in hues
you didn't recognise; never your island,
always your skerry – 'unable to see

the romance of the thing for the thing itself'.
That, airing his house, the rancour
would catch as far as the common;

and what you found in the garage was scrap:
not the showpiece I'd imagined but the pin
pulled out, a car returned to the sum of its parts.

Driving now through the cloughs at dusk
I am struck by the things I can't let go;
that some things weal on the body like braille –

the sight of you just home from the milk-house
matted and choking, your raw nose streaming,
gutting the fridge in two clean strokes –
like a swimmer striking out for land.

The Diomedes

Summers he would leave for Alaska,
working the crabbers as deckhand or galley;
autumns returning with cold-weather stories of
clam catchers, fur trappers, and the twin isles
of Diomede: two miles and a continent between them;
and how, in winter, when the straits froze over,
the islanders could walk from one to the other,
crossing the ice-sheet to see family, swap
scrimshaw, the season's stories, or marry,
passing the Date Line that ran through the channel,
and so stepping between days as they went.

As far as I know he never went back;
if he had he'd have learned that
only the bravest now track on foot,
the winter ice no longer reliable,
for walrus, ski-plane or the human step,
leaving the skin boats alone to wait for the summer,
to edge themselves into the melt-water.

Even now, there's something to his story
I find difficult to fathom. At home, in London,
listening to my neighbours' raised voices
or catching the girl opposite dressing,
I wonder, what it is we will do to be neighbourly,
how part of us longs for it to matter that much,
to be willing to nudge our small boat into the waves,
or set foot on the winter ice,
to be half-way from home, in no safety,
unsure if we're headed for tomorrow or yesterday.

A.B. JACKSON

Andrew Buchanan Jackson was born in Glasgow in 1965 and raised in the town of Bramhall, Cheshire. At the age of 11 his family moved to Cupar in Fife where he developed an interest in poetry at high school. He studied English Literature at Edinburgh University and after abandoning one complete manuscript in 1995, he finally published *Fire Stations* (Anvil Press, 2003) which won the Forward Prize for Best First Collection. A limited edition pamphlet, *Apocrypha*, is due from Donut Press in 2010. He works for the NHS in Glasgow. Jackson's work is concerned with the metaphysical: the interaction between mind and body, imagination and nature, religious icons and animals. A gothic sensibility coupled with a dry wit underlies the poems, which are often formal, condensed, and highly tuned. Geoffrey Hill and Sylvia Plath are among his major influences, as are the psychoanalytic works of C.G. Jung. Striking language, numinous imagery and an elegiac, but sometimes playful tone are the keynotes in Jackson's poetry.

A Ring

1

You and I could be, knowing just this much –

in times of flood, clamber to the roof;
wear day-glo orange, holler. Train your sight
on tiny omens. Take them as a truth.

On orchard walls, new buds and barbed wire.
In the cat's jaws, game, as we're in love.

2

The kitchen table, the bed where we move
to serve and share the long meal of a kiss –

the lost and found debris of togetherness:
wine bottles, underwear, dead birds, amethyst –

the granny wallpaper: identical ships
on their small identical pedestals of sea.

3

With both of us asleep, the room wakes up,
a durable masque of curtains, ashtrays, cups.
They see what lies between us, face to face:

an hourglass – a space dividing profiles.

Let's taunt our eyes eternally with this,
let's always cancel one or other out.

4

Fuzzy, undefined, we look again –

our city stands, a forest of alarms,
TV aerials, dogs chewing footballs;
a broken sign which reads: *Salvation Arm.*

Invisible, the rainbow's other half,
the sister-arc that ploughs beneath the earth.

Lauder's Bar

Sir Harry smiles from every wall.
Rain turns to sleet and falls
on three taxis planted in the rank.
A bus emblazoned *Glasgow via Reykjavik
to the USA & Canada* stands

empty opposite. Some bright spark
has amended a scrawled *UVF*
to *LOVE* in the gents' toilets.
Milling around, fake-fur coats
and shirts the colour of Opal Fruits.

Hands flare from various cuffs.
The papers are full of 'LUNAR ICE'
and far-out possibilities for life.
I'm smashed. There is no us.

Foxes

A passion fuelled by foxes cannot last.
Our joiners cobbled up this mirrored bliss.
A skater's weight will force a pond's collapse.
Fox-love is a game of hit or miss.

I'll throw them chicken wings, a slice of beef.
Porch lights will ignite when foxes run.
Our garden is a pool of disbelief.
Vermin have their holes in kingdom come.

The synaesthete sees colour in a word;
a tune is bitter almond, orange peel.
A fox's nose is cleaner than a sword.
Our kiss was burning bibles on a wheel.

Hail, as foxes gnaw their daily bread,
the winter pavement serving as a dish.
We snuffled out our boundaries in bed.
Christ send me, quick, another night like this.

Star

Home, in split seconds:
a cloudless, non-carnivorous sky,
morning star – all

I remember. As sacrifice,
this jam-jar of water
poured in the River Eden;

by Tentsmuir,
seaweed thrown to the sea.
Once more

I dream my unborn daughter:
within her palm,
one sand-grain's infinite

coastline becomes one handful, becomes
the whole inhabited land.

from **Apocrypha**

Adam lay miraculous,
unconscious with drink.
In a dream, he named whiskies

by nose, palate, finish:
brine and limes, a delicate
peat-reek, Weetabix.

Plasticine, emulsion paint,
amyl nitrate. A warm horse.
Kippers, treacle toffee, grassy

with green grape...
the work was endless.
Jalapeno peppers, tobacco notes...

Adam rose with a rough tongue
and heartbroken.

                    *

Abraham wielded a watering can.
With star-mangled fervour
he sprinkled the Arctic, the Sahara.

Five years later, a riot of wild
orchids and tropical liana
convulsed the Arndale shopping centre.

Moths fled their equator.
With twelve-inch tongues uncoiled
they drilled for glacial nectar.

Some species perished: inverted
atmospheres, increased cloud cover
snuffed the jewelled frog, the grail spider.

When moonlight wobbled
Abraham knocked a nail through it.

                    *

Daniel's ear, awash with voices:
the high voltage
war council of thunderclouds,

crackling theomania. Words
flashed their gold leaf,
a self-swallowing

knotwork of new gospel.
Daniel stormed a lions' enclosure
armed with roast chicken –

once bitten, twice bitten,
his mortal star on marijuana,
unlucky in Leo. His horoscope

foresaw this day, the dark
stranger dressed entirely in fire.

                    *

Gethsemane: a grassy knoll
fringed with prize daffodils.
Special forces

interrogated molehills,
dusted breadcrumbs, entertained
appleseed possibilities.

Mary gathered soil samples,
odd bits of mown flesh
to reconstruct a mugshot, a man's

pith and pip. At dusk, children
followed a loop of new law,
ran rings around roses, roses –

the scrambled air command; a sole
surviving god, his wow and flutter.

ANTHONY JOSEPH

Anthony Joseph was born in Trinidad and has lived in the UK since 1989. He holds an MA in Creative Writing from Goldsmiths College, University of London, where he is also completing a PhD with an interest in experimental Caribbean poetry and life writing. He is the author of three collections: *Desafinado* (1994), *Teragaton* (1998) and *Bird Head Son* (Salt Publishing, 2009). His spoken word CD *Liquid Textology* appeared in 2005 and his 'afro-psychedelic-noir' novel *The African Origins of UFOs* followed in 2006. In 2005, he was the British Council's Poet in Residence at California State University, Los Angeles. He is also a lecturer in Creative Writing at Birkbeck College and at Goldsmiths College. Joseph is well-known for his spoken word performances, often accompanied by his jazz quartet The Spasm Band whose debut album *Legge de Lion* was released in 2007. His work fuses his Caribbean background with an experimental aesthetic. He has been described as 'the leader of the black avant-garde in Britain' and cites his main influences as surrealism, jazz and the rhythms of Trinidadian speech and music.

Conductors of his Mystery
(for Albert Joseph)

The day my father came back from the sea
   he was broke and handsome
I saw him walking across the savannah
   and knew at once it was him.
His soulful stride, the grace of his hat,
   the serifs of his name
   ~ fluttering ~
     in my mouth.

In his bachelor's room in El Socorro that year
he played his 8-tracks through a sawed-off speaker box.
   The coil would rattle an the cone would hop
but women from the coconut groves
  still came to hear
   his traveller's tales.

Shop he say he build by Goose Lane junction.
    But it rough from fabricated timber string.
        Picka foot jook wood
    like what Datsun ship in.

And in this snackette he sold   red mango,
    mints and tamarind.
Its wire mesh grill hid his suffer well tough.
    Till the shop bust,
        and he knock out the boards
        and roam east
        to Enterprise village.

Shack he say he build same cross-cut lumber.
    Wood he say he stitch same carap bush.
Roof he say he throw same galvanise. He got
    ambitious with wood
                in his middle ages.

That night I spent there,
        with the cicadas in that clear village sky,
even though each room was still unfinished
    and each sadness hid. I was with
    my father
    and I would've stayed
    if he had asked.

Brown suede,
    8 eye high
    desert boots.   Beige
gabardine bells with the 2 inch folds.
He was myth.   The legend of him.
Once I touched the nape of his boot
    to see if my father was real.
Beyond the brown edges of photographs
    and the songs we sang
        to sing him back
            from the sweep and sea agonies
            of his distance.

Landslide scars. He sent no letters.

189

His small hands were for the fine work of his carpentry.
   His fingers to trace the pitch pine's grain.
      And the raised rivers of his veins,
         the thick rings of his charisma,
            the scars – the maps of his palms –
      were the sweet conductors
                     of his mystery.

   Aiyé Olokun.

He came back smelling of the sea.

The Cinema

Frizzle-neck chickens pick padlocks under the cinema.
Midday Saturday when it hot in the coop
an that chicken shit start to buzz from the chopping board
      when man watchin Chen Sing kick-up.

In the cinema the ground build tilt, the wall shaky-shaky.
Sound bounce round like few hundred radio
                     tumblin down.
The film stock zog-up zog-up
            (like chicken did scratch it)
It jagged and it bruise
            when man watchin *Shaolin Temple*.
And the soundtrack get contaminate
with San Juan taxi horn and bicycle engine,
   the market shout and the dub wax pump,
            the heifers in the abattoir bawlin!
The pie man's slappin palm. Every coconut head that slash,
      each cuss an cut an planass pass
get mix with the Sheng Fan death grip.
But the seat-back break from balcony to pit,
the screen heng like curtain that twist,
         an kick missin instep
         like chicken missin neck.

The Myst

My brother become the Myst that night. He put his boots on.

He fixed his mask. He slid a brittle edged Gilpin cutlass into the
sheath he pulled from his belt. Nanobyte salt kept the edge well
grim and his under arm grip hid his cow-itch pouch as he ran
through the bush upper Kandahar hill.

He had been planning this arrival since May. And now his bulk
was proper, his gullet root tough. For months I watched, when he
let me, and when he didn't, see me peep, as he assembled his
implements. For the suit, he dyed and synthesised tarpaulin; pure
black with sandbox root. His gloves he proofed with Banga seed
heart, his jackboot steel he sanded off sheen. Bois canon bush did
his dada head: dread. The mask made last with perforated pigskin
leather waxed and moulded on his sleeping head with shallow holes
for hooks and eyes.

I saw him churn old iron on the riverbank. Saw when he swam
under floodgate with a single column of breath, and came back
hours later with handfuls of armoured cascadura, whose scales he
sharpened to blades. He sharpened his toes. With calabash milk he
poisoned the tips.

He drunk duck egg, nog and cowheel porridge, till the muscle to
leap in his legs grew across the width of one of five rivers. His
cryptic grip was wire bent, his speed through jungle elastic. His
cutlass slap would spin heads around, his battle stance was brute
and bad-minded.

Sudden so the sky get dim and snarling when he put his mask on,
and he mount the steep incline
        like a lizard.

LUKE KENNARD

Luke Kennard was born in Kingston upon Thames in 1981 and grew up in Luton. He has a PhD in English from the University of Exeter and lectures in creative writing at the University of Birmingham. He won an Eric Gregory Award in 2005 and his first collection of prose poems *The Solex Brothers* was published later that year by Stride. His second collection *The Harbour Beyond the Movie* was published by Salt in 2007 and was shortlisted for the Forward Prize for Best Collection, making him the youngest poet ever to be shortlisted for that award. A third collection *The Migraine Hotel* followed in 2009. His criticism has appeared in *Poetry London* and the *Times Literary Supplement*.

Kennard's work comprises a sort of chimerical opera of fabulous characters and their put-upon sidekicks. Around half his work is in the prose poem form. Though dreamlike, his poems emerge from awake imaginings of parallel realities, where creatures and objects speak and people indulge in improbable behaviour.

Chorus

The choir hadn't left him alone since the first day of summer;
He awoke to find them stationed around his bed.

One day the choir arrived without warning or explanation,
Sang the choir in four-part harmony, handing him toast.

On his first day back at work, the choir stood at his desk,
Singing, *The choir are making his professional life impossible.*

Two weeks later his partner left him for an osteopath.
Hannah cannot stand the choir any longer, they sang.

That night he pummelled the choristers with his fists;
He beats the choir in frustration, but though they are bruised

And bleeding at the lip, they sing with redoubled vigour, sang the choir.
Then they sang, *He cannot get to sleep, he cannot get to sleep,*

He cannot get to sleep, in perfect fifths, until he fell asleep.
In time you may even grow fond of us, they sang, quietly.

Daughters of the Lonesome Isle
(for Annabelle)

When I reach the station, Marcus is asleep.
Someone has thrown his hat into the bin.
He won't wake, so I board the train alone.

The window tastes like a river on my tongue.
'Annabelle?' I ask the opposite woman.
'No,' she says. 'Sorry, honey.'

Stupid Marcus, falling asleep like that.
But in the city it is snowing,
And I love snow more than anything.

Little stalls flank the cobbles:
£20 – Your past redefined
As manifest destiny. All symbolism

Subtle! Unsentimental! Hard-won!
But I don't like the look of the gypsy's
Typewriter. By the doughnut wagon:

All Your Secret Desires Engraved on the Head of a Pin!
Tradition dictates that you then shove the pin
Into someone you love for good luck.

A crow lands on the doughnut wagon.
'A crow in the snow!' cries a little girl.
The crow regards her with disdain.

'Crows are great, aren't they?' I say.
'Do you like crows too?
It really is kind of you to listen to me.'

A man plays piano with his tongue.
A harlequin paints a cream pie in watercolour
By the quay. I guess... Oh, I don't know.

I sit down by the darkened alleyway.
A charcoal overcoat flashes past me.
'Annabelle?' I say. 'Annabelle?'

The Forms of Despair

We returned from the war happier, arms around our shadows –
Who claimed to be older than us. They told great jokes

And lay around barefoot, hair precisely
Unkempt, cigarettes hissing and glowing like Christmas lights.

Only our fiancées were tired and bothersome,
Having forgotten how to love, or vice versa.

Some had moved to factories in other cities,
Others, when pressed, said, 'No one's forcing you to put up with me.'

We went skating with our shadows,
Huddled under fir trees drinking sausage tea.

Inquisitive sheep collected around our camp;
It was good to be among the ice storm and the believers.

We described the funny pages to Simon – who had lost both his eyes
But the jokes didn't work so well in description.

Instrumental #3

Curse those *Untitleds*:
Restaurants serving cookery books;
The gift of wrapping paper –

Yet somehow the lamps are lit,
And most of the blood is fake blood.
I don't remember getting up this morning:

The fridge is full of food and charming
Theatrical light. Brinksmanship
Would have us remember its ends,

But history abhors a brinkman:
'He's really more of an antihero
Spiking his coffee in a cinema diner.'

Nevertheless, there are compensations:
Coffee at the language schools of the marina;
The quality of canvas sails in dusk light.

Tonight doctors prescribing Get Well Soon cards
Glance at their watches or assistants
Who glance at their watches and say,

'It's getting late, Doctor.
What's another word for beautiful?
Would you describe me as perceptive?

What is the word "is"?' Language is the butter
You rub on a pirate. Language is the key I stick in your eye.
I would sooner have no tongue than nothing to say.

Scarecrow

I kissed the scarecrow: the scarecrow was cold and inert and tasted of sawdust. It was damn silly. Abelard took the photographs and advised me as to how I should kiss the scarecrow – with a hand on its shoulder, for instance.

After the shoot I purchased an *Avian Guide* from an unmanned stall, placing a note in a rusty can. The guide began:

> *Every bird that flits across our path contains a pea-sized brain which the bird uses for navigation, muscle control, detection of predators and tweeting.*

On its way to my pocket a ten pence piece glinted in the moonlight. I checked the date (1992) and the tiny but unmissable chink one micron to the left of the Queen's earring. This very coin had turned up in my change during most – if not all – moments of significance in my life to date.

I went to sit by the river to reflect on what its arrival might portend on this occasion, but was immediately seized, bound hand and foot and carried into town. 'Like scarecrows, do you?' said the grubby-faced men.

During my trial the judge's contact microphone kept losing power. 'Foul... Unnatural... Halcyon... Porous...' he said.

Next day they attached me to a post in the middle of an oceanic cornfield and left me for dead. A crow landed on my shoulder and whispered, 'You do realise, old thing, that we're not actually the *least* bit scared of you?'

NICK LAIRD

Born in County Tyrone in 1975, **Nick Laird** was educated at Cambridge and worked as a lawyer for six years before leaving to write full-time. He has published two collections with Faber & Faber, *To a Fault* (2005) and *On Purpose* (2007) and has also published two novels. He has won several prizes for his fiction and poetry, including an Eric Gregory Award, the Rooney Prize for Irish Literature, the Ireland Chair of Poetry Award, the Betty Trask Prize, a Somerset Maugham award and the Geoffrey Faber Memorial Prize. He has lived in London, Warsaw and Rome and was recently an adjunct professor at Columbia University in New York. Laird's ambitious and varied first collection met a number of influences head-on. Formal yet discursive, the poems are political in a broad sense and there is a focus on foreign travel and dislocation. *On Purpose* was a more complex and stylistically congruous book which pointed the way to the softer edge which typifies his most recent work.

Adeline

The smallest one among them
tasted air and named it breath.
The others lopped her silver hair
with garden shears – she wept

all through the second hymn
and then they hid her duffel coat
and so she ran the two streets home
to where they said they couldn't see her,

no. Her brother's glasses trapped the sun
and made his eyes alive with fire.
Each colour had a different flavour.
She ran the taps to free the rivers,

begged her eldest sister let her
count the galaxy of freckles.
No one ever missed her
with their spit or snowballs,

open hand or closed. She stayed
so still, she was so good,
they laid her body on the doorstep
like a sandbag for the flood.

Donna

Her younger brother stole across the river
to boost beer-kegs from the Royal Hotel
and float them back across the river.
In accordance with all classical myth,
he hadn't bargained on the current.
The weirgate dredged him, dead.

Music was heaven to Donna, heaven
overheard on earth, sifting down from
the shifting spheres or an open window,
the hi-hat moon. Heaven, with the heat
of evening, and her singing coming down
the stairs. Billie or Nina or Dinah.

Pug

I

Bruiser, batface, baby bear,
bounce in your moon suit
of apricot fur with some fluff
in your mouth or a twig or a feather.

Emperors bored you.

You with the prize-winning ears,
who grew from a glove
to a moccasin slipper
and have taken to secrecy

recently, worming in
under the furniture.

To discover you here
is to keep still and listen.

The settee begins wheezing.

II

Hogarth loved the fact
that for your first half-year
you hardly differed from a rabbit.
When you're over-excited

you tend to get hiccups.

You squeak when you yawn
and your tongue is unfurled
in a semi-circle, salmon-pink
on coastal rock, that trilobite

embedded in the slate
roof of your open mouth,
perfect for the mascot
of the House of Orange.

Your weapon of choice is the sneeze.

III

Above the winter garden
a hair-thin moon, reflecting.
You are open as a haiku,
all *karumi*, hint and sigh.

The Buddha would've liked you.

Watch us from your separate dream
then pad across to clamber through
the plastic flap and plant your paws
four-square again on grass, like this.

Your hackles bristle and you ridge
your back and bark and bark and bark,
at shadows and the fence,
at everything behind the fence,

the cuttings and the railway foxes.

The Hall of Medium Harmony

In lieu of a Gideon bible
          the bedside table drawer
has a *Lonely Planet Guide to China*
          and a year-old *Autotrader*.

You skim through the soft-tops, the imports,
          the salvage & breakers,
then pick up the book. Over there
          they are eight hours ahead

so it must be approximately dawn
          in the Forbidden City,
where something might evade the guides
          already at the entrance,

might glide right past the lion-dogs
          on guard, asleep in bronze,
might fire the dew on the golden tiles,
          ignite each phoenix on its ridge.

Light. Nine-thousand nine-hundred
          and ninety-nine rooms
begin to warm under its palm.
          Here, in the book, is a diagram.

There is the Hall of Union and Peace.
          The Hall of Medium Harmony.
The Meridian Gate. The Imperial Library.
          The inner golden bridges.

You fidget. You are, you admit, one of
          the earth's more nervous passengers.
But this is different, a reasonable space.
          In the palace of an afternoon

a child-king hiding in the curtain
          listening. For a second apart
from the turn of the thing, for a second
          forgetting the narrative's forfeit –

how nothing can outlast its loss,
  that solace is found, if at all,
in the silence that follows each footstep
  let fall on the black lacquer floor

of the now, of the here, where you are,
  in the sunlight, blinking, abroad.

The Eventual

Your hands surprising at the station,
shinycold and taut as plumskin, late.

It could have been All Hallow's Eve:
me kidding, ripping open Cox's pippins,

you sombre, the counter in the kitchen,
water in the basin dammed with apples.

*

Like a bag of unlabelled bulbs,
the fireworks wanted the precise

release of soluble tablets,
to flash their toothless yawn, and shut,

anemone-abruptly, on such a glossy dark
the laundered hail was frictionless and filmic.

*

If a long retreat was both giving in to gravity
and growing up, if Jumping Jack Flash

and the Catherine Wheel signed themselves
to the eventual, then things called true

were caught and missed by you,
trepanned windfalls, ghost trains home.

SARAH LAW

Sarah Law was born in Norwich in 1967. She studied English Literature in Cambridge and London and subsequently taught part-time at the University of East Anglia and also worked as the administrator of the Julian Centre, a visitor centre dedicated to medieval mystic Julian of Norwich. Her first and second poetry collections, *Bliss Tangle* and *The Lady Chapel*, were published by Stride in 1999 and 2004. *Perihelion* and *Ascension Notes* followed from Shearsman in 2006 and 2009. Since 2007 she has lived in London, where she lectures at London Metropolitan University and for the Open University.

Law's work is broadly split between a textured, linguistically innovative style and a more conventional and formal lyric approach. Though sometimes introspective, her enigmatic poetry has a lavish and numinous quality, and George Szirtes has noted her tendency to be 'ecstatic, mystical, playful, sensuous and deliciously intelligent. And behind these qualities there is an intense joy.'

Phase Transitions

It's the softness of the shifts which take her;
          a branch trembles imperceptibly
                    and the piled snow falls

Light clarifies into ice,
          sweet pink, at the point of dissolution,
                    becomes sudden water

A sun-drenched fence is as if breathing;
          a clutch of blue-white butterflies
                    lift into the sky

A lucky clover spins,
          splayed out in the air
               the wind takes it

One carnation blooms
        the blush of its petals
                tinged with gold

And she is as if flying
        rescued from the gruel of the mountain
                where, in the far distance,
                        the whole earth turns.

Breathing

Had I studied under other masters
I would own names for the difference of breaths
which seize us, in our differences of mood,
manner, or address.
                There is the bellows breath,
the pant of salty exertion, good or ill,
which energises, warms of imminent end
while yet excelling. I have breathed like this
bending, snakelike, into the sky, or hacking
the roots for the drift of a fire at night.

There is the shining skull, the no-death breath,
casting out puffs of destruction like old fluff
expulsed from the nostrils. I have snorted thus,
sitting ramrod in the dusty aisles; ever-preparing,
ever intending to fly.
                These breaths are archetypes,
tricksy, alchemic, promising the end of oceans.

There is the staretz breath, the eastern, orthodox,
and other: *Jesus son of God* (breathe in) *have
mercy for my sin* (breathe out). This slows the pulse
to petitionary rhythm. Bending heartward
on the meditator's bench. Where the old adepts
sucked for a thousand years or more
at the lozenge of traditional recourse.

Children are quick breathers. The animal,
the snake, the smart bee breath, hummings
and hissings tuning up their pipes.
My use of air is clearly not unique. But
I can't dispel the clarity of lucent inspiration;
a pace within myself yet not from me
as I am in mind. My robes are coarse;
my skin swims air like satin. It's pure,
a heavy outflow, costing gold to raw:
kaleidoscopic mothering, or more.

Parisian

Darling, you are divided like a king.
The art that kept these centuries intact
copies for us now the vital moments.
You, in your suit, crash-landing in ink
as each woman wrings her hands, reflects
that the dive has nothing on a platform,
a roundly stopped clock, a schoolgirl's hat.
There's a chicken in the basement.
Nothing is stable. Ascetics are marching
through this sumptuous city, arresting
silvered eyes and swathes of waist.
One day you order this; a genius paints
my face in afterglow, and your wealth is sealed
in this room with its bloom of hidden veins.

from Stretch: A Yoga Sequence

Easy Posture

Glass-bottled in the classroom of the world.
Head is happy with her easy posture, tulipped
in a peaceful sheath. Rain comes. And all
the plugged-up roots of distemper, tempting
irascible rejoinder. Ladies, it ain't easy at all
to stop your head from rolling. You have to keep it
light in a net, remember to breathe it out of the net
thinking it might do good. Your old vest's
a collapsible ship. Remember those heart-string bags?
This is the universe now. Don't settle, don't strain.
Snow comes, blanketing you for quiet grieving.
Glass-bottomed in the blue reef of the girl,
watch the coral, accreting in varying weaves.
Shiver of birthing, sea-sigh horses.

A Gem for Women

Because you can never seem to get those eight hours
rushing like a dirty wave into the foam which holds
your mind almost together on the subatomic level
I am telling you now, do the pose. Its chest-opening
offers a valve for the wound you harbour, pout
all you like against the curve of fate, gives pump
to the nature of the stamp you face, the tax
of give and take away, and the tenuous strain
sieving half the impediments away in loose blood.
A vague etymology for your favourite circuits, pony
blonde tail quipping in the dust: of small swimming children
in the might-have-been, the weathering meals,
cowering stomps of cessation. Train the mind to expect
less weal, less woe. Like an oyster park.

205

FRANCES LEVISTON

Frances Leviston was born in Edinburgh in 1982 and grew up in Sheffield. She read English at St Hilda's College, Oxford, and received an MA in Writing from Sheffield Hallam University. Her pamphlet *Lighter* (Mews Press, 2004) was a Poetry Book Society Pamphlet Choice, and her first collection, *Public Dream* (Picador, 2007), was shortlisted for the T.S. Eliot Prize and the Forward Prize for Best First Collection. She won an Eric Gregory Award in 2006. She has worked as a bookseller, a secretary and a snowboarding instructor, and has reviewed poetry for the *Guardian*. Leviston's poems are measured and attentive, at times observational, in other moments, metaphysical. She is interested in elemental subject matter: the hidden or shifting dimensions of air, wood, water. Paul Batchelor commented that her poems 'draw their power from a tension between the seen and the unseen, the familiar and the uncanny, the quotidian and the spiritual'.

The Zombie Library

In gallon jars, years of damsons rest
against the glass, contingent organs
sunk in the blue formaldehyde
of supermarket gin,
breathing one life out, another in.

Whatever throb of husbandry
long-handed their labels and shelved them here
in the cool of the cellar, for a rainy day,
hasn't been back since '94;
another phantom child of a future,

the perfect occasion, failed to appear.
Frozen heads of billionaires
are waiting still in a rented hangar's
ventilator-hiss of ice
to be summoned back from dreamlessness,

and out of the desert's
durational sifting *from* and *towards*,

clay funereal offerings rise
with seals unbroken,
their friezes crude, their contents petrified.

Sight

That winter drift-trapped in the house,
learning the campfire of flesh and the endless
tether the mind ranges upon,

I came into the living room and saw
a glass jug suspended in the air, six feet clear
of the carpet, tipped. There were no wires,

no mirror tricks. The whole world hung
on whatever invisible hook or hand
was keeping it tilted, empty, gleaming.

I stepped towards it, as if in a dream. It fell
as the rain falls, suddenly out of
the sky's indifference, and shattered at once.

The Gaps

And then they revealed that solids were not solid
That a wall was not solid
That it consisted of molecules fixed and vibrating
Some distance apart, as did the flesh

That solidity was really the likelihood
Of stuff not falling
Between two chairs, down the gaps

And that walking through the wall was not impossible
That it could be like
Slipping between pine trunks into a forest
Which had looked from the road impermeable
But was where something lived

207

And that one could peer back from the gloom towards the light
A different creature
With tender eyes, with an ear for water

Moon

Startled by the moon in the middle of the day,
same blue as the sky, like a crater in it,
for the first time in years I think of the flag
still flying there, of the men whose lives are fastened to it
even though the rest of us have turned away,

and I think of all the places I've been
in love, or happy, where I'll never go again
and probably couldn't find – that linden tree in Boston
I was lying under, watching summer's college kids
lope across the grass on their muscled brown legs,
when I suddenly headed for home.

There are bones inside my body I've never seen.

Scandinavia

I think I could be happy there, north of fame, in light
unbroken; blending the imagined hours' horizons into sky, sky
through soft-heaped fields, unclaimed, their rims forever
reforming at the wind's deft caprice. I could try

to live as a glass of water, utterly clear and somehow
restrained, a sip that tells you nothing
but perpetuates the being-there; could sit, lie, settle down, the white
of one idea entirely lost upon another, as rain is lost

in the shift of the sea, as a single consecrated face
drowns in the swell of the Saturday host, and the notion of loving
that one critically more than any other flake in a flurry
melts, flows back to folly's pool, the lucid public dream.

GWYNETH LEWIS

Gwyneth Lewis was born into a Welsh-speaking family in Cardiff. She was the inaugural National Poet of Wales in 2005-06. *Chaotic Angels* (Bloodaxe, 2005) collects her first three books of poetry in English (*Parables & Faxes, Zero Gravity* and *Keeping Mum*). Her most recent poetry title is *A Hospital Odyssey* (Bloodaxe, 2010), a phantasmagorical epic poem on illness and healing. She has also published collections of poetry in Welsh and two books of non-fiction, *Sunbathing in the Rain: A Cheerful Book on Depression* and *Two in a Boat: A Marital Voyage*. She is an award-winning playwright for radio and has written three libretti for Welsh National Opera. Now a freelance writer, she is writing a new version of the Clytemnestra story for the stage and currently spending two years in the USA.

Though not a formalist, Lewis often makes use of metre and rhyme. She used to make television documentaries, which she suggests has lent a narrative directness to the poems. *Parables & Faxes* was a fascinatingly original and complex debut and, like many poets, her work has loosened and opened into a less implicit and more self-aware, narrative-driven style.

Prayer for Horizon

I wish you, first, an unimpeded view
with a boundary in it, between seen and unseen,
a line to hold onto when you're feeling sick,
something to aim for but which retreats
as fast as you travel. May you stand undeceived
and see, not a line, but a curve of the earth:
an elegant offing that leads beyond fear
out to Vasco's discoveries. It's three –
visible, sensible, rational – lines
for what we may calculate and what we can't.

In fog, I wish you mercury sight,
artificial horizon, so that you know
where not to be, quickly. I wish you the gift
of knowing where your own knowing ends.

And finally, I ask: when you reach
the event horizon from which your light
will no longer reach us and space, highly curved,
will hide you for ever, that you watch me arrive-
you shouldn't see me, but you will –
marching with flashing lighthouses, buoys,
to the edge of your singularity
with fleets of full-rigged ceremonial ships
and acres of scintillating sea.

A Golf-Course Resurrection

Mid morning, above the main road's roar
the fairway's splendid – eighteen holes
high on a mountain, which should be all slope,
too steep for a stretch of evenness or poise.
By logic this layout shouldn't work at all
but all the best places are untenable
and the greens are kind as mercy, the course
an airy, open paradox.

The golfers move like penitents,
shouldering bags and counting strokes
towards the justices of handicap and par.
The wind, as sharp as blessing, brings its own tears.
Just out of sight is the mess below:
deconsecrated chapels, the gutted phurnacite,
tips reshaped by crustacean JCBs,
tracts of black bracken that spent the night on fire.

There is a light of last things here.
These men have been translated from the grime
of working the furnace with its sulphur and fire
into primary colours and leisurewear.

They talk of angles, swings and spins.
Their eyes sprout crows' feet as they squint to see
parabolas and arcs, an abstract vision, difficult to learn,
harder to master, but the chosen ones
know what it is to play without the ball
when – white on white – against the Beacons' snow
the point goes missing, yet they carry on
with a sharper focus on their toughest hole,
steer clear of the bunkers, of their own despair,
sinking impossible shots with the softest of putts
still accurate, scoring an albatross
as around them the lark and the kestrel ride
on extravagant fountains of visible air.

Night Passage to Nantucket

Those days night ferries travelled blind
and, once they were over Nantucket Bar,
used a single searchlight to pick out buoys
and find the channel. I sat outside,
watched the light swinging as if it could feel
the port side cans and starboard cones,
reading the fairway by floodlit braille.

My patients fumble for every word.
I refuse them the searchlight, sit on my hands
as they drift towards their most dangerous sands.
I must stay quiet. They have to learn
to distrust car headlights, that a landing star
is a plane. They need new marks
for self-navigation, to know where they are.

Memorial Sweater

I'm starting my magnum opus: it will be
my memorial sweater.
I can't see yet how it will end
but it starts with ribbing made of rain
on circular needles, so that the sleeves,
when they wear out, can be replaced
like choruses: Raglan cheers or batwing sighs,
depending on circumstance. I do know
I'll have shoes for pockets, the soles worn out
from dancing, I hope, to inherited tunes
and some new. I'll have a Hall of Fame:
a panel in Aran with cameos
of Milton, Herbert. I'd like a boat
in the story – if you can knit,
splicing comes easy – and a sea
of triple waves for voyages.
I'll have a computer linked to the eyes
of Hawaiian telescopes, so I can view
the mottle of early nebulae,
which will be a large feature of my work.
I'd like it to be a pleasure to wear,
not tight round the neck or under the arms.
I want Moorish whispering galleries
and orange groves, the breath of moss,
the occasional desert... I must start soon.
It's cooling and, as evening comes on
terrified, I hear soft whirrs:
the pollen-heavy moths of time.

JOHN McAULIFFE

John McAuliffe was born in 1973 and grew up in Listowel, Co. Kerry. He studied English in Galway and in 2000 won the RTE Poet of the Future Award. He has published two collections with the Gallery Press, *A Better Life*, which was shortlisted for the Forward Prize for Best First Collection in 2002, and *Next Door*, which was published in 2007. He has worked as a teacher and lecturer in Cork and London, writes regularly about contemporary and 20th-century poetry and directed the Poetry Now Festival in Dún Laoghaire from 2003 to 2007. He now lives in Manchester where he co-directs the University of Manchester's Centre for New Writing and edits the online journal *The Manchester Review*. McAuliffe's poems are often formal and they yoke together different kinds of language while staying grounded in speech, using traditional forms or rhyme. They are often concerned with ways of thinking about place and displacement, looking at places (Ireland and England, town and country, domestic and public) as adjacent, not opposed spaces.

Flood

The trees, up to their waists in earth,
up to their oxters in water, are for once insecure;
even the dumb animals have gathered on the mounds
they call hills cast of Gort.

I'm stranded in the low haggard cottage
practising philosophy and maths
and keeping a weather eye on the range

when you tiptoe into the bedroom's flood-plain
and floor me with linked tables of flotsam,
plantation ecology, train-times and lovage

and you drown out the tree-dwelling bird,
the land's flat liquid veins, the sounds
of rain on deepening rock-bottomed lakes, and the pure
ferocity of weather, its grey currents of light.

You Can See

how rows start here – ours was a windy autumn day
when I couldn't tell the birds from the leaves,
the red of the leaves, the red of the robin's breast.

Light faded, we walked down the arcade
flanked by pale statues of gods, horses and men,
the Triton fountain's intermittent spray

predictable as our arrival
at this or that exact spot, our yawns at the grotto
mimicked by the bridges' tiny *O*s.

When we could barely see the big house glow,
a sign asked us to admire the view
and you found a shortcut to the streets of shops,

that eat money like air,
into which we disappeared, like swimmers
entering their proper element.

Tinnitus

My father's tinnitus is like the hiss off a water cooler
only louder. And it doesn't just stop like, say, a hand-dryer – the worst is
it comes and goes. Or you shine a light on it
And it looks permanent as the sea,

a tideless sea that won't go away. The masker
he's been prescribed *is* a machine, an arc of white noise
that blacks out a lot
but can't absorb the interference totally

any more than you or I – taking the air,
stirring milk into coffee, daydreaming through the six o'clock news,
trying to sleep on a wet night –
can simply switch off what's always there, a particular memory

nagging away, the erosive splash off a little river
wearing through the road, say, on the Connor Pass,
a day out, through which he'd accelerate
in the flash, orange Capri.

The Electric Jar

Knowing its occult property,
its charge of static electricity,
a scholar in Leiden,
trying out new instruments, not a theory,
had air blown

into a dome of amber
from which he ran a damp wire
through a gunbarrel
to a jar of water,
tapping a charge so reliable

it drew a crowd
who, for an open-air experiment,
held the wire and formed a circuit.
The idea, the instrument,
gripped and tethered

the curious and obedient
like revealed truth
or the shockproof future
that belongs to whatever power
draws such subjects to it,

occupying both town hall
and city street –
even as it solves, for all,
the black hole
that flows around their feet.

CHRIS McCABE

Chris McCabe was born in Liverpool in 1977. His first collection *The Hutton Inquiry* was published by Salt in 2005. He is a regular performer of his poetry, has a poem on the Oxfam CD *Lifelines* and recorded a CD for The Poetry Archive. His second collection *Zeppelins* was published in 2008 and a pamphlet called *The Borrowed Notebook* (Landfill) followed in 2009. He works as a Joint Librarian of the Poetry Library at the Royal Festival Hall in London and lives with his wife and son.

McCabe's poems draw upon a wide range of sources and influences, both traditional and innovative. Experimental in approach, his poetry is both political and humorous. Overheard speech patterns are often woven into a tense fabric of human experience adrift in the city, creating what Iain Sinclair has described in his work as 'a topography restored by love'. An absorbing performer, McCabe's multifarious approach to poetry makes him an urgent and impressive writer.

Radio

A connection subtle as fish skull shadows,
of leaves on the patio –

a near-silent patter of distant claws:
soon you will not be alone.

Remember this: family close and hushed
and forbidden to speak,

omphalos box – make a wish –
all the words were sweet wrappers

melted down with the heat of promise.
You could warm your hands

around the vowels of the BBC –
all those things you could never say.

Each of us connected to each of us
like rosary beads strung out in the night

arriving at just this place,
camp as showbusiness

or pink champagne,
a dream of a swimming pool –

close your eyes and you could be
in any place the voice comes back from,

these mawkish arias of chance
and you thought: *I want more of this.*

Digital removed what was nasal
in the mucous turning of the dial

when you switched it off
static like city lights

flickered behind your eyes

Do you remember the first time? Small hands upturned
to hold the shrapnel that fell from above

pattered silver inside your ears.

That night you dreamt snow started to fall
on the new foil gloves you wore.

The Essex Fox

I needed air and went to do the community circuit at two
in the morning. Didn't see so much as a shadow of another.

Barracks of endless terraces & not one with a light on.
Brandless wafer of the forked church.

Like an airport attaché case the first fox stops.
Another moves in the shape of the night it is not.

Skewered kebab for brush, casino-token eyes.
They wait in a row of children's suits

at the gates of tomorrow morning's work.

Weightless I found them & hung them here.

Poem in Black Ink

Looked up poetry in the *Yellow Pages* & it just dripped –
put me through to Melvyn Bragg's office which connected to this.

A childish chant: get your DNA out for the labs.
The staff in the *Costcutter* taped the note back together –

it was accepted (despite the Queen's hair bouffed into a hedge).
As Johnny Cash got older he started to look

like a bronchial Orville dressed all in black.
The card arrived: you both make such a lovely couple

in the marriage-blend of semiotics & witchcraft.

Be happy.

The Thames swirled & crashed against the steps
like a drunk creeping up to bed –

leaves dunked & drowned & submerged:
amethysts in mist as we kissed.

There are no ropes in the twigs of a hedge
and fighting is controlling the Body Politic –

now that people can see far back from their eyes
to be aware of the lights on cars.

The under 25s raise their voice to integrity
– Australian Question Intonation –

when you ask what they do for a job.
So when it all kicks off on the bus

you're just a child again, a figure
positioned in a red Corgi,

a battered face in the street on a Saturday night
scrunched & crushed into a scotch bonnet.

The icicles start to melt from the satellite
as the London Signal reconnects –

all was quick around us that night
but we have since forgotten & lapsed

like days of endless breakfast radio.
Laptops on thighs negating their sex –

lambs in latex on the abattoir ride.
When we stop to eat at the estate agent window

our reflections are bigger that the house we rent.
Try the Penelope-sophistry of this aphorism:

she said that she would only remarry
if they came to reinvent the Rag & Bone man.

As chestnuts button-up September's streets:
keep two in the palm for stress-relief.

Lemon Blue

We grabbed the handles of the shimmering zimmer of chance –
someone offered a box of matches called LEMON BLUE
from the stall that sold flint wheels attached to plastic steps
ridged to a range of coloured cylinders of gas. I cursed
my sloped brother of history – why hadn't he copyrighted fire?
Then came a text to say he was with whiskey & dancing to light.
I placed the phone face down on the Las Vegas beermat,
on the albino feline that never made Top Cat. So I said
to the one with only numbers behind their thoughts:
Give me something cloned to sell, to profit the sons of my only son.

HELEN MACDONALD

Born in Surrey in 1970, **Helen Macdonald** read English Literature at Cambridge before working in conservation and falconry in the UK and UAE. Based now at the Department of History and Philosophy of Science at the University of Cambridge, she works on the cultural histories and geographies of nature, particularly those relating to amateur natural history, hunting, the history of ecology, and the relationship between nature and the military in the 20th century. An early pamphlet *Simple Objects* (Poetical Histories) was followed by a selection in *Etruscan Reader I*. Etruscan Books published her first full collection in 2001.

Macdonald's work is airbound, concerned with the air, airwaves and the creatures which populate it. The richly textural *Shaler's Fish* has rightly been hailed 'a modern classic' in the innovative poetry world. Her poems set technical and scientific vocabularies against and through lyric poetry in provisional attempts to articulate the ways we orient ourselves in and against the natural world.

Poem

Between her wings the novitiate
conjures blocks from the palms of her hands.
Some fall, some rise to create their own mistakes
blossoming in little liege-struck parentheses of air
and cement, blood and spittle. They survive like
open chitin, small frequencies, with pearls and tines
in circuits, dust to small versions of nothing
ventured, nothing gained, and that sets a smile
to prey upon her face, where the dirt is.
The wings are black, of course: she'd assumed
they'd be off-white, a kind of shabby perfection,
but the thumbs and the long, emarginated curves,
the complex slings of cord and muscle that flare
at her shoulders are not. They're black. Not
that this is a bad thing, she decides, at once. It means

I can't be seen at night. And during the day, I'll hide.
I'm good at that. There are parts of the air so thin
you can slip inside them, and then, with the wings
hitched and the coverts raised, each little feather
with its four tiny muscles erect and the air between
burred with the warmth from her back, she'd sleep.
Never wanted to be nocturnal. But dusk
and dawn are enough: larks sing in the dark, and
I know the blackbirds do, too. I shan't see reptiles
she thought, with sadness, but then if I lived in Ireland,
nor would I then. St Patrick kicked them out. Or at least
St Patrick in that form of an icesheet. She shivers. How
various then, these theories of the world. Paper
at her feet, wet cobbles, white fletchings & vowels
swans, verbs, the headlines all the swans' invention,
showers of thrips and crowds, the last
in their progress less certain of meeting
each other than of the water running under
their feet. Concerned, she drops a block; it breaks
to fifteen dice, one watchface, a cabbage white, two
Yale keys & a small vial of perfume. Tester. Unlabelled
of course, she sniffs. And cabbage whites? As if.
Dropped blocks for disorder, for curt treatment
the demiurge despoiled. Across the water, Debussy,
high definition porn & the diplomat's own smooth language
stroking all matters of pasture and selvage up to his own
sweet ends, no matter what the ends themselves
Delft animals, styles, fat corn to be pushed to the heel.
He might turn for the time to respect what is gathered: prime
miracles just numbers to be signed. Wrapped in gauze. Sealed
with a print. Stored for faith. Those tiny blue hooves
and tiny flowers. A prospect, a roof, and above, in clouds,
a miniature graze of indigo, ghost against the craze. Some
human error, some mimic tacked the receded features.
And polity, and the white parsimony it calls to mind. Later,
in clocks and patches, with roundels glued to the eye,
her blocks are minded to sing. Blisters. Forks. The corkscrew
faltering fall of pipits through air. And seeds are never
never, and the lures all remain: tiny, panicky gods,
covering their eyes while the fire escape burns.
I love you, parsimony, he cries,
throwing his arms wide

MIR

A fragment of paint, a carrying bolt
DERA had missed & the threat of rain
so prolonged that the dictation of miracles
was abandoned. These simplicities were useless to me.
though war was all there was to see; scat and hesitancy

the brilliance of a star, the sapphire's boxed array
the cobra beside the stone & all I saw
was the nought on the scales as the snake moved, not the crowds
nor the pigeon-egg diamond in the hilt of the vizier's armory
the lock of hair or the hand of bronze to kiss

only egrets, white through lignite and soft hydrocarbons
and each wing a scant line of cartilage broken into ribs
of light and shade. Every time the line progressed like silk
iron deer, tin diamond and blue sky over Topkapi
dismembering the fortuity of travel one stop and bracketing

this was the world as it existed for our amusement
satisfactions snipped from empirical brochures entire
Ginza, Hadramaut, Nazca in six by four, milled, screened
& bleached to cuttle-ink by months of sun and wind
there are twelve, including the pyramids,

the tower in Paris, the bowed milk of the Opera
House and the silver heaped about Bilbao
the thin crenellations of a wall about hills
and the lights of a city west of an inland sea.
No distinction is offered; these are tokens only.

Your farewell is only the cuttings looking at me
their derivation is both more than ours and lessening;
the marketable and the promise of these cities both.
Either could be plain; though bells are ringing, it is only
the changes they are practising, fringes meshing into an airy

October night. And overhead a point of light travelling away
from the setting sun, the falling station describing its sere arc
before it passes behind clouds and enters the shadow of the world.

Jack

where diviners are hauling water is a bump of turf
and a cloud caul low over old heather scurf, sleep.
Dodder wrapt and a mimic fit to klepe greenshank
cotton blowing eastward, a match-mime set in as ore
shoulders sunk, heavy as rain and thistlewool merlin
blinking at the roll of weather. New roles settle, ticking
gently at the yaw singing out an arc overland

a whisper of suspicious music like the stars are dead
and the real fact of succession is dripped over rock in a sincere bid
to stay. But there is no stay. There is ice at the steady damage
patterned ground and small burrows where air laps and falls
an emergency environment at the instant where the jack comes
parabellum of delicacy and mores

violent spoils as manuscript through drier air
manifest as movement

the video slips & marshalled antics fade

Earth Station

Caught the push for describing the personal and segregated it.
Remarked on it as interest in power for memory's sake, stepping out
each step discarding metaphorical intent, each print filling with water
where laminates of carbon threw steep bubbles of air & sense

to an intermediate, grave position cowled by a stack of cumulus
white phragmites extending thirty miles out to the far ridge
whose new dishes proliferate on unlikely chalk, child of bullet time
wading through new sedge, watching the commsat's ink-point above

constructing a beautiful personal cosmology from the inclination
of space and communicative links, where the dishes' upturned curves
represent immortality and such, so that nights long they could be watched
as the band of microwave radiation pushed up through low cloud

as ravens slope-soaring on the updraught from the dish's face some nights
in tears, drawing with greasy pen on the glass new lines between the ridge
and the point of light high above, then moving back and thinking less;
Kent sodium-dark to the east, and the sky rising to night in the west

attenuating to empyreal black and its soft dust, description:
the day breaking below vision, the arc of light
dishes half-buried in fog and the sky raising itself at dawn
static carbon on the generator exhausts & the feedlines coming in

speech in wires he laughed and returned the compliment
because they were speaking for him, as they always had done

PATRICK McGUINNESS

Patrick McGuinness was born in Tunisia in 1968 of Belgian and Anglo-Irish parents and was brought up in Belgium, France, Iran, Venezuela and Romania. His collections are *The Canals of Mars* (2004) and *Jilted City* (2010), both from Carcanet, and a pamphlet, *19th Century Blues* (2007). He won an Eric Gregory Award in 1998, *Poetry*'s Levinson Prize in 2003 and the Poetry Business Prize in 2006. He lives in Caernarfon, North Wales, and works in Oxford where he is a Fellow of St Anne's College and Professor of French and Comparative Literature. He has written academic books, a novel, and edited the works of T.E. Hulme and the modernist poet Lynette Roberts. His translation of Mallarmé's *For Anatole's Tomb* appeared in 2003 and was a Poetry Book Society Recommended Translation. *The Canals of Mars* had been translated into Italian and Czech and a *Selected Poems* for the North American readership appears in 2011 from Véhicule Press in Montreal.

McGuinness's poetry 'explores transition and translation, the afterlife of absences'. He is a careful poet, influenced by travel and he guilefully matches ideas of place with metaphysical conceits.

Heroes

> *I think the sun, the moon*
> *and some of the stars are*
> *kept on their tracks*
> *by this Person's equilibrium*
>> Lil, in Ed Dorn's *Gunslinger*

That 'some' – only some – that measure in all
things, even when the praise outsoars the praised
but is never good enough, still falls
short though it takes in a world, entire skies

to give the airy Slinger ballast
and close his image in her words. Un-
bridled praise, but she holds back: no limits,
only frontiers for this superhuman

cowboy, slender in the sunlight of her eye.
Red suns burn to white. As she sees him leave,
saddling is talking horse, she thinks he'll fly
to join the things she can compare him with.

Dust

Form and form-giver, light and light-bearer,

mistaken for air, for light by the eye,

flies wingless, lighter than what it bears

Stored in the eye, makes sight substance,

guides the pen, the brush, thickens dimensions;

shorelines hinge on it, feathers aspire to it

form and form-giver, translates the sun

a bauble turns it and turns in it

leaves coil in it, shine like coins in it

disappears and is lighter than disappearance

The Age of the Empty Chair

In Monet's *The Beach at Trouville*, it is week one of the Franco-Prussian
        war.
The chair lodges in the sand between two women. One reads, the other

points her face at the emptying beach. The chair belongs to no one,
it is a found chair, a *trouvaille*, and there is never one chair too many

but one sitter too few. A flag rigid on its pole indicates
a swelling in the air, or something stronger, and the rent waves,

delicate turmoils of spume and lace, are distant cousins of the revolution
bound into the ebb and flow it breaks free of, then breaks back into.

There is sand in the paint; the place is mixed into its making
and even the brushstrokes replicate the water's peaks as they take

the light: roofs pell-mell across a city skyline, flashpoints in the sun.
The chair suggests all that can be suggested about change, but it
      remains

apart from it: the way a sail suggests the wind, the way a shell holds
a recording of the waves even as the waves turn around it.

Montreal

Un hiver dans un hiver... a winter within a winter.
The idea holds but the English lets the wordplay go:

a universe within a universe, a symmetry of
interleaving lives that, like the leaves themselves,

tells of precision married off to transience,
form that finds fulfilment in anonymity.

The snow starts soft and intimate as marrow,
climbs down winter's ladder, and finishes

as mud or mulch as tyres and gritters
mash it back to its beginnings.

It is as if something in ourselves had burst
into the air; an explosion of all our privacies.

Blue

Azur! Azur! Azur! Azur!
MALLARMÉ

(In memory of Malcolm Bowie)

Azure! Azure! Azure! Azure!... all that was before:
before we rode it in planes or used it to park satellites,
or as ethereal landfill for our emissions. All the best skies

these days are polluted: jet fuel-refracted intricacies
of dead air and carbon-dazzle, cyanose confetti
that we mistake for light as we mistake mirrors

for what they show us of ourselves. But the thought
of all that emptiness, its promise of fresh starts, persists...
and though aftermaths look much the same

we never think of them as happening in the sky.
We never think of them as *starting* in the sky:
only beginnings are possible in such virgin air,

we think, harvesting new breath from frictionless
blue fields, those oxygen plantations with their Boeing
ploughlines and their furrows of weightless tilth.

But each square of it is Heathrow or JFK, tailbacks
of landing lights, control-tower static, log-jams of conditioned
air and shredded cumulus. First breath, first light: the original

repetitions, and the sun all the more intricate in its dying back
for the furnace it was at the beginning. And it's beginnings
that we dream of as we observe the blue, the great illusion

that every day it starts again from zero, that perfect world-
shaped formula for all or nothing: *O*

KONA MACPHEE

Kona Macphee was born in London in 1969 and grew up in Australia, where she worked in a range of occupations including composer, violinist and motorcycle mechanic. Eventually she took up robotics and computer science, which brought her to Cambridge as a graduate student in 1995. She now lives in the town of Crieff in Scotland. She received an Eric Gregory Award for her poetry in 1998. Her first collection, *Tails*, was published by Bloodaxe in 2004, and her second collection, *Perfect Blue*, in 2010.

Macphee brings a scientist's brain and eye to poetry. A varied poet, strong rhythm is her most consistent strategy, whether in her sometimes song-like formal pieces, or in the repetitive structures of cadenced verse. She is especially good at capturing the atmospheres (sometimes tranquil, sometimes malicious), as opposed to the physicality, of places. Her shorter poems employ an enviable and delicate concision.

Melbourne, evening, summertime –

the flies settling, passing the torch
of insect purpose to moths, mosquitoes
(the night-shift's proletariat); the sun
now tucking in until the morning, furling
the eucalpyt linen of clean blue ranges
to its chin; the murmured benedicite
of late sea breezes to the exorcised heat;

and we, alone on lawns, or jointly laid
in the mitred corners of urban parks,
curled in deckchairs, swingchairs, armchairs,
rocked on bayside boats, or dieselling home
on end-of-workday tractors as the mendicant sky
sums up its last small change of sun,

we find our warmth in evening's cool,
see drawn like sweat our gentlest selves,
are loosed to float on the slow emotions
stirred by twilight and the rightness of things.

Shrew

the tapered nose, an otoscope for a wheatsheaf's ear

lips that don't meet over tiny scimitar teeth

caviar eye-dots, sunk like the knots where buttons were

four clawed feet, screwed into hooks that catch air

fur in tandem streaks of sleek and spiked cat-spit

a splut of puce intestine, looking glued on, no blood

the fine fuse of the tail, that won't be re-lit

Pheasant and astronomers
(for GTR)

Burnished, finicky, picking his headbob way
across the asphalt path, into the leafy scrub
behind the twelve-pane window of our office,

we can't not watch his colours in the sunlight.
Our measures and projections fall aside
as coarsest calculus to his most perfect curve;

so we observe.
                    Can such a day-star brave
the midnight sky whose glaring spectral eyes
seethe down the invert shrinkage of a telescope,

or does he sleep all clouded in the hedgerows'
straight-line rays of green restraint to roads
that sling his slow kin cockeyed in the gutter?

On foot and unconcerned, he patters out of view,
out of our world again; the sunlit room
falls just a lumen dimmer with his passing.

Terminus

A raven's restless mechanism
ticks on the signal box. Below,
midday sinuates the sheets of air
that work their quavering mesmerism,
dazing the land to stillness. Here
beside the fenceline's silted flow,

wheatstalks perpendict the lines
whose rusting railtops flash quick bronze
with flicking skinks, the sleepers, stones,
slowly weathering beneath them. Signs
have lost their lettering, blank as bones.
A peppercorn tree, some kurrajongs,

slip their roots beneath the rails
and scatter leaves and shadows. Boles
that brace the sky-flecked roof are scored
with tracks of borers, spiralled trails
that dwindle, disappear, record
a distant passage. Quick patrols

of ants dissect a fallen moth,
freighting it piecewise down the run
of pheromones that won't outlast
their usefulness. Green overgrowth
lies heavily, like something cast
to drip and dry in midday sun.

Perspective's engine hauls the eyes
along the single-gauge, the groove
of jumbling rocks, which slant toward
a station hidden past the sliced
horizon. Here, no train to board.
The hot air shimmers. Nothing moves.

Waltz

He grips the gather of her waist
and pours her like a ewer into dance.
The blacklist swells of bust and bustle
brim with white-laced imminence –

her body, known by sortilege
alone, its volumes undisclosed,
tonight approximately gauged
through darkness and their civil sleeping-clothes.

PETER MANSON

Peter Manson lives in Glasgow, where he was born in 1969. His books include *For the Good of Liars* (Barque Press, 2006) and *Between Cup and Lip* (Miami University Press, 2008). A prose book, *Adjunct: an Undigest*, was published by Edinburgh Review in 2005. He studied English at Glasgow University and was the Judith E. Wilson Visiting Fellow in Poetry at Girton College, Cambridge in 2005-06. He has worked as a proof-reader and editor and more recently as a Support Officer for the Land Register in Glasgow. For a number of years, he co-edited the experimental/ modernist poetry magazine *Object Permanence*, an imprint revived as a pamphlet publisher in 2001. He published a booklet of adaptations from the poems of the 19th-century French poet Stéphane Mallarmé and is working on a complete, annotated translation of Mallarmé's *Poésies*.

Manson's work is concerned with ambiguity and fluidity of language, whether everyday speech or philosophical dialogue. He is interested in the possibilities of 'found language' and has commented that 'Poetry is what happens when a reader can no longer refer a piece of language back to a speaker to unpack its ambiguities.'

Hymn to Light

Rock away   hold all
at dimpled bay
rose fashioned of textile block, shining through.
The sun has set firm, carrying light westward
to benefit unseen eyes. Ears stop deaf to allusion.
My heart scares itself to a knock on the throat.

In April, after the clocks go forward
light vies with inner blankness to project
the rice white arc rising careless of impact
on lives climbed into for sanctuary.

I still enter the forest, innocent of roadkill,
trace handwritten entries in the log for warmth:

they will no more touch back than the white wrist
hiding the poem conduct me back to silence.

Light slows to walking speed in a gel
the upturned life dilates on and reverts.
Desire is comic, nothing like this blind-spot:
the shadow cast by a star, of the sun, on me.

In Vitro
(after Mallarmé)

Exploded from the vent
of ephemeral glassware
rather than garlanding its bitter vigil
the neck breaks off, uncut.

I know well two mouths never drank –
not my mother's, no lover of hers –
never with this Chimera,
me, sylph of the Petri dish!

A decanter that's tasted no wine
but long widowhood
grudges with dying breath

– o funereal kiss! –
that the dark
should spawn roses.

Poem

At the end of fear, a halter in furnished gaps
synthesis of matter and flailing
gives over to you an axiom from which to bend.
Solid though half the achievement is, enter other doubt
hardening over the eyes' pencilled-in benison
to undo all known good at one belting pulse

and pack the encultured face off to memory camp.
Reversing back out of what ignorance took for a short-cut
but drew out nine years to a hundred, rejected frame by frame,
the incline so steep at the cusp that the back-seat driver spilled
his surplus on retro cobbles in the Merchant City,
the vehicle, a subject particle
going itself forth, allied with lost potential,
plutonic drag trashed by looking with contacts in
to body gone, gives up the smashed-up leer,
an item in the cold crowd God does not compute.

Four Darks in Red

The pain is near celibate in the bridal tune
our new, wild process rotting in the wrong
case.
            I stood it though, and thought
not that I died then in the smell of bonus
brought on as violent asthma in a burning month
to stammer clear of, canted.
                            Singular as mud
the flyspeck paints a generation out.

A learned support to the left breast speak hardly
at all now, sing.
                    Lift the maquette up, broken
to the blue yolk-bound solution
of a deep-rooted sleep problem.

In ear the events bid high in a run on hollow gold
brought forward along the jaw
by the headlamp negating contrast
to pulverise effort headstrong in the fur
(fit draped in cinnabar
moth that you choke on gladly)

and only for so long
let this name come to the fore
as a paradigm's endgame.

Familiars

(for Maggie Graham)

in the nowhere unrecognised as such at the top right
the brain does not patch over, not the blind spot
no cat ever leaped out of, bordered by what you know
or that second learned at the centre of night vision

is a holding cell where everything permitted and more
bleeds, called by the pulse at the scar boundary
names you would wish on no one. Eskimos
build in the ischaemic loss, where it is warmer

out than in. Give them that, Greenland
looks big on a map. Literally nothing doing
where once what you see gently gave out
a shock in itself to halt speech and flash

the return of halting on all possible moves.
Your mother wouldn't teach you to knit
but someone did, part of the head an amulet
too keen to wait to be written, barely

a kitten on the keys, it is trying to help.
We bury the dead or else would extend empathy
without prejudice to the inanimate.
Shot down in giving up, your ghost

does just what ghosts do, won't be told
you didn't die. Knit it a woollen hat.
It blocks a high road into the beloved
who would be stateless, but for it.

D.S. MARRIOTT

D.S. Marriott was born in Nottingham in 1963 and grew up in Gedling. He is a professor in the History of Consciousness at the University of California, Santa Cruz, where he now lives. His first collection, *Incognegro* (Salt Publishing), appeared in 2006, and his second collection, *Hoodoo Voodoo*, came out from Shearsman in 2008. He has published two critical books, *On Black Men* (Columbia, 2000) and *Haunted Life* (Rutgers University Press, 2007). He is currently at work on his third poetry manuscript, *The Bloods*. Although Marriott's full collections appeared fairly recently, he published a number of smaller publications in his 20s and 30s and *Incognegro* contains both new and earlier work (sometimes heavily revised). This earlier work displayed the influence of the Cambridge school of poetry, though his work is now markedly varied in style, though driven by a dense but taut lyricism. Although not the focus of his earlier work, the subject of race has become central to both his poetic and critical writing in the last decade. The crossovers and divides between classical and popular culture are another apparent interest.

The Day Ena Died

The words were often calibrated to hurt
all casings removed –
the eyes crimping – lightless –
at ease only when the wreckage burned.

The voice – corrugated, galvanised –
hard in its bleak certainty,
unhurried in its cobbled seething;
so thick dactyls could clog-hop on it

or haul hammers to the seams.
Even from this distance, I recall:
losing my grease-smeared grip
as the news reached me at the sink,

the mug breaking like the wrecked walls
of that final dismal script,
the hole too big to be fitted or shaped,
as they hammered in the bolt, tolled the change.

Under the wreckage the immortal
grimace – how odd to believe it no
longer thickening or swathe? – and how Violet hated it:
the black hairnet shroud holding back the years.

Tap

A sick and tired-looking Bill 'Bojangles' Robinson dances lightly and quickly up the steps to the house. Shirley opens the door and invites him in. He sits down slowly, wearily, as if the act required great effort. She looks at him with a calm, almost malicious intensity, as indifferent to this show of weakness as to the bodily collapse it represents. Uncle Bo, her once, glorious edifice, no longer able to bear the load, as cameled now by her screen legend as a morning shadow by sunlight.

The room is unnaturally warm. The furniture and walls a uniform high pink. Shirley exits the room tap dancing only to return, a moment later, with a tray of drinks. She approaches Uncle Bo as if she were on a battlefield, dancing with all the grace and beauty given her, her ringlets flashing like a dying star, he the dark that surrounds it. He sits mute, mesmerised, with a measured smile, like Oedipus searching for his eyes in Gaza.

The colours are of fall,
the airports unvaried after the hotel lobbies & cafeterias,
and the jim crow cars I missed
        running barefoot in the dark,
    taking part of me away
as I led the line
        tapping quick steps on a table.

Footprints sparkle in the darkness.
The air thick with corn liquor,
the putrid mouths holler.
I passed through the swamp of white faces and burnt cork

so footloose on the slats & hinges,
I slip-slid through the mud giddy, unhinged.
            It was a jig without a history.

Something deeper than skin
the whites sitting doubled over,
            their hands slapping their knees,
or coiling their arms into rope as my legs ran amok;
their blacked-up faces
    in shock as if I were a smear in the pigment,
or a limp trying to disguise itself in the firm thrusts.

Then came Shirley,
    rehearsing the shooting
        demanding the flash and bursts
            through the backstage era,
    onto the freeways riding through the night...

She covered my loins with dimples and laughter –
I couldn't get enough of the towns, cities, and theatres
or this rote version of myself clumsy, unable to stand.
                No touching, no danger. But even then,
    when we danced on unshattered legs,
                I felt a noose closing:
the weight of the past tap tapping on my crippled legs.

My dances were syllabaries:
hard-won movements whipping the air,
loose-limbed flings towards freedom,
        jigs blazing in the blood
    along the hips, knees, ankles, shoulders, and elbows, –
even when I played the darky I was never blackened.

Now when my soul trembles
under the moon
in the light of my nighttime mind,
in the blur of form and memory,
nothing moves my body but gravity –
I mean, I arrive limping, my heart stumbles,
like a child who can't walk yet,
ready to carry all the weight of those years,
    about to leap, headlong, onto the stage,
        and stamp this arrhythmia out of my body...

239

Over the Black Mountains

The shore of the lake comes first,
bringing the dark closer to the roof of the valley.
The appalled blood
of the landscape almost a sickness inside her.
The frozen surface, ice-braided,
clear like her memory of winter,
summoning demons through the wind-swept hills,
loading trucks from another era in frosted fields,
thinning her longing down to a glint on the railings.
The graveyards of plague,
and the sorrows of children buried waistdeep in the sod,
and the dead, silting caves and reedbeds,
strewn amid the cairns, poured down the gullies' throat.

There was the gossip of the villagers,
appalled by the homes abandoned to the stranded eyes of sheep,
and fog so thick rain could only make it porous
as clouds spat out their disgust on the mountains.
If only she could take everything back,
reverse the daily roadkills underfoot,
the flesh astounded by the bones' collapse,
by the ease with which it is mastered. Fragile; struck.
It is not the cold and silence hard like flint,
nor the loneliness black as pitch,
but the creeping decay that shrives her,
of lumbering toward a dark without will, unaware.

The shore of the lake comes first,
bringing gamesmen, tourists, keepers, and peasants.
Sunset hid its modesty
behind a few curtains of red cloud
as she drives past imagining the night's wolf eye
and the flash of knives in the forest.
The streets are filled with sadness.
The look on her face naked, alone
knowing this is the ship she steers,
as darkness spreads on the waves of her devotion.
Lost, the moon gaunt in the windscreen,
and no effusive wish to go home
and reengage the wars from her lack of attrition.

The shore of the lake comes first,
but her skin was not a road for children
and her love turned out for the pharmacies
whenever her legs failed to reach the ground.
Only when god was near and the dogs barked,
did she remember the deeds but there was no one near to inherit
        them.

SAM MEEKINGS

Sam Meekings was born in 1981 and grew up on the South coast of England before studying at Oxford and Edinburgh universities. He has spent a number of years living in various parts of China, working as a teacher and editor, and is currently employed by Oxford University Press in Shanghai. His debut collection of poetry, *The Bestiary*, was published by Polygon in 2008, while his novel based on Chinese history and folklore, *Under Fishbone Clouds*, appeared from Birlinn in 2009.

Meekings' poems often hinge upon overlooked points of human interaction with the natural world and the feeling of being lost or out of place in the present. The work in his first collection is mostly comprised of responses to the natural environment, often informed by an interest in historical records. The poems are generally short, clear lyrics with brief, definitive titles. His forthcoming second collection focuses on his time and experiences in China, with particular emphasis on displacement and mass migration.

Describing Angels to the Blind

Acronychal mosquitoes lolloping
like strange machines patented from erotic daydreams.
They whistle in B flat, rattling the cutlery;
their breath is fingers in the plug socket.

Their wings are lopsided like dislocated shoulder blades
or the feel of another tongue sucked into your mouth.
They are the things that as a child you were not allowed to touch;
their voices table-salt on paper–cuts.

They carry the reek of moths sautéed in the lampshade,
of dredged-up reservoirs and spoiled meat;
their faces are the pumice stone you take to your feet.

Their language is a live catfish wriggling through your hands
or a tic or twitch you can't control,
their half-human faces a fit of giggles at a funeral.

Bees

King Ethelbert of Kent met the missionaries
in the open air, fearing their incantations
would raise bones from his whispering fields.

Instead their honey breath drew up stones
into his fledgling cities, like bees breaking ranks
around a perfect slab of dribbling comb.

Men watched them weave a hive of ghosts
from the charred tang of thick shadows.
Pale palms and bleach-rim haloes poured

from the stained-glass, stretching the light
past eyes staring up, amazed at the vast sky
being compiled, brick by brick above them.

Migration

Finger-pinched scales mark the pale seams of dumplings
steaming in bamboo baskets or between chopsticks,
feeding men wearing dusty suits and dusty skin.
They debate cranes, beer, steel, bricks and next week's shifts.

They will not talk of home – fields where shadows bite,
where fish sing, where their wages travel by post.
They will not talk of pasts or provinces or wives.
This is what it means to live your life as a ghost.

The hardest work is forgetting – fighting free
from the tug and current, the pull of memory.

Work that might be torn apart without warning
by a single dumpling – one bite of the dough
is like firecrackers on Spring Festival morning,
filling mouths full of sparks, and heads full of home.

Depth

It seems like days before his eyes adjust
to the aubergine glow of the hugging dark,
feeling as though he is floating in phlegm:
bent knees pressed up to his twisted neck
in the roaring accordion of the whale's gut.

Jonah's world is composed of textures,
of shudders and damp echoes
tugging through his cold, aching body
and more fish frantically flapping in
every time the whale sings or swallows.

This is the depth to which we test ourselves,
he repeats. Soon his own wild shouts
join the booming chamber music.
His talking to God is similar to the tuning
of crackly CBs, late into lonely nights,

when solitary figures send cautious words
into the clumsy deep of rolling sound
and listen for something to return;
tentative voices testing the water,
each one prisoner of hearts and tongues.

SINÉAD MORRISSEY

Sinéad Morrissey was born in 1972 in Portadown, Co. Armagh, Northern Ireland. She has published four collections with Carcanet: *There Was Fire in Vancouver* (1996), *Between Here and There* (2002), *The State of the Prisons* (2005) and *Through the Square Window* (2009), the last two both shortlisted for the T.S. Eliot Prize. She was the 2002 Poetry International Writer in Residence at the Royal Festival Hall. Having lived and worked in Japan and New Zealand, she now lives in Northern Ireland where she is currently Writer in Residence at Queen's University, Belfast. She was selected by the British Council to take part in the Writers' Train Project in China in 2003. In 2007 she was awarded a Lannan Literary Fellowship and in 2008 she won the National Poetry Competition. A distinctive reader, who recites her poems by heart, Morrissey is a questing poet of place and interpersonal struggle. Her main themes include individual identity and foreign landscape. She is fond of scrutinising totemic objects in her poems and an interest in the supernatural adds poignancy to her work.

from China

5

Evening. Beijing. And farewell to Mao's mausoleum
through the glass, ablaze in the nerves of the Square of Heaven
like everlasting Christmas. The bus forces us on:
another station, another train, another city, another season.
Advertising flickers in the waiting room. That night I dive like a
       child –
borne aloft by the train's engine, or like one born again in its mild
motion, the shunt and click of the carriages over the sidings
the soporific tenderness of a language I do not recognise –
and re-surface at nine, an hour beyond breakfast time.
The mine wheels, factories, fish farms, and allotments
battling for space between slack-blackened tenements
have receded now into the north. Here the sky is unfolding the blue
cloth of itself on a new country, or on a country which never grew

old to begin with. Spinach, pak choi, cabbage greens, lettuce,
geese sunning themselves among shiny brown cowls of the lotus
and an echo-less emptiness, a sense of perspective too wide
and too high for the eye to take in. Two crows collide
in a rice field, then are flung backwards out of their war
as the train pushes on. We loiter like Oliver in the dining car.
Brunch comes as simmering bowls of noodles, under a film
of oil, and we sit watching the landscape unfurl like a newsreel
into history. By noon, foothills are banking to the south.
By two, we're approaching a network of tunnels blasted out
of the Xi'an Qin Mountains. Blackness falls clean as a guillotine
on the children in pairs by the trackside, and then again
on the man and his son who will walk all afternoon into evening
before they are home. We enter Sichuan without rupturing
any visible line of division, though dinner at five is brimming with chillies:
dried and diced and fried with the seeds inside, while the extraordinary
Sichuan pepper balloons into flavour under our tongues. And all along
darkness is gathering itself in. I see a boy and a woman
lit up by the flare of a crop fire, but can no longer believe in them.
Windows have turned into mirrors the length of the train.
Hours pass, and there is only my white face, strained
in its hopelessness, my failure to catch the day in my hands like a fish
and have it always. The train descends from the soil terraces.
Electricity switches the world back on: town after coal-dusted town
streams by in the rain, revealing its backdoor self, its backyard frown,
until all converge in a dayglo glare at the end of the line and we merge
with our destination. We have been dropped to the bottom of somewhere
blurred and industrial, where the yellow of the Yangtze meets the green
of its tributary, the city with a name like the din of a smithy: Chongqing.

Shadows in Siberia According to Kapuściński

Are upright –
cast not by sunlight but by frozen breath:

we breathe
and are enveloped in an outline

and when we pass,
this outline stays suspended, not tethered

to our ankles
as our sun-shadows are. A boy was here –

fantastically dressed
against the arctic frost like an heirloom glass

in bubblewrap –
he has disappeared into the portico

of himself. Not even Alice,
with her knack for finding weaknesses

in the shellac
of this world, left so deft a calling card.

'Love, the nightwatch...'

Love, the nightwatch, gloved and gowned, attended.
Your father held my hand. His hands grew bruised
and for days afterwards wore a green and purple coverlet

when he held you to the light, held your delicate, dented
head, thumbed-in like a water font. They used
stopwatches, clipcharts, the distant hoofbeats of a heart

(divined, it seemed, by radio, so your call fell interwined
with taxicabs, police reports, the weather blowing showery
from the north) and a beautiful fine white cane,

carved into a fish hook. I was a haystack the children climbed
and ruined, collapsing almost imperceptibly
at first, then caving in spectacularly as you stuttered and came

– crook-shouldered, blue, believable, beyond me –
in a thunder of blood, in a flood-plain of intimate stains.

On Waitakere Dam

(for Charles Brown)

You wanted to up-end the boat
and set it on the lake we lived by
because no one would know,
It was lavish with silverfish and looked
defeated, humped on its secret
like a hand. There was nowhere to go to

but the magnet of the middle lake
where a vapour sat wide as Australia –
as sovereign, as separate, as intimate
with daylight, as ignorant
of clocks and raincoats and boats.
It threw a soft, unwatchable shimmer

we would not be human in.
You dismantled a sky
as you tipped the boat over,
the nest of a possum was robbed.
The hull settled outside-in
as you inverted the universe.

We bobbed in the reeds.
The trees lay down their crowns
beneath us, an underwater canvas
of spectacular women. Above us
the crowds of their branches were cold.
Black swans were nesting in the nesting place,

trees reared to the rim of vision –
we slid on to the centre. At night,
with no lights for miles, the lake
would glitter with the Southern Cross.
It smiled at us
with a million silver teeth.

We'd heard it roar with rain
and watched it coughing eels
over the dam's brim,
too water-sore to keep them any longer.
They fell flinching themselves
into s's or n's.

And now we sat stilled in a boat
in the centre, under the lake's shroud,
and the listening
was for the car of the caretaker –
weaving down from the Nihotipu Dam
with Handel or Bach on the radio.

DALJIT NAGRA

Born in London and raised there and in Sheffield, **Daljit Nagra** comes from a Sikh Punjabi background and currently lives in North West London where he works in a secondary school. His first collection *Look We Have Coming to Dover!* was published by Faber in 2008 and went on to win the Forward Prize for Best First Collection and *South Bank Show* Decibel Award. It was nominated for the Costa Poetry Award and the *Guardian* First Book Award. The title-poem had won the Forward Prize for Best Individual Poem in 2004. His second collection, *Tippoo Sultan's Incredible White-Man Eating Tiger-Toy Machine!!!*, is due from Faber in 2011.

Nagra's poems reflect his background both in their content and their innovative blend of Punjabi and English. He explores the English tradition from an Indian migrant's perspective so that conventional forms and uses of language are suited to a modern sensibility. The work represents multiple perspectives on key issues to modern Indians living in Britain: caste and class, the interactions between first and second generation migrants. His poems are mostly divided between character monologues and more rigid narratives with complex syntax.

Look We Have Coming to Dover!

> *So various, so beautiful, so new...*
> MATTHEW ARNOLD, 'Dover Beach'

Stowed in the sea to invade
the alfresco lash of a diesel-breeze
ratcheting speed into the tide, brunt with
gobfuls of surf phlegmed by cushy come-and-go
tourists prow'd on the cruisers, lording the ministered waves.

Seagull and shoal life
vexing their blarnies upon our huddled
camouflage past the vast crumble of scummed
cliffs, scramming on mulch as thunder unbladders
yobbish rain and wind on our escape hutched in a Bedford van.

Seasons or years we reap
inland, unclocked by the national eye
or stabs in the back, teemed for breathing
sweeps of grass through the whistling asthma of parks,
burdened, ennobled – poling sparks across pylon and pylon.

Swarms of us, grafting in
the black within shot of the moon's
spotlight, banking on the miracle of sun:
span its rainbow, passport us to life. Only then
can it be human to hoick ourselves, bare-faced for the clear.

Imagine my love and I,
our sundry others, Blair'd in the cash
of our beeswax'd cars, our crash clothes, free,
we raise our charged glasses over unparasol'd tables
East, babbling our lingoes, flecked by the chalk of Britannia!

This Be the Pukka Verse

Ah the Raj! Our mother-incarnate Victoria
Imperatrix rules the sceptred sphere as she oversees
legions of maiden 'fishing fleets' breaking wave
after wave for that 'heaven-born' Etonian. Smoke
from cheroots, fetes on lawns, dances by moonlight
at Alice in Wonderland no the Viceroy the Viceroy's ball!
Lock, stock and bobbing along on palanquins to gothic
verandahs where dawn Himalayas through Poobong-mist,
the topi-and-khaki shikar, Tally ho! with swagger-sticks
for boars in dead-leaf hush, by Amritsar a bang!bang!
bagging the flamiest tiger! Jackals, panthers,
leopards, pig-sticking, Kipling, Tatler, Tollygunge,
High Jinks and howdahs for mansion whacking banks,
mock-paddocks with sheep and deer, and the basso of evensong,
poppy-pods, housey housey and hammocks under the Milky Way...
Tromping home trumps – here come the cummerbund sahibs
tipsy with stiff upper lips for burra pegs of brandy pawnee,
pink gin and the Jaldi punkawallaaahhhh! on six-meal

days with tiffin and bobotie pie and peacocks
and humps and tongue and the croquet and polo and yaboos,
Ootacamund, and the twirling of sabre-curved
mustachios for octoroons panting in gunna-green fields
and ayahs akimbo and breathless zenanas behind
bazaars where the nautch and the sun never sets when mango's
the bride-bed of lingam-light in a jolly good land overflowing
with silk and spice and all the gems of the earth!
Er darling, it's not quiiite the koh-i-noor but would you...
(on a train that's steaming and hooting on time through a tunnel)
Ooo darling a diamond! You make me feel so alive.

University

On the settling of birds, this man blesses

                                                    his daughter.

She'll split fast for Paddington, then slide

                                                    east
which may as well be the black beyond

                                                    of Calcutta.

The low long curving train opening its

                                                    mouth
gulps from his hands her bags to a far-side

                                                    seat.
He gawps from his thin-rivered, working

                                                    town.

The train roars, the tracks beyond humped

                                                    with light.
The rucksack'd man with whom her eyes

                                                    meet...
Five birds pluck their wings off the train

                                                    and fly.

Our Town with the Whole of India!

Our town in England with the whole of India sundering
out of its temples, mandirs and mosques for the customised
streets. Our parade, clad in cloak-orange with banners
and tridents, chanting from station to station for Vasaikhi
over Easter. Our full moon madness for Eidh with free
pavement tandooris and legless dancing to boostered
cars. Our Guy Fawkes' Diwali – a kingdom of rockets
for the Odysseus-trials of Rama who arrowed the jungle
foe to re-palace the Penelope-faith of his Sita.

Our Sunrise Radio with its lip sync of Bollywood lovers
pumping through the rows of emporium cubby holes
whilst bhangra beats slam where the hagglers roar
at the pulled-up back-of-the-lorry cut-price stalls.
Sitar shimmerings drip down the furbishly columned
gold store. Askance is the peaceful Pizza Hut...
A Somali cab joint, been there forever, with smiley
guitar licks where reggae played before Caribbeans
disappeared, where years before Teddy Boys jived.

Our cafés with the brickwork trays of saffron sweets,
brass woks frying flamingo-pink syrup-tunnelled
jalebis networking crustily into their familied-webs.
Reveries of incense scent the beefless counter where
bloodied men sling out skinned legs and breasts
into thin bags topped with the proof of giblets.
Stepped road displays – chock-full of ripe karela,
okra, aubergine – sunshined with mango, pineapple,
lychee. Factory walkers prayer-toss the river of

sponging swans with chapattis. A posse brightens
on park-shots of Bacardi – waxing for the bronze
eye-full of girls. The girls slim their skirts after college
blowing dreams into pink bubble gums at neck-
descending and tight-neck sari-mannequins. Their grannies
point for poled yards of silk for own-made styles.
The mother of the runaway daughter, in the marriage
bureau, weeps over the plush catalogues glossed
with tuxedo-boys from the whole of our India!

CAITRÍONA O'REILLY

Caitríona O'Reilly was born in Dublin in 1973. She took BA and PhD degrees in Archaeology and English at Trinity College, Dublin, and was awarded the Rooney Prize for Irish Literature for her debut poetry collection, *The Nowhere Birds* (Bloodaxe, 2001). She has also held the Harper-Wood Studentship from St John's College, Cambridge. Her second collection, *The Sea Cabinet*, followed in 2006 and was shortlisted for the *Irish Times* Poetry Now Award. Her poetry can also be found in *The Wake Forest Irish Poetry Series Vol.1*. She is a widely published critic, has written for BBC Radio 4 and has published some fiction and collaborated with artist Isabel Nolan. A contributing editor of the Irish poetry journal *Metre*, in 2008 she became editor of *Poetry Ireland Review*. Childhood and the sea are two recurring subjects in O'Reilly's rich and imagistic work. Praising her debut, Michael Longley noted that her 'work is seldom less than beautifully intricate, there is an amplitude here, an exuberance which jousts in a thrilling way with her particular refinements.'

Octopus

Mariners call them devil fish,
noting the eerie symmetry
of those nervy serpentine arms.
They resemble nothing so much
as a man's cowled head and shoulders.
Mostly they are sessile, and shy
as monsters, waiting in rock-clefts
or coral for a swimming meal.

They have long since abandoned their
skulls to the depths, and go naked
in this soft element, made of
a brain-sac and elephant eye.
The tenderness of their huge heads
makes them tremble at the shameful
intimacy of the killing
those ropes of sticky muscle do.

Females festoon their cavern roofs
with garlands of ripening eggs
and stay to tickle them and die.
Their reproductive holocaust
leaves them pallid and empty. Shoals
of shad and krill, like sheet lightning,
and the ravenous angelfish
consume their flesh before they die.

Calculus

Here is the letter I wanted to write, the one
that shows me succumbing to the light's blandishments

like a Vermeer housewife, my silk skirts swollen
as mariposa tulips, my complexion milky.

I collect fine words the way others collect birds' eggs:
for kestrels' I have *roseapple*; for wrens' *pearlwort*.

Were it not that my natural disposition is hurried,
you'd have me convinced the most beautiful word in the language

is *haemostasis*, which means the stopping of clocks,
the scientific observation of what ticks on in an interval

during which I am detained by shadows, those details
(again) you'd have me accrue: the copper moth's clownish flight

in my yard, how the sweet pea tethers itself to those
scalene strings I've pinned to the wall. Each day at noon

I drive another nail in to mark the day's high-water moment,
the sun's clumsy arabesque in that makeshift analemma

I've sketched on the floor: your regard's incalculable angle.

The Lure

(FROM A Quartet for the Falcon)

Snared in a mode of seeing,
the raptor's eyes unseel again.

Not an outline scarfing the blue wind
but several worlds unscrolling:

the chemical plant's logical conduits
glitter like the keys of a flute

while brown earth casts up
bones of its lost alluvial people:

shards of Delft in a Dutch landscape.
Abandoned churches ride the horizon

like high ships. She is caught in the rigging –
such details as flowers in dark grass,

calligraphic wings imped by a scribe
to *fiat lux*, or mantling their Marian prey.

Over a bleached Segovian plain the eye
seeks its eagle like the sky's pupil.

Aguila, describing a brutal circle.
Slow clouds tumble from the cooling stacks.

Anchor, tear-drop and cut diamond –
now her sentimental silhouette descends

to a swung horseshoe bound in leather.
It is the World, the Flesh, the Devil.

Pandora's Box

I might lift the eaves again
and startle a small room still lit from within
and finger the traces I left there.

The considerations of days
lurk behind porous walls.
They cling there like stains.

Carpets soaked in the seepage of dreams,
flakes of skin
piled on surfaces as thick as dust.

There's a head-shape in the pillow
like a big fingerprint.
Memories flutter up like insects –

small shrieks, minor crimes inside
an inked-up window-pane
with clotted stars,

and now, outside the shut box,
this black beach with an ocean on it
breathing in waves,

tiered like plate glass,
and the whole world at night-time
a wide sea full of starfish waiting to be caught.

ALICE OSWALD

Alice Oswald was born in 1966 and now lives in Dartington, Devon. She trained as a classicist and has worked as a gardener. Her first collection of poetry, *The Thing in the Gap-stone Stile* (OUP, 1996), won the Forward Prize for Best First Collection and was shortlisted for the T.S. Eliot Prize, an award she subsequently won with *Dart* (Faber & Faber, 2002), a book-length poem which combines verse and prose and tells the story of the River Dart in Devon. *Woods etc.* was published by Faber in 2005 and was shortlisted for the Forward Prize and the T.S. Eliot Prize. In 2007, her poem 'Dunt' won the Forward Prize for Best Single Poem. Her most recent publications from Faber are *Weeds and Wild Flowers*, illustrated by Jessica Greenman (2009), and *A Sleepwalk on the Severn* (2009), a poetic drama for several voices.

Predominantly a nature poet, Oswald's two miscellaneous collections have been augmented by a number of other projects. The modes of writing most associated with her work – the formal, the dramatic monologue, the pastoral – veil a wider range of styles, for Oswald can also be quirky or intriguingly spare in her writing.

Field

Easternight, the mind's midwinter

I stood in the big field behind the house
at the centre of all visible darkness

a brick of earth, a block of sky,
there lay the world, wedged
between its premise and its conclusion

some star let go a small sound on a thread.

almost midnight – I could feel the earth's
soaking darkness squeeze and fill its darkness,
everything spinning into the spasm of midnight

and for a moment, this high field unhorizoned
hung upon nothing, barking for its owner

burial, widowed, moonless, seeping

docks, grasses, small windflowers, weepholes, wires

A Greyhound in the Evening
After a Long Day of Rain

Two black critical matching crows,
calling a ricochet, eating its answer,

dipped
    home

and a minute later
the ground was a wave and the sky wouldn't float.

*

With a task and a rake,
with a clay-slow boot and a yellow mack,
I bolted for shelter under the black strake dripping of timber,

summer of rain, summer of green rain
coming everywhere all day down
through a hole in my foot.

*

Listen Listen Listen Listen

*

They are returning to the rain's den,
the grey folk, rolling up their veils,
taking the steel taps out of their tips and heels.

Grass lifts, hedge breathes,
rose shakes its hair,
birds bring out all their washed songs,
puddles like long knives flash on the roads.

*

And evening is come with a late sun unloading a silence,
tiny begin-agains dancing on the night's edge.

But what I want to know is
whose is the great grey wicker-limbed hound,
like a stepping on coal, going softly away...

Shamrock Café

Last night I thought I'd stop
at the Shamrock café, behind the shop.

It was dead quiet, only me,
my serviette and my cup of tea,

and I was looking at buying one
of the prints on the walls of Neanderthal Man

when I heard this tremulous moaning, just
what a gale beginning or a gust

of a hurricane would make at sea.
I threw an anxious glance at my tea.

There to my horror, was a small
row-boat sinking in a whorl,

and round about the rim a foam
of tea waves crashing in the gloom,

which I drank. All unawares,
a fat girl came to the foot of the stairs

and stood there, with one hand
on the banister, swinging around.

Woods etc.

footfall, which is a means so steady
and in small sections wanders through the mind
unnoticed, because it beats constantly,
sweeping together the loose tacks of sound

I remember walking once into increasing
woods, my hearing like a widening wound.
first your voice and then the rustling ceasing.
the last glow of rain dead in the ground

that my feet kept time with the sun's imaginary
changing position, hoping it would rise
suddenly from scattered parts of my body
into the upturned apses of my eyes.

no clearing in that quiet, no change at all.
in my throat the little mercury line
that regulates my speech began to fall
rapidly the endless length of my spine

KATHERINE PIERPOINT

Born in Northampton, **Katherine Pierpoint** read German and French at the University of Exeter and now lives in Canterbury, Kent. She worked in publishing and television before becoming a full-time writer, editor and poetry translator. Her work won a Somerset Maugham Award from the Society of Authors and she was the *Sunday Times* Young Writer of the Year. Her recent projects include translating the contemporary Mexican poet Coral Bracho, working with the Poetry Translation Centre in London. Her first collection, *Truffle Beds*, was published by Faber & Faber in 1995 and was shortlisted for the T.S. Eliot Prize. Her poem 'Buffalo Calf' was shortlisted for the Forward Prize for Best Individual Poem in 2005. She is currently finishing her second collection of poems. Pierpoint has the knack of shifting gear and style, sometimes within a poem. *Truffle Beds* was a varied and powerful debut, mixing poems of childhood and relationships with nature poetry and poems employing clever conceits.

Waterbuffalo

Waterbuffalo walk, they walk as if in sleep to the water,
Hip-gloss of light rolls on each black ball-joint and belly, bulk-head,
shiny as something melting.

Shiny as melting
these slow-strung beasts recline, recline
    into the water, their knees give –

bodies turning   they go down like a wall   like slow death
they half-coil onto one side,
    sigh,   and fold
into the water,
paying themselves out
through the oilskin surface, and begin to glide.

The water moves, brown and muscular.
Mosquito larvae wring themselves along,
and curds of sickness stir in the mud.

Far out in the cooler water the buffalo rest, silent,
each a live head set on that table,
with a rack of horn, warm at the root, risen ringed and scaly from
        the skull;
throat held out flat, and chin on the water,
their dark blocks of bodies turned to weightless light.

Burning the door

This cut and thrown heap
is ready. Its dry leaves, shrunken, point to earth,
but they turn and rattle like the tearing-up of flames

and I've forked and lifted,
provoked it all,
to break the bundle's dreamlife.

I've carried an old door out, and
it's set just ajar now, to the ground;
its dark green street-paint faces inwards, to the heap.

First match to a twist of paper
makes smoke roll like wood-shavings.
A single black-footed flame climbs
limber round the twig-joints;
it tumbles upwards, birdlike, through the bush,
to dither at the open top.

The brushwood is clasped
    on one dancing spot,
dissolved in a fierceness.

A pockmark of heat works up under the paint.
Flames bite a hole quick-alive
    which breathes itself wider,
and smoke bounds through, as
the door is opened from its own centre
by the fire. Fire unpeels things

like an orange,
but goes on opening them, long past the skin,
thumbing them round and round, in a falling-away,
fraying things out and down to nothing.

Later that evening, how little ash a big door is become,
dull driftmat of silver. Hot dust
with red feelers. Many tiny sunsets moving.
The ashes stir like breathed-on down,
and the last blown spot of heat crawls round
like a baby's wandering edge of consciousness.

Burnt right through
and untouchably soft,
wood still holds its grain-pattern of growth
the way newsprint shows on a blackened page,
or a single word can skewer a life
like a red name shot lengthways in a stick of rock.

Frame and form withdrawn now,
this door has walked away,
right through itself.

One hinge is fallen open, like a wing.
One hinge has fallen
very softly closed.

Cats Are Otherwise

Cat steps into the house; courteous,
But still privately electrified by the garden. His fur,
Plump with light as the breastfeathers of the young god of air,
Implies brush-bruised geraniums, and herbs:
Fruitmusk webs of blackcurrant groves
Rusting slowly in an old sun:
A slow-unrolling afternoon
Asleep on the warm earth, above fresh bird-bones.

Cats know control as the basis of magic.
They are our slimmer selves,
That peel doors open to slip out – all eyes – and are gone;
May or may not report back
The easy cruelties of the perfectly adapted, the over-civilised.

When they yawn, a hot zigzag rose blown open
Amazes with its pinkness.
The yawn seems bigger than their whole head, like a snake's.
Two eyes slip, soft yolks on a bone brink, right back into their ears.

Cats may not care to offer up each thought. We look on them;
And remain, like children on the stairs at a dinner party,
Acknowledged by that other world,
Yet uninvited; and so not fully present.

Plumbline

This body of loved music leans close in, to breathe directly in your
        nostrils;
A bullish mass, viewed from below, underlines the summer sky,
It unclasps a fluid pouch of a bass line;
A soft kick in the pocket;
Idling yet full
Bass line, ploughing the loam of the smaller self;
Spreading it, like knees.
The boom swings deep across the boat towards you,
The tinkling curtain parts and up it comes, the
Lowing bass line, head to the rolling ground,
A tiger's cough, disarming:
Not which way to run, but whether, to this
Push and pull of sound from the ring of surrounding hills.

Thick turning cable, taproot and sinew of sound;
Young hooves pestling on old mud,
One warm thunder without threat,
The beat and the note loping together in three dimensions,
Screwing right down to a never-sticking point.

And the soft-shell underparts of the music, not bone nor flesh,
Endlessly sailing up from dark to light;
Rhythm of the hung moment,
Gathering on the swung edge of the outer arc,
        breasting the rim between forward and plummet...
Somewhere an armadillo rolls over and smiles at the sun.

The first time I felt like this I was a small child
Making butter curls in a summer room,
Skimming the meek shining ingot in its white dish;
Judging the amount just right,
Counting the warm oily waves, ribbed in gold.
A soft cairn of butter for chosen guests, who would offer
Curls of richness to one another on the miniature knife,
Its worn horn handle, yet blunt-bladed innocence;
The rich mineral bite of parsley.
I hadn't yet seen John Belushi's eyebrows,
But maybe if I had, I'd've understood.

And back slides the music, round to the probing nub;
That funnelling bass line, fluxing dark,
Centripetal suction nudging the notes out and back,
Warm waves that lift the feet from the sandbank,
And place them exactly one firm foot away – deft implantation;
No consonants, no cormorants in this sea of folding inflections,
Alluvial sound and sunk bullion; moody slippage,
Confluent domes, warm running spine of woven ovals.
Come, soft-bucking sea, we crave a boon, a boon.

CLARE POLLARD

Clare Pollard was born in Bolton in 1978 and currently lives in East London. She has published three collections with Bloodaxe, *The Heavy Petting Zoo* (1998), *Bedtime* (2002) and *Look, Clare! Look!* (2005), with a fourth due in 2011. Her first play, *The Weather* (Faber & Faber, 2004) premièred at the Royal Court Theatre. She works as a broadcaster, teacher and editor. Her documentary for radio, *My Male Muse*, was a Radio 4 Pick of the Year, and she is a Royal Literary Fund Literary Fellow at Essex University. With James Byrne, she co-edited the recent Bloodaxe anthology of younger British and Irish poets, *Voice Recognition: 21 poets for the 21st century* (2009).

Pollard was a prodigy – the poems in her first book were mostly written when she was still at school and describe teenage life. Unlike many early starters, she has continued and developed through her 20s and into her early 30s. Themes run throughout each book, including the struggles of youth, Englishness, the worlds of bed and tourism. The third collection contains a moving sequence about her father's death. Her newer work is darker and more attuned to natural elements.

Puppetry

It comes quietly, is something spilt,
a cup of tea nudged over whilst I slept;
a leakage of silence that weeps through sludge
my skull cups like a preciousness.

It is the chemicals, my doctor says:
they puppet me, softly drip from my mind
to soak through muscle's petticoats; the heart's damp walls.
A silt of hurt is backing up my veins.

To wake to this, in this crotch-scented bed,
this skin, a *day*, is fear. I watch my strings –
translucent tendons – web the wobbling air
above my slump, and who in hell will pull?

It is an effort, to lift up the foot,
one knee, a thigh; to sway in my sad sweat.
In the kitchen, a voice thrown onto me
squeaks: *yes*, *of course*, *oh*, *just had a big night*,

and I pop pills from pharmacies and hippies.
So many puppeteers! They slug it out.
The wind's a wolf; the sun its greasy eye.
No, none of that, this is not imagery...

it is not tea, or puppetry, or beasts,
this is me sniping snide remarks at you
for no reason, and you saying: you're twisted,
and walking out with a frown like real life.

I wash up, staring out at next door's kid,
her dolls, and think on death, but I soon scare
that it is just like this. Things bleed.
I think, no, *know*, my soul is not my soul.

Fears of a Hypochondriac Insomniac

I know the poetry of sickness –
ailment to zymosis,
and recall it, feverish, in blinded dark,
awake again: the alarm claiming 3:14
in figures neon as blood on a light-box,
your heart's *slump*, *slump* thrumming near my bent ear,
the window open to ambulance sirens and possible screams.

Can I hear your breath? Or is that the trick of gas
whispering through slender copper pipes?
Your guts gurgle like a radiator, your heart
scares me, with its stop, start.
The opacity of our bodies alarms me, their capacity for lies
            and secrets:
marrow gammy as old spunk in the femur,
histamines threatening hissy fits beneath our skin,

wrong signals crackling through acetylchline,
aneurysms, ulcers,
the arteries thickening like moss-plush gutters.
The lung my hand is pressed above
could catch a darkness, like the shadow of a hawk
above a furrowed field of harvest mice.
A clot, like an inky full-stop, could nudge up to the heart.

Your body jerks a jolt, slams up
like some mad professor's monstrous creation
electrified alive by storm-light –
my mouth crawls needily near your ear:
'Are you all right? Are you okay?'
Yes, you say,
it was just one of those dreams where you fall.

And I know we have it all,
that elsewhere in this town loved ones are stretched out on stretchers,
in corridors, with clean floors that smell of swimming pools,
steadying themselves on eyefuls
of white walls and Magritte prints,
and waiting for one of the not-enough-beds
with fear they have a right to.

And I know my life is perfect, or near perfect,
that anything better is a beautiful dream –
like God, or The One – but no more.
I have writing, you, my health –
so why this wakefulness: insomnia
diseased with hypochondria,
these morbid X-rays I imagine of your sleep-slowed body?

It is luck's fault, for giving you to me,
for all this bounty, fluke and preciousness.
For leaving me nothing to long for but this, *now*, for longer.
Bodies we love must always be taken,
and at night I wait for the signs I don't want,
hooked round your body, its mess of cartilage and capillary,
a very human shield.

Where your bone skims the skin,
at clavicle, hip and heel,
and where veins thread at your wrists, brow and penis –

these places provoke suffocating grief, for what I'll lose.
Last week, you confessed you had been scared shitless
that some humdrum ache was actually cancerous.
My mortal love, what fucking fools we are.

The Panther

Frayed now, tongue-worn, the legend tells
that my parents – young and expecting me –
walked beneath drizzle, nests, blood-sprays of berries,
breath-clouds mushrooming as they plotted their future,
when the woods convulsed with a pitiless roar
and thicket shook with the rage of a dark engine,
of dragons, of demons; of hunger made meat.
They ran all the way back to their bungalow.
A week later she heard the growl on radio:
If you hear this sound, beware.
It is a panther about to attack...

As a small girl, I pored over theories:
big cats as escapees from menageries,
Victorian travelling circuses, prehistory, death...
I found a picture: *Melanistic Leopard*,
the eye like a chalk-pit or toad spawn,
teeth the sour colour of lambswool in the jaw.
And at dusk I sensed them out there; other –
the Beasts of Bolton, Bodmin, the Fen Tiger –
nuzzling a deer's bowels, careful as burglars.

In this city, now, I had forgotten them
in the scuffle of commonplace violence:
the friend beaten for a bike, his eye
popped out like a tiny moon; the needle-tracked
crackwhores smearing dung on our stair-well;
the lean dark men in hoods who may have guns.
But tonight, as I swallowed some small rejection,
I found myself willing it true:
longing caught in my throat for a panther's leap into view,
like the opposite of disappointment.

JACOB POLLEY

Jacob Polley was born in Cumbria in 1975. A selection of his work was first published as part of a county council pamphlet publishing initiative in 2000. In 2002 he was poet in residence at the Wordsworth Trust and he won an Eric Gregory Award in the same year. His first book, *The Brink*, was a Poetry Book Society Choice and shortlisted for the T.S. Eliot Prize. His second, *Little Gods*, was a Poetry Book Society Recommendation in 2006. He was a Visiting Fellow at Trinity College, Cambridge, in 2005-07, and has written film scripts and a novel, *Talk of the Town*. He has also collaborated with film-makers, theatre designers and artists.

Polley grew up near Carlisle in an area he describes as 'a bit of a borderland where the urban quickly runs into the rural, which is itself full of the un-lyrical, the abandoned, the rusty, polluted and dirty'. These landscapes often crop up in his somewhat timeless poems which are in the main elemental and honed, with a darker taint, and of which Charles Bainbridge commented, 'there is a certain cutback virtue throughout, a belief in a restrained language and the transforming possibilities of description and metaphor'.

The Bridge

The trees are leaking shadows
Where they stand upon the hill
And as we walk the mountain throws
A deeper creeping chill

I hold her hard hand tighter
For we've turned away from home
And my apron blazes like hers
In the blue encroaching gloom

Where are we going mother
Somewhere we haven't been before
The river's spent its silver
The day's a bolted door

You'll get nothing back tomorrow
You touched or heard or saw
The bridge we cross is sorrow's
And this is sorrow's law

All you hold you hold to lose
And standing cold inside you
Such unfathomed black knowing pools
Cannot be added to

Rain

as fishing nets, a wedding dress,
rain that defies rain's downwardness
and spools past the windows, frame by frame –
film after film of Edwardian rain.
Rain as a haunting, rain's ghost-train.
Rain bleeding black from the cracks in bricked-up chimneybreasts;
rain's wall-maps, rain's damp lands, outlined in great stains.

Old rain, the same rain, my father's father's cold rain
taken up like a tune, confessed
to the city, hurried into the drains
and the dark and piped under playgrounds and cold-frames.
From the hills comes rain as more river, not falling
but fattening – bales of newspapers, abandoned books,
hemp ropes, rotten logs and fungi: rain feeds.

From the top bar of a five-bar gate hangs
the green world stilled in a water seed,
while the river slides by, echoing and echoey.
Rain as lost shoes; drinkers huddled like rooks.
Rain that's put paid, done you out of a day. Rain's patter,
rain's slang; rain's bespittling of the spiders' webs.
Rain's pillars of smoke, rain's rooms outside the room

you watch from as rain runs through its embodiments –
a bride swinging like a bell, a lunch-hour factory crowd,
the shadow of a matchstick girl: the smudgy, underdeveloped dead
rain remembers as spaces it once rained around.

Rain's pencil-leads, rain's sketchiness,
rain writing, but whatever it tries to read back
drowned out. Rain's inconsequence to the sea.

A few pins drop, then rain's loosened like hair,
or it steps with the night clean out of the air.
Rain's sound is the sound of the day undone,
the rustle of cellophane, someone and no one.
But at dawn, in the silence just after the rain,
the wet black earth of the bare field lies –
frankincense for you and me.

The Crow

Once Cain had done for Abel
he peeled off his gloves,
rolled them up tight
and set them alight.
It was then they were blackened into life,
already at the wind's throat.

The North-South Divide

fills with flood-water;
the bows of Scotland lift clear
of the Atlantic, cod roam
the East Anglian plains; kelp
throttles Sherwood, the chimneys
of the Midlands slowly barnacle,
Cumbria tilts;
congers lie in catacombs
cold-wiring our relics,
our kings' bones;
a whale hangs a moment
singing in the vault

of St Paul's; men dive
through their Southern libraries,
where crabs unpick the calfskin
of our histories;
Stratford-under-Avon
is swanless and rip-tidal,
hagfish haunt Leicester Square,
anglerfish twinkle
through Trafalgar's oyster beds.
Look from Manchester
out to sea: the South you knew
from quiz shows and road maps,
from nursery rhymes and bad news
is gathering a storm
to its heaving,
gull-broached,
heavy-breakered bosom.

The Turn

You pull the front door to
    by the cold horseshoe
for all the luck in the world has left you.

The weir shuttles sticks,
    the ignorant owl cries *who?*
You're dressed in weeds, now you've swallowed her echo,
    the moon facing you over the fields.

You drip like a cave-wall
    so hard have you swallowed,
so far down does her cold echo roll.

The night smells of matchboxes, chimneys, milk,
    rosehips, apples and river silt.
But your heart, your heart, your sackless heart,
    cringes, blind, in its burrow.

DIANA POOLEY

Diana Pooley was brought up in the Queensland outback and worked as an artist and art lecturer in Brisbane and in London, where she has lived for many years. Her poems have taken awards in the Essex Poetry Competition and in the *Mslexia* Competition and have been published in various journals. Her first collection, *Like This* (Salt Publishing), came out in 2009. Her paintings and sculptures are held in collections in England and Australia. Animals, especially horses in her childhood, have been important to her throughout her life. The contrast in her poetry between "real" and "unreal" may be brought about by the sense of displacement of the immigrant. Pooley writes in a number of modes: her narrative poems about her outback childhood are clear, colourful and inviting; she also writes unsettling snapshots often set in and around the art world; a third strain employs playful conceits with fantastical twists and juxtapositions.

The Bird

He sat for a week two storeys up
looking out of his kitchen window,
a bottle of Indian ink to his right
on the drainer of the sink,
his drawing board over a shelf
and a piece of old singlet on his lap
for wiping the fine steel nib
as he drew the tops of the buildings
of his town. He left a lot of paper bare
for sky, but mainly for the bird –
just an outline at the beginning;
then he covered the breast
with stipple and rows of cross-hatch,
the tail with loops in close parallel
and the wingtips with arabesques.

Its back sagged only a little at first,
then the head sank with the weight
of flourishes on the comb,
but the bird didn't start to drop
until he had nearly finished
putting a dot on the 'v'
of every other overlapping feather.

Listen Amelio,

this is how you make a painting of the night:
fix your easel, set out your palette, brushes,
maulstick – everything – the way I taught you.
When the tower clock begins to strike at noon
come to this drawer. Take out the black silk scarf
I keep between these little bags of loosestrife
and eyebright. Blindfold yourself, tying the knot
above your pigtail, and paint. You'll be finished
by two. Have a break, then bring in some ochre;
grind it well. Now I must be off; the sun's up
and the lunette above the cross in St Paul's
needs retouching. Pass me those wings. There,
on the hook under my red cloak. Tomorrow
I'll show you how to use them and you will find
they are essential if you're working on birds,
angels, insects, dragons or flying horses.

Inscriptions

It took him ages to bury his old dog – the soil was all clay
and dry and hard; and ages to cut into the thin trunk of the gidgee:
the P of Popeye and the R.I.P. with serifs, the cross
like the one he saw in his Arthur Mee, inside a long, thin oval.

It takes him ages to bury his old dog – the soil is all clay
and dry and hard; and ages to cut into the thin trunk of the gidgee:
the D of Dagwood and the R.I.P. with serifs, the cross
like one he saw as a boy in Arthur Mee, inside a long, thin oval.

And when he's used up all the trees in the scrub across the claypan
he'll lie back in his long canvas chair on the veranda,
watch them through the dust jiggling upside-down in mirage.

Now he's used up all the trees in the scrub across the claypan.
He lies back in his long canvas chair on the veranda,
watches them through the dust jiggling upside-down in mirage.

Back at Pathungra

The house had been left half-painted. Except for strips
by the gate where clumps of dried-out Mitchell grass stood
the garden was just beaten-down soil and rat holes.
A wall-vase in the dining room had turned red with dust;
so had the seats of chairs Dad didn't use. A bunch of ginger cats
kept their eyes on us, panicked if they got in,
flew up the wire mesh of the kitchen doors and spat.
No poddy lambs or calves dithered at the back steps; no joeys
upside-down in old potato bags hung from the rails;
there wasn't a dog. Sheep came to water at the bore, but no horses.

That Christmas Eve, once the heat of the day had eased up,
Judith and I drove into the paddock behind the shearing shed.
Though the channels were dry, trees of all sorts grew there.
We propped branches all along the veranda, strung them
with tinsel and I put her new toys out. When a paintbox turned up
she made a picture on the inside cover of *The Grazier*:
Santa Claus in the snow, with a sun that was a whirl of thick red.

King

We propped the dried-out carcass of a bullock
up against a gidgee tree, the skeleton
more or less of a piece with the wrinkled sheet
of brown hide that had been facing up away
from the ground. Both of us ignored the underside
which shed dust and crumbs of innards. I hooked
the horns onto a branch so the white-faced head
joined up with the neck. Jane used a forky stick
for a hind leg, placed three pebbles in a row
between the ears, flicked her plaits and said 'I now
pronounce you king of all.' We left to water
our ponies at the creek beyond the claypan;
I looked back at him all hunched-up in the shade
and said perhaps he'd make the rain come soon.

RICHARD PRICE

Richard Price was born in 1966 and grew up in Renfrewshire. He trained as a journalist at Napier College, Edinburgh before studying English and Librarianship at the University of Strathclyde, Glasgow. He has a PhD on the 20th-century novelist Neil M. Gunn. In the 1990s he co-edited several poetry magazines and was co-founder of Vennel Press. He has published many pamphlets and collaborated with musicians and on various art projects, including artists' books, digital installation and sculpture. His collections include *Lucky Day* (2005), *Greenfields* (2007) and *Rays* (2009), all published by Carcanet. His work has been translated into several languages. He is Head of Modern British Collections at the British Library.

Price is the youngest of the Informationist group of poets that includes Robert Crawford, David Kinloch, W.N. Herbert and others, whose central idea was that 'poetry can be about anything; sound and visuality can be foregrounded'. Price likes to write in sequences, skilfully building an atmosphere across texts, and he is interested in the process of information flow, such as specialist vocabularies and scientific reporting.

from A Spelthorne Bird List

Cormorants

They did not pass the test. Just past the school for private girls, in coats of strips of black blazers, they colonise the flooded pits.

Mallards

A delicate dad caught dabbling in Debbie Duck's drawer – a green glossy popsock caught at head and neck, lycra in chestnut for his chest, grey the rest. In the brown uniform of a money warden his chosen takes five ducklings through their mocks.

Heron

A greying Senior Lecturer in Fish Studies (Thames Valley), he stands in frozen hop concentration, regarding a lectern only he can see. Still, he gets results. He's hoping for a chair.

Song thrush

Its shirt in ill-advised off-white, customised with blotches of crank-oil, a thrush prods the temporary car park. He/she almost forgets to repeat itself, but on a scaffold a song finds it and finds it again.

Wake up and sleep

Drowsy finalising the blueprint,
drowsy verifying the footprint.
Drowsy in data entry,
drowsy on checkpoint sentry,
drowsy and missing the asset-stripping on Dead Street.

Half-asleep, fingertipping the spreadsheet,
thumbing the defective directory
of on-the-mind on-the-mend half-attended ex's.
Half-asleep and just holding on
to the handholds in the homemade purgatory
of six-of-one custody fro-and-to vexes.
Half asleep quoting chapter and hexes
from the ratified sleepwalking directive.

Wake up outside your conscientious waking dream,
wake up and sleep.
Wake up outside your ache, your late luscious just-what-it-seems,
wake up and sleep.
Wake up to the what-happened, wake up to the casehardened,
wake up between look and leap.
Wake up in the shatter and decade-seep,
wake up and sleep.

Say goodnight to shaking –
there's a wake in over-waking.
Scowls and scarlatina are the stories in the clinic cantina:
more at the morgue does tend to mean less.
Owls and the ocarina are glories in the night arena
but leave them for a week, I guess.
(Sleep's demeanour improves life's fever –
you need to nod to get to yes.)

Peace and quiet for the codes and the kids,
for the didn't-halfs and the nearly-dids. Rest your roads, your well-rids.
Peace and quiet for the sky-deep, ocean-high equation.
No tended-baggage advantage-adage panic profiticians. No palpitations.
Peace and quiet for the offence-taking nations-within-nations.
Peace. Not a peep. Please,
sleep.

Languor's whispers

*

Straps stripped,
tans' stripes,
laps and lips, lush
soft locks.

Languor's whispers
to longing, listening.

*

The release

of play and please,
quietly now allowed.

Two
perfects the crowd.

*

A lick, a life.
The lyric lazed within,
the link

of glow and glimpse,
the jewels
of just ourselves.

*

Lying in.

Lambency from shirk,
the glints
from whys and whines
(work), the shoosh
of sigh-by-sigh
drumming of the hum.

*

Friendless.

Hand-in-hand's routine
routed, de-planned:
forwarder, franker, fresher,
serious leisure.

Louts – us –
dedicated layabouts,
blunt
and blameless (would-be).

*

Touch, and touch's could-be
deep shallows, lap
and kiss, sense-sipping lips,
finger-tips.

*

The taste-sniff
sniff-taste
hear of here,
the see

of near-bounded, no,
the near-boundless sea.

*

Touch, touch, touch.

Hopes, love, luck,
perfect just,
a right too much.

SALLY READ

Sally Read has published two books of poems with Bloodaxe: *The Point of Splitting* (2005), which was shortlisted for the Jerwood Aldeburgh Prize for best first collection, and *Broken Sleep* (2009). Her work has also been translated into Italian. In 2001 she was the recipient of an Eric Gregory Award. She is a teacher of English and creative writing and was formerly a psychiatric nurse. Married with a daughter, she lives between Suffolk and Santa Marinella, Rome. Working as a nurse has clearly informed Read's work, which is very much located in the physical: the body and its machinations as metaphor for psychological states. She spends part of the year in Italy and the context it provides – of beauty and violence (she has witnessed, second-hand, a lot of Mafia-type vendettas in Sardinia) – plays into the fascination of how to interact with physical facts in the physical world. Sex, illness and violence are recurring themes in her poetry. Her second book contains some of the most moving and original poems on motherhood of recent years.

Fog

On the slung ropes of sail-boats
fog succumbs to globules, teeters
along a helm. Here there's no
winter, just white days. Ships,
skirting the harbour, steady
with panic-filled lights.
My daughter's a stunned weight
on my shoulder, bouncing
a complacent second after
each tread. Now we are two.
The scar purses to a thin
brown line. The uterus shrinks.
But these damp days –
the same way old sailors
complain of the screws

in their knees – there's a bright
snaggle of pain, as if something
were left inside. And she observes
blandly the splintered jetty
strutting off into nothing, as though
she weren't quite here still.
As though she observed it all
in rapt safety, from an attic window.

Mastectomy

It's an effortful, uneven line
across your chest, a bashed lip
blood's still vacant from:
Touch it.

My fingers quiver, though you tell me
it's still numb: two more years
till nerves yawn and crackle.
In place of abundant flesh,
there's space and bone. A long,
misjudged step – like missing
a stone stair in the country dark –
and I lose a breath, and all my hands'
bones murmur at the loss.
I rest my palm deep into it,
study your new form, tipped
like a half-loaded boat.
My silence runs and gains;
and that's it. Outside, a brittle

cold unclinches: snow on the Eastern
Plains till, incrementally
and with a hiss of dryness
the world's wiped white. Little
sinkers meandering down,
each their own sailing, selfish,
thoughtless weight, many times
lighter than my hands.

Mafia Flowers

4 A.M., you're called to the blindness of a country night
where you only tell the mute space of your eyes,
awkward step, formless breath.

The farmhouse is lit: a cage of day. Every lamp
and overhead jammed on, the unshakeable light
of a hundred suns. The white haired man's

vertical in the middle of the room, eyes popped
of meaning like a baked fish. Red hands covering
his mouth in the first fresh jump of shock,

though the florist's van came in daylight, innocent,
at the regular hour of eight. *'Why'd you wait so long
to call?' 'There were more than I'd reckoned.'*

The room's bright as a butcher's shop with blooms.
Not blooms, not flowers. Wrought, dyed, compressed
funeral wreaths. Dense, satin-sashed circles,

and one spelling his name in rusty chrysanths.
It's propped on his straight chair, another's laid
on the bed, another on the sports section

at the folding table, more overwhelm the floor.
Tight daisies in fanciful blue, salmony pink,
hawkish yellow, heaving the scent and stickiness

of God's nature, amassed beyond wonder.
The colours of Gabriel's miraculous, oily wings
(as fleshed out by men). You take your cap off,

bedazzled at the light, at this man's funeral
and the man not dead. You walk the creaking wreaths,
pretending notes, pour grappa to restore his voice,

bag them like bodies, flick switches one by one
to a dim bedside lamp, so as you step out into the cold
the moon reasserts itself calmly on stones,

the natural order of things. But as you drive,
you can't shake the image of the man slunk in his chair
– crazy – refusing to wake his brothers or tell a soul

of this visitation. The daylight and angels and wreaths
are his – whatever crime he may or may not have done –
as if he conjured each flower himself; he stinks of them.

The same as if 14-year-old Mary had gone running
to Elizabeth, broad-sided by her elaborate tale, saying
it was nothing of her idea and she'd as soon forget it.

Too late. Already the gold congeals above her head,
and Elizabeth's eyeing her warily, her flesh
and blood womb leaping in fear.

On the main road the dawn develops, grey
as sanity, the town is a host of cool witnesses
waking, and as you turn into your lane

there's an almighty rightness you're still
clinging to a month on
when news of his death is delivered.

The Death-Bell

(Orosei, Sardegna)

Again, my house reduced to one lit square,
lamp dipping defeatedly as the heater cranks back up.
My small co-ordinates: a glass of the good stuff
(so thick it's black), a book, when the bell slams
back and forth. The muscular weight of that sally
dragging in the gong's whale-like reluctance
and delay. Each bronze hit slugging out to the last
wave, till air's congealed, struggling to swallow
sound. I'm prevailed upon: the night ploughed up;
the book a smooth palm in my lap; window
devoid of skyscrapers, lights, diluting cars.
All minds marshalled to a stranger's dying:

the awful struggle to still a heart that retches,
retches, long after the ghost's given up by exhausted
wife and daughters. Well now, some muscle has wrung
out years, to silence. The air still smells of it.
But before we all relax, at ease, the bell starts up again
(blood seeped back to some upended arm)
and rung as if this random ringer is trying to beat
a shape out of a lumbering iron when he might as well
forge a horseshoe from the sea.

Instruction

Check: water, soap, a folded sheet, a shroud.
Close cubicle curtains; light's swallowed
in hospital green. Our man lies dense
with gravity: an arm, his head, at angles
as if dropped from a great height. There is
a fogged mermaid from shoulder to wrist,
nicotine-stained teeth, nails dug with dirt –
a labourer then, one for the women.
A smooth drain to ivory is overtaking
from the feet. Wash him, swiftly, praising
in murmurs like your mother used,
undressing you when asleep. Dry carefully.
If he complained at the damp when alive, dry
again. Remove teeth, all tags, rip off elastoplast –
careful now, each cell is snuffing its lights,
but black blood still spurts. Now,
the shroud (opaque, choirboy ruff), fasten
it on him, comb his hair to the right. Now
he could be anyone. Now wrap in the sheet,
like a parcel, start at his feet. Swaddle (not
tight nor too loose) – it's an art, sheafing
this bundle of untied, heavy sticks. Hesitate
before covering his face, bandaging warm
wet recesses of eyes, mouth. Your hands
will prick – an animal sniffing last traces
of life. Cradle the head, bind it with tape

and when it lolls, lovingly against your chest,
lower it gently as a bowl brimmed with water.
Collect tags, teeth, washbowl. Open
the window, let the soul fly. Through
green curtains the day will tear: cabs, sun-
glare, rain. Remember to check:
tidied bed, emptied cabinet, sheeted form –
observe him recede to the flux between seconds,
the slowness of sand. Don't loiter. Slide
back into the ward's slipstream; pick up
your pace immediately.

DERYN REES-JONES

Deryn Rees-Jones read English at the University College of North Wales, Bangor, followed by doctoral research at Birkbeck college and she now lectures in literature at Liverpool University. She won an Eric Gregory Award in 1993 and her first collection, *The Memory Tray*, was published by Seren in 1994 and was shortlisted for the Forward Prize for Best First Collection. Her second collection, *Signs Around a Dead Body*, was a Poetry Book Society Special Commendation. *Quiver* was a book-length poem published by Seren in 2004. A pamphlet, *Falls & Finds*, appeared from Shoestring in 2008. She is also the author of a monograph on the work of Carol Ann Duffy and co-editor, with Alison Mark, of *Contemporary Women's Poetry*. Her collection of essays, *Consorting with Angels*, was published by Bloodaxe in 2005 with a companion anthology, *Modern Women Poets*. A narrative poet, Rees-Jones has said her presiding theme is 'an interest in female subjectivity, with a particular interest in memory and identity', though her early poetry is often playful or comic, and in her most recent work, there is a clear interest in scientific themes.

Trilobite

Remember, as a child, how someone would shout Catch!
and too old to refuse, and too young not to –
the body's coordinates not quite set

this object, moving in an arc towards you
somehow created you, trembling, outstretched?
That's how it came to me, this trilobite,

a present from the underworld, a stern familiar
hopelessly far-fetched. What it wanted from me
I never knew, its hard parts being its only parts,

the three parts of its crossways nature
cephalos, thorax, pigidium
as later, now, I've learned to call them,

carrying a memory of itself like water
as my fingers moved on its captive body,
the feathery stone of its cool guitar.

It reminded me of a woodlouse, too,
the honesty of small, friendly things.
But the metallic gleam of its smoothed edges

were taut and innocent as an unfired gun.
So it bedded in, leaving behind a gleaming trail
as a biro bleeding in a pocket might,

a puff of ink from a hounded squid.
And my skin shimmered
with its silvery threads, and my breath quickened

as it wrote my body, left a garden of knowing in damp tattoos.
The further I threw it, the closer it came.
Sometimes, alone, I'd ask it questions

stroke it like a secret pet
How deep is the ocean? What's the blueness of blue?
How is the earth as you lie inside it?

It would reply in a voice both
high-pitched and enduring, or
whisper like a ghost till silence remained.

And left me only when I'd learned to love it,
small as a bullethole,
in the place where it pressed itself

its fossil colours close to my heart.
Last night, unable to sleep
it nudged its way back into my life,

pulling me from the fragrant pillow
to perch again on my naked shoulders,
to drop like a coin in my offered hand.

Beside me, my husband slept.
And the fact of its presence, its subtle truth,
was something to touch,

like the wounds of Christ.
Its transformation as I went to kiss it,
a wafer on the pushed-out tongue.

My Father's Hair

For it has stood up like a coxcomb before a fight.
For it is whiter than lace on a bobbin or snow on a bough.
For in his youth it was auburn, leading to blackness.
For it has a grave insouciance,
What they call in Sassoon's 'a natural air'.
For it has resisted gels and lotions, brilliantine, mousses.
For it has been photographed, ridiculed,
Admired, swept back.
For it speaks the language of wild things, everywhere.
For it has suffered the barbary of barbers, and my mother.
For it has been tamed with deerstalkers,
Baseball and camouflage caps.
For it is something of a pirate or an admiral.
It is a spark transmitter and a Special Constable,
It is Harrier, Jumpjet, parachute, Chinook.
For it is salt on an eyelash, fresh from the sea.
For it is loved by many women of the district,
And is piped aboard the sternest of vessels.
For it cannot be mentioned, the pot of *Vitalis*
She gave him on their honeymoon.
For its mind is as fast as light, the elastic stretch
Of a falling star. It is not anybody's servant.
For we will say nothing of Delilah and Seville.
It is both gravel path and skating rink.
It is velvet, it is epaulettes. It is sunrise, it is sunset.
O my father's hair! It is an unsung hero!
But because of the sickness, or the cure for the sickness,
It lies like an angel's on the pillow:
Long white strands, like wings, or long white wings, like hair.

from **Quiver**

A Visitation

Here, in a patch of darkness in the Bluebird where I sit,
Liverpool opens like a rent in time. The centuries elide

to a collage of water, newspaper print.
The songs of the slaves with their branded foreheads

rise to the heavens in a shift of pain,
and then the refugees take up their song,

abandoned in an unknown port.
Choleric children shake and cry.

The angel of history throws back her shoulders,
her violet eyes look forwards and back.

And for the first time in a long time I feel that I could weep
as daytime's colours slip

inside each other, disappear.
I press the buzzer as instructed,

and the slow world turns.
I give a last look back at the roughed up night,

hold its memories close:
a street lamp, a dog bark,

orange, unearthly, bleak.

NEIL ROLLINSON

Neil Rollinson was born in Yorkshire. He has been the recipient of a Cholmondeley Award and an Arts Council Award. His poem 'Constellations' was a winner of the National Poetry Competition. His first collection, *A Spillage of Mercury*, appeared in 1996. Two further collections have followed, *Spanish Fly* in 2001 and *Demolition* in 2006, all published by Cape Poetry. Rollinson founded the internet literature magazine Boomerang which he designed and edited for six years, and has himself created and exhibited animated poetry at galleries in Paris and Turin. Rollinson's first book was notable for its frank and explicit erotic poems but he has written, in a style which the critic Justin Quinn described as 'the piling up of whimsical metaphor with a tone of languorous pleasure', on a variety of themes including the sensual pleasures of food, physics and astronomy, and sport and apocryphal myth. Rollinson rarely employs metrical form or rhyme, but his free verse narratives have conversational charm and he can also write lyric poems with impressive delicacy.

Dreamtime

We rock through a canopy of lime leaves,
a cargo of pungent secretaries lounging
in blouses, dozy bankers in mohair
cursing the weather; the cattle run, the 7.31
from Peckham to Putney. It's so humid
you could grow bananas in here. We snooze
in the heat, headphones hiss like cicadas.
By the Half Moon Tavern, a wasp, drawn
by a promise of sweat and the sweet
dampness of typists, flies through a window.
It lurches and swaggers, drunk on midsummer
pollen, up and down the aisle, everyone
wide awake now; a buzz of anxiety runs
through the bus. It hits the front window
and dithers a moment, dazed in the sunlight.
I wipe the sweat off my face and watch it

butt the window again, frustrated, the gardens
of Herne Hill pressed in glass, like his Permian
brothers sealed in amber. My neighbour rolls up
her *South London Press* and hammers it flat;
a yellow smudge on the glass, honey
and cider, the sweetness of local plum trees.
We breathe again, and doze in the hothouse.
The suburbs slide by like dreamtime,
all the way to Brixton where we rouse ourselves
and head for the Tube, yawning in unison.

Constellations

Beyond the house, where the woods
dwindle to a few stray trees, my father
walks on the lake with a hammer.

He's never seen so many stars,
and wonders why
with all that light in the sky

it doesn't cast a single shadow.
He takes a few blows at the ice, and drops
a sackful of bricks

and kittens into the hole, listens
a moment to the stillness of deep winter,
the hugeness of sky, the bubbles of warm

oxygen breaking under his feet,
like the fizz in a lemonade; the creaking
of ice as it settles itself.

His father's at home, coaxing voices
out of a crystal set, a concert from London.
Ghosts in a stone.

My father doesn't like that, he prefers
the magic of landscapes, of icicles
growing like fangs from the gutters of houses,

the map of the constellations. He turns on the bank
and looks at the sky, Orion rising over Bradford,
Cassiopeia's bold W, asking Who, What, When

and Why? And down in the lake, the sudden
star-burst of four kittens under a lid of ice,
heading to the four corners of nowhere.

Between Bradford and Pudsey

The long drive home,
the jaundice
of yellow street-lights
gilding the car,
and then
between Bradford
and Pudsey, a frenzy
of white horses
loose from their field,
skating the black road,
drunk as fairground horses,
their eyes wild
in the headlights.
Dad slows to a crawl
at the roundabout,
the horses scatter:
a merry-go-round exploding
in slow motion,
all the horses
off their poles,
an instinct gathers them
and they sprint down
the ring road in a
welter of hoof sparks,
panic driving them
deeper and deeper
into their nightmare:
Thornbury, Laisterdyke,
Dudley Hill.

Long Exposure
(for Phil Huntley)

You're out all night in Dartmoor's freezing cold
and can't believe how silent it is, how dark
without a moon; you can hardly see
the boots on your feet. You sit on a stool,
the camera perched, owl-like, on its tripod.
The shutter is open all night, its aperture shrunk
to barely a pinprick, drinking the scenery
bit by bit. You think of the photons falling
invisibly onto the stock, like snow on a pond,
infinitesimal quanta of light fixing the landscape,
capturing detail you can only imagine
in this pitch-black scrub land.
You walk away for a cigarette, the single flare
of a match head could ruin your work.
At half past two you take a cloth and wipe
the condensation off the lens, knowing the camera
will make a ghost of you. You watch the stars,
and think of the Earth turning, you've seen
the Dog Star rise above the hill and fall from view,
you imagine the sun sweeping the globe,
the tide of dawn rushing towards you, already
over the Urals, the west of Afghanistan, people
rising for breakfast, and those in its shadow
drifting to bed, streetlights all over the western
seaboard flickering on. At five o'clock, before
dawn, you let the shutter fall, and pack your gear.
As you drive home you watch the first light
develop the moors, early sunlight racing west
across the frosted counties of England.

JACOB SAM-LA ROSE

Jacob Sam-La Rose was born in London in 1976. His pamphlet *Communion* was a Poetry Book Society Pamphlet Choice in 2006 and praised for its 'evocation of contemporary Britain', and his first full collection is forthcoming in 2011. He was managing director of a web development studio before becoming a freelance writer and editor. He is the Artistic Director of the London Teenage Poetry SLAM, Editor-in-Chief of Metaroar. com, and an editor for flipped eye press. He also facilitates a range of literature-in-education, creative writing and spoken word programmes through schools, arts centres and other institutions.

There are two major strands within Sam-la Rose's work: one is the personal narrative of family, friends and work, which makes comment on subjects such as city life and racial identity; his other style of writing (see 'Blacktop Universe') is woozier, more elliptical and influenced by contemporary American poets such as Terrance Hayes (whose anagrammatic form Sam-la Rose uses in 'Plummeting').

The Beautiful

They live in worlds
where light has been tamed.

It does what it's told – pools
like piling syrup, tethered and kind.

It coddles, shines and buffs
their skins; knows how to dance

with the dark. Our light is harder–
                       wild, unruly,

unafraid to brandish its teeth.
Paints everything as is. Under its gaze

there are things we cannot hide.

Blacktop Universe

the court marked out like
a star-map / each shot launching

a satellite into orbit / rising / lofty /
tarmac spangled with the salt

of exertion / with each bounce /
each elbowed jook / each shimmying

hip / each jangling near miss /
each phrase of patter-jazz footfall / a world

was born / and to extend the metaphor /
I guess that made us gods

A Life in Dreams

There have been teeth
        falling loose from their sockets
        like a shower of petals or bones.

There has been treacle;
        attempts to run against a gravity wound so tight
        that single steps were futile,
        a travelling nowhere,
                a running on the spot,
                        a fanged leer and a gnarled hand
        inching ever closer.

There have been glorious revolutions in unnamed countries,
        wars against tyrants,
        troops like legions of swarming beetles.
        There have been blades, flashing at the sun.

Once or twice, a fluency in kung fu.

Up has mostly been up,
        though has been convincingly turned
        on its head.

There have been drives down unfamiliar streets,
        the front of a car crumpled
                like denim pulled fresh from the wash.
        Once, a mobile home.

There have been more than a few kisses. School
        classrooms and corridors.
                A hiding place in a primary attic.

There have been clothes, forgotten
        and remembered too late.
        A numbness of gums.

Weightlessness.
        Unassisted flight.
        Falling but never hitting the ground.
        Fear
                as solid and real
                as table tops or bed-frames.

There has been silence,

the power of sound cleft from the mouth,
        the jaw gummed with quiet, the throat
        emptied of ammunition.

There has been love.

There have been messages
        passed back and forth between hemispheres, metaphors
        like acres of fortune cookies.

All this, behind shuttered and fluttering eyes
        and, I'd wager, some of the best,
        where everything moved like snowfall
        and time itself was as delicate as a snowflake,
                melting on the tongue.

Plummeting

He works it, hard as a mule:
left, right, launch-step, discipline like a lump
of lead in his pocket he can melt
into gold. Keeps on until the sky turns plum,
sporting a corona of sweat like a plume
of peacock's feathers, stoking the fire in each lung
as proof against the failing light and time
passing; left, right, launch-step, pelting
ball at hoop, deep bone-ache for the sweet line
from hand to flawless, unimpeachable plunge.
The rim's wide mouth, mute.

ANTONY ROWLAND

Antony Rowland was born in Bradford in 1970. His first poetry collection, *The Land of Green Ginger*, was published by Salt in 2008. Since studying at Hull and Leeds he has taught literature and creative writing at the University of Salford. A selection of his work appeared in *New Poetries III* (Carcanet, 2002). He received an Eric Gregory Award in 2000, and a Learning Northwest Award in 2001. Like many writers connected to Leeds University in recent decades, Rowland engages with recent European history and class issues, but he adds a distinctively gastronomic edge, as several of the poems in his first book are bravura takes on culinary subjects, such as a diatribe against cucumbers and an elegy for pomfret cakes. Travels throughout Europe also inform many of his poems. His work exists in the middle ground between mainstream and innovative writing, linguistically challenging but fascinating in its complexity and ambitious diction.

Lésvos

The candles only make us see the dark
more clearly, a nightmare head
clapped by the shuttles.
Spoondrift lovers spoon by the wind's edge
where Orpheus's skull
lolled around inlets, rosy fingers
as dextrous as pilliwinks
in the torturous sun.

A Turkish minaret piggybacks
Greek Molyvos, spoon-baits
through the rock to the mackerel.
An Orthodox congregation
slowpokes to the church,
past these strung octopi,
salting Mussolinis,
the wind-chimes of unseen kri-kri.

We gentoo seaward,
as if at an absent ship or the breeze
that colours the wheat.
Gull-roosts dribble the Aegean,
the dipping mist. Swallows collect.
I have not found you again and you
are closer to the Styx than a skimmed pebble.
The sun hods the sky, the armies of nimbus.

Damrak

White rabbits greet the eve of September
on Rokin, a street which leaves a hole
in Amsterdam. Our temporary home
is shabby as the fubs in *The Flying Dutchman*;
our carpets are the texture of droog brood.
In our rucksack, a nibble of cracker packets.
Autumn comes with a creeping hush.

This city is a giddy kipper.
This bridge is lekker in an icing of stream.
Crepuscular roads of water are
dreamed by seekers of skunk;
fingers twitch in bottomless pockets.
Dante's waterways concentricised Hell;
the lidless eyes of tourists pass.

Your face as grey as an absent tulip,
we grace Damrak, stationed by a rusp of canals.
A heron freezes the obelisk of a barge.
Pigeons boozle loose air in Singel.
ECUs rise like metaphysical bees
from these thin roofs atop with hooks.
The single sun is a Gogh, ocherous.

The waiters are as elusive as ciscos
in the brown bar, The Three Quarks, marking
the discos of Dam Square. Round the Vondelpark:
flesh, sand and guitars, all bad.

The fat porks glisten in the Indian heat.
In the Twin Pigs, banana bunches peek
like yellow spiders over the bowls.

We have forgotten your mother for a night
but the hotel is still the edge of a nightmare.
Our nostrils pickle with Damrak's sough
as, reflecting neon, mushrooms and windows,
our owner gnomes on Warmoesstraat
with Sunday smiles and hosepipes.
An aubade of dealers flushes the cobbles.

Pie

Will you go to the pie-feast?
(DODSLEY, 1550)

Singing herb singe roast vapours Fray: Saturday
pie-floater in Rawson market; waxy peas island
gelatine-coated pink flush before comic stall.
Passionate friendship wanted with a Bentos,
good sense of meat to gravy ratio. Slim,
attractive suet looking for pudding love
with like-minded crust: no tin wasters;
Swiss-slapped pâté on the brawn of pigley
-pie, ridged with needle precision and oh,
so delicately browned at the knobs, bow-tie
at the centre hot-puddled, pie *de pundio*,
fayre buttys of Porke smyte with Vele welcome.
Mint-chopped sausage baguette found abandoned:
police are savouring bent *expenditum*
at Bolton Priory in pyis et pastellis. Pie-purrs
undercut by cholesterol scam: police support nut diet.
Sought in attractive wastes of Uppermill: chips just so,
clay-coloured dish Delia-thick in hot top-slick
– 'That's not a pie, it's boo-gloop with a bin lid' –
pastry chocked round oval but peels off faced with fork.
'Hote pies, hote! Goode gees and grys, Gowe dyne, Gowe!'
Bramble for afters? No, two would be spoiling us.
Policy wonks hit pies with fat tax, fatties

304

who puttis fast at their vly pyiss, headlines
Yorkshire chippies' favourite rag, *The Fryer*.
Finger buffet threat to national health:
Blair's babes weaned on focaccia and lamb's lettuce
forced into Mowbray tour of the bow-walled pie,
northern one-portion growlers and stand-pies
that stand–pipe Robert's pie-house in Bradford:
Jerry bombs cobweb the glass but daily displays
defiantly steam. 'Every puff,' puffed Priestley,
'was defying Hitler. Keep your pie level
to avoid ungelled gravy dribble incident.'
The Fryer pastes the government's attempt
to ration meat dripping – 'Animal fat
for the dominant race. Animal fat
for the dominant county within that race.'
Cold balls lovingly brisked with milk yolk: Sunday chow
brought family together not gristle niblets
in bad butchers' pork cast-offs. Bison pies
go missing in Salford posse mix up. Small shops'
warmers in sausage roll chaffage scandal:
police inspect gluten levels, mustard lovers,
cuckoo mayonnaise run off with sheer pie.

Golem

We come from beyond the Slovak pail
to find snails on nippy streets
the Sunday rain washed the Vltava plain.
A cat roils a washing line with drops
watching us pale from the CSA plane.
A dog nips at our shadows, barking for sun
and the balmy simplicity of Czech afternoons
but it is as warm as when Rabbi Löw glued
his golem together from Vltava turf.

With you in a pivnice, chilled by wine
bubbling with the graves of Vysehrad
engraved in your camera, a tomb
for the embarrassment of tourists.

You long for foxes in the Southern Cemetery,
not the thin, spooky statues heavening here.
Your arm gooses when I brush it
by a mausoleum, your lilac smile
like light frosted on the white walls.

We sit like fish as a street boy slips
a backpacker's bag from a Coke café.
The velvet revolution is a trail
of brown amok in our red and white cups.
As we eat ice cream in Wenceslas Square
(neither square, nor good),
Russian bears pause in the National Museum,
frozen in a language I can barely understand.
Take my hand. Feel the sundae heat.

JAMES SHEARD

James Sheard was born in Cyprus in 1962 and grew up abroad, mainly in Singapore and Germany. He has made a living as a freelance tutor and trainer in language and communication skills, and has lived in Hamburg and Helsinki. He is currently a Lecturer in Creative Writing at Keele University. His pamphlet, *Hotel Mastbosch* (Mews Press, 2003), a result of his MA Writing at Sheffield Hallam University, was a Poetry Book Society Pamphlet Choice. His collection, *Scattering Eva* (Cape Poetry, 2005), was shortlisted for a Forward Prize for Best First Collection and a Glen Dimplex Award.

Sheard has a strong interest in poetic 'Europeanness' and academic interest in the literary qualities of the translated poem. His poems are often concerned with moments at which the individual finds him-/herself conscious of the artefacts and movements of history, often as a result of minor moments of intimacy. He generally switches between the short image-led poem and the dramatic-narrative lyric.

Four Mirrors

He bought four mirrors
from a sale of kitsch fitments –
silvered plastic tricked up
for a warping of bodies and light.

It was wrong to hang them foursquare
down the dead cream walls of renting,
placed to catch the phone
and his fakir stillness.

Because he bulged; skinned over
with the pierced stone eye of a lizard;
and bent into strychnine loops
of mixed fruits and kaleidoscoping.

Sometimes he rippled like a washboard,
and found ribs, a whole history
of sidesteps and shifting;

or raised a thickwalled cup
which flared out like a medium
spewing cheesecloth, in that moment
before the sceptics rise
and pounce.

Cargo Cult

In an imperfect incense
of soil and old candles
the kept objects sit
on split grey shelving –
dull cones of lead, broken tools,
bits of strange bracketry.

For a while I fake
the slimfingered expertise
of a collector turning porcelain,
before letting my square hands
hang and rust.

Tumbled here like cargo
from the metal perfection
of a distant father, pinning me
between fool and acolyte,

between turning and waiting
a quiet unscowling moment longer
for him to return

and tell me what these things were
and why it was they mattered.

The Lost Testimony of R. Catesby

The gentler tortours are to be first usid unto him, et sic per gradus
ad ima tenditur

JAMES I to Fawkes' Interrogators

The night had that distant glitter of marcasite.
We rode northwest,
steaming off our chain of horses.

I fumbled largesse at the waystations;
struck fresh reins from the nervous hands of ostlers.
It seemed the turf peeled back,
and the bones of recusant England
tore loose beneath us.

We had left women to watch
the hurdles and quartering-tables;
ravel up the tawdry miracles of the scaffoldside.
Lips might twitch in a held-up head;
blood shape a face on a cornhusk.

They slammed the fact of Reformation shut
on Guido's hands. Those thick fingers
cut tapers, drew maps, bent barrelhoops
an extra inch. He told me once

we had lived too long
as spiders in the curtains.

Now I think of his strength
decaying like dead powder;
of dim ships slipping back into Biscay fog,
carrying their sour cargo
of questions
and instruments.

Café Verdi

We feel rough and pitted as promenade rails,
our talk a slapdash glosswork
between the slack voltage of the sea
and our backboard of facts and old houses.

Our planes and angles are set awry,
a hasty laying of seafront flagstones
or the cafe rising in a drunken hedron
of glass and grey weathering.

We soon trace the offsquare weave of cheap napkins,
consider *ciabatta and cheddar*. The waiter's
Welsh-Italian makes arcs and tangents,
the stumbles of an acrobat.

I have new blueprints to unfold.
A tracery of new alignments to knucklelock
above the tabletop. Hands to circle intersections
of clarity and need.

But she traces a more faded line.
Brief lives of the rockpool creatures.
The bright-eyeing of market treats.
Squabbling daytrips to misjudged threepoints
in the tight inland lanes.

So as Verdi assembles his playhouse
from primaries and angled tubing
I tell her of the climbing frame
which, as children, we would dress
with bolts of threaded straw.
Then crawl in
and call it home.

ZOË SKOULDING

Zoë Skoulding was born in 1967 and has lived in north Wales since 1991, having previously lived else-where in the UK as well as Belgium and India. Her collections include *The Mirror Trade* (Seren, 2004), *Dark Wires*, with Ian Davidson (West House Books, 2007) and *Remains of a Future City* (Seren, 2008). She holds an AHRC Fellowship in poetry at Bangor University and runs the university's part-time literature and writing courses. She is a co-editor of *Skald* and editor of the quarterly *Poetry Wales*. She has been involved in music projects, notably Parking Non-Stop, whose album *Species Corridor* was released in 2008. Some of her performances juxtapose poetry and field recordings as a means of exploring acoustic and linguistic connections between places.

Skoulding is a poet informed by both traditional and innovative writing and especially interested in extended metaphor, as in the city poems in her second book. Ideas of place are important in her work: Ian Gregson commented that her poems suggest 'an equivalent in spatiality of inter-textuality – that places can only be understood in relation to each other and never in isolation'.

Trappist Brewers

They smile and glide as if time means nothing,
as if there are no billboards outside the sleepy town
showing how Chimay is drunk in Tokyo.

From their glassed-in cloisters they remember
how power, prayer and alcohol flooded the veins
of the oldest maps. The road from the abbey leads

to the town square, where the bells ring slightly
out of tune, tinny and distinct, marking out
each quarter hour while nothing changes.

Wild rabbit from the fields below melts
into plums and onions; the cheese is creamy,
dipped in salt. Remembering that rich, slow drunkenness

back home, I will buy the same beer
under bland fluorescent light
and drink it from the wrong glass,

searching its bitter velvet for a footstep on stone,
an off-key chime or a white scut
disappearing into the woods.

History

The poem lying in a suitcase on the fourth floor
describes the attic as a head with closed eyes,

a ship of creaking boards with trunks
adrift in elsewhere, half-way across the sea,

each box still packed with objects reassembled
as signs growing cold: envelopes like folded wings,

ostrich eggs, lies and invitations, letters,
dresses of dead aunts all locked in

but ready to leave on the first breath
out of there. Line by line it tracks

glances scattered in the street below,
roofs sloping this way and that, heads and

tails of coins clinking in a pocket, wind
under the eaves – restlessly, as if a gust of air

could blow it into the dust of this page.

Preselis with Brussels Street Map

Up Europalaan under blue
        reach of sky   bare feet in spongy moss
I need a map to tell me where I'm
not   along the Avenue de Stalingrad
              squeal of a meadow pipit

skimming
        over rue de l'Empereur
tread softly on the streets   the sheep trails
        between bird call and bleat echo
a street folds across two languages   here and there

Wheel tracks into crashed grass
        might lead to somewhere
           a small bar sleepily open

or nothing but wind
        and ponies wheeling out of sight
over Kolonienstraat   rue de la Loi

          at Rondpoint circle a bale of wire
then over a fence and into the dry white branches
     kestrel elevations
   of the European Quarter

under the vertigo of power   parched grasses pull apart
       where voles run without names
in a mesh of body scent
       that writes the ground with movement
              as a map the size of itself

New Year

Open the door to birds crossing at all angles. Sun
strikes glitter like old data transferred

uncorrupted into the present, winter written white.
Revolving in a current of air, you stub your toes

on glass, one foot wedged in a triumphal arch
you can never pass through twice, or with too much.

Turn a page on its hinge, a rectangle the size of
yourself to step through, print blurred to grey

buildings made to frame each door. Trapped wings
beat in the gap between seconds, galeforce then gone.

Docks

in ultragreen the sunset on
          rust glows
still in the haven

                    limbs rise and sink to the pitch of
          an ear over the sway
                    balancing the
          small loss of your face left
                    behind
                              the city's weight

                              slides out to sea as iron
                    steps out on water a loose
                              bolt a gap in the door
                    a rusted girder or an arm
                    tattooed way below deck

                    the light gone
                              we assemble our-
                    selves in muster stations

CATHERINE SMITH

Catherine Smith was born in Windsor in 1962, graduated from Bradford University in 1983 and worked as an Information / Research Officer in London before having children and taking an MA at Sussex University, where she now teaches on various creative writing courses. Her first publication *The New Bride* (Smith/Doorstop) was shortlisted for the Forward Prize for Best First Collection and her first full collection *The Butcher's Hands* earned her a place on the *Mslexia* 'Ten Best Women Poets' list and also the Poetry Book Society's Next Generation promotion of 2004. Her third collection, *Lip*, was shortlisted for the Forward Prize in 2008. Smith most commonly writes about the body. Dreams and erotic fantasy – 'dangerous pleasures' as she puts it – feature in her work. She can be visceral too, and has created a string of untrustworthy and badly behaved character personae. Rachel Campbell-Johnson said of Smith, 'Her scary, unsettling voice seems unexpected in poetry. It cuts her free of the crowd.'

The Set of Optics You Wouldn't Let Me Buy in Portobello Road Market, September 1984

Remember how I fell in love with them,
displayed on a stall by a wall-eyed dealer
sucking morosely on his Turkish cigar?
How they glinted in the weak sunlight
amongst the tarnished soup tureens,
the scratched fob-watches? My hand went out
instinctively to trace the inscriptions –
whisky, gin, vermouth. Oh that word, vermouth –
evenings in a silk kimono, louche, bohemian,
sipping my drink, listening to Rachmaninov,
living the life I deserved. I'd have fixed them
above my desk in my high-ceilinged study
with its polished floors, I'd sit on
a green and gold Lloyd Loom chair,
overlooking a lush jungle of a garden.

That glug of spirits, the satisfying *ah, ah, ah*.
My own private bar. Look, if I'd bought them
I'd have stayed out of sleazy cafés and pubs
and drifted round my Hampstead flat,
thin and mysterious; I'd have written
that trilogy of exquisite novels, I'd be
taking a call from my agent to say
the film rights had been sold for megabucks,
darling, and when could we do lunch?
Remember how I fell in love with them?
My hand went out. Oh, that word. Vermouth.

Wonders

> *(Julia Pastrana, a bearded woman, was billed as 'the ugliest woman in the world' by her 'manager', Mr Lent. The couple later married.)*

The earth is cooling now. All day they've sweated
in the August heat, his Wonders,
twenty-seven rescued freaks. Prodded
by ignorant children, they've proffered
limbs and faces, caused women to faint.
Only he sees their beauty, the human template
twisted by Satan or God.

He tends them carefully, his strange flock,
bidding them good-night by name –
Angus the Lobster Boy, Pedro the Wart-Man.
His dog barks as he tucks up Martha and Mary,
twitching their shared hip. He checks the locks
on the caravans, as the stars burn
above the French village, miles from civilisation.

And Julia waits patiently at their polished table.
She's lowered the lamps,
brushed and oiled her beard, the way he likes.
Tonight they'll play cribbage into the early hours,
he'll smoke three cheroots, she'll chide him
in her tiny voice. He'll unbutton her,
lay her flat, sleep deeply on her hair-shirt skin.

Picnic

This way. He punches in the code;
five to midnight – the monitors glowing
like fish-tanks. The Veuve Cliquot
has roused them, their fingers
laced as he leads her to his manager's desk.
eases her clothes away like packaging,
kneels between her shaking legs.
She hardly murmurs even though
she's pressed against the in-tray –
this is an act of worship, but also unholy,
the desecration of the temple, the gods
will be angry with them forever.
Afterwards you ask *Are you hungry?*
They sit by the office fridge, and gorge
on Louise's strawberries, Geoff's garlic Boursin,
Mary's half-bottle of Pinot Grigio.
They lick their fingers clean, kiss,
the cheese sweetening their breath.
She remembers her first picnic –
lemonade bubbles exploding in her mouth;
my mother's shoulders burned, thistles
pricking her through the wool blanket.
The songs in the long grass, swaying,
sandwich crusts curled in the heat
and the soft curdling of egg and cress.

The Fathers

All over the city, women in restaurants,
cafés, bars, wait for their fathers.
The women sip coffee, or wine, pretend to read.
Some fathers arrive promptly, smiling –
dressed as policemen, or in flannel pyjamas.
Sometimes the father is a priest
in a cassock stained with candle wax.

317

One or two have pockets gritty with sand
from Cornish holidays. One father
flourishes a fledgling sparrow, damp
and frightened, from an ironed handkerchief.
One wears a taffeta dress, fishnets and stilettos,
rubs the stubble under his make-up.
They bring spaniels, Shetland ponies, anacondas,
they bring yellowed photographs
whose edges curl like wilting cabbages.
One father has blue ghosts of numbers
inked on his wrist. There are times the fathers
have been dead or absent for so long
the women hardly recognise them; some
talk rapidly in Polish or Greek and the women
shift on their chairs. A few sign cheques,
others blag a tenner. One smells of wood-shavings
and presents the woman with a dolls' house.
They might tell the women *You're getting fat*
or Put some meat on your bones, girl.
Some women leave arm in arm with their fathers,
huddled against the cold air, and window shop
for turquoise sequinned slippers or angelfish
hanging like jewels in bright tanks. Others
part with a kiss that misses a cheek – lint
left on coats, and buttons done up wrong.

JEAN SPRACKLAND

Jean Sprackland was born in Burton-on-Trent in 1962 and studied Philosophy and English at the University of Kent at Canterbury, then taught for a few years before beginning to write poetry at the age of 30. Her first book *Tattoos for Mothers Day* (Spike) was shortlisted for the 1998 Forward Prize for Best First Collection, and *Hard Water* (Cape Poetry) was shortlisted for both the T.S. Eliot Prize and the Whitbread Poetry Award. Her third collection, *Tilt* (Cape Poetry), was the winner of the 2007 Costa Poetry Award. She also works in education, training and consultancy for organisations including the Poetry Society and the Poetry Archive.

Sprackland is a narrative writer of the concise and the colloquial, who composes poems which describe unusual happenings in the familiar landscapes of childhood, home and memory. Jules Smith has written of her work that it 'shifts perceptions by continually juxtaposing the surprising and the visionary against the familiar and everyday'.

The Way Down

Forget the path.
Hack through gorse and blackthorn
and walk into the stream.

The thing about a stream is
it knows where it's going, has a gift
for finding the shortest route.

A path can lose its nerve,
peter out into bog or bracken, divide
inscrutably in two. I've stood at that place

and weighed the choices, weighed
and checked again, while mist crawls
over the mountain like sleep.

When the stream divides
both streamlets are equally sure.
Each plays its own game – the slick of moss,

the sudden race over a sill of rock –
and each, if you let it,
will carry you down.

Bracken

Lives by its own rules, obeys
a single imperative: *Swarm*

Can smell the space a mile away
where trees have been cleared

Claims squatters' rights
from Norway to Tasmania

and has been seen through telescopes
on the surface of Venus

Closes over the heads of children
where they lie waiting to be found

Spins long curled arguments
tentative as fists

that drink in confidence
thicken into dogma

grow brown and esoteric
waiting for the moment

to pounce on the accident
of the discarded match

An Old Friend Comes to Stay

She rings from a station
somewhere south of Heaven, north of here.
Guess what? I'm down for the weekend.
A sleeping bag on the sofa will do.
I'd forgotten the precise smoky register
of her voice, how close it is to jazz.

Good thing I kept her Indian cotton skirt,
the one I took when she died.
She arrives without luggage, wearing
temporary garments unsuitable for October.
She bundles the skirt to her face,
breathing its lost scent. I lend her
a red sweater – she was always glamorous in red –
but the wool makes her skin itch.
Bodies are so treacherous, she says,
allergies, wrinkles, wind…
I want to talk about the day we buried her
but it seems impossibly rude

so I ask has she got plans,
people to look up, business to finish?
She says by Christ she could murder a brandy and Coke.
The band is loud and loose, the sax man
half her age, leather jeans and a ponytail.
I come back from the bar, and he's rolling her a cigarette.
She's telling him she's spent five years as pure spirit,
she's missed the pleasures of the flesh.

Well what did I think she'd want,
a day out at the Albert Dock?
She's travelled so far to get here
and forty-eight hours can be very short.
I'll get off home and leave the door on the latch.

Hands

She peels cod fillets off the slab,
dips them in batter, drops them
one by one into the storm of hot fat.
I watch her scrubbed hands,
elegant at the work

and think of the hands of the midwife
stroking wet hair from my face as I sobbed and cursed,
calling me Sweetheart and wheeling in more gas,
hauling out at last my slippery fish of a son.
He was all silence and milky blue. She took him away
and brought him back breathing,
wrapped in a white sheet. By then
I loved her like my own mother.

I stand here speechless in the steam and banter,
as she makes hospital corners of my hot paper parcel.

JOHN STAMMERS

John Stammers was born and bred in London. He read philosophy at King's College. His first collection, *Panoramic Lounge-bar* (Picador, 2001), won the Forward Prize for Best First Collection and was short-listed for the Whitbread Poetry Award. His second collection, *Stolen Love Behaviour* (Picador, 2005), was a Poetry Book Society Choice and shortlisted for the T.S. Eliot Prize and the Forward Prize for Best Collection. His third collection is *Interior Night* (Picador, 2010). He was Judith E. Wilson Fellow at the University of Cambridge in 2002-03. He is convenor of the British and Irish Contemporary Poetry Conference. He teaches creative writing and lives in London with his wife and sons.

August Kleinzahler noted that Stammers writes 'some of the most memorable love poetry of his generation'. He has written poems on popular music and cinema and employs various modes of parlance: joshing, plaintive, self-mocking and peppers his poems with jargon and words from other languages. Frank O'Hara's mix of iconography is a notable influence, with its fusion of multiple dictions, but Stammers also has a delicate side and his work leaps from the fabulous to pastiche to taut formal pieces.

Mary Brunton

Let us walk to the waterfall before lunch
and sail the paper boats we made yesterday;
let us not put away that afternoon of losses
when the August sunshine belted onto the Kerry slate roof
and cooked the lichen to fine, sallow dust.
From out of nowhere, I saw you shatter
the blank white page to an angle
and all my flat earth certitudes fell away,
as any waterfall collapses into its pool.
You see, I wanted to believe more than you thought,
but the plain fact of how your fingers
worked the terrible geometries into being
frightened me, the way a child is frightened
by death without knowing why.

This, though, was a coming into the world.
It had not occurred to me to think
you would know how to do such a thing.
You showed me the proper way of it
and so you are changed to me and I to you,
the way that creases remain always
in a sheet of paper that has once been folded.

A Younger Woman

The long huts hunched above the Arctic circle.
The slow veil of sunshine failed and failed
onto the solid earth. In this un-place
insects froze to a halt and dropped from the air
as individual sleet; hail ball-bearings fired
onto the marble ground with a crack yet leaving no crack;
icicles pierced sheet steel when they fell.
                              A single stove per hut
around which, nightly, the zeks would lie in a decaying spiral
like the orbit of a Soviet space hulk.
Daybreak, they would haul out the lumpen bundles
of those next to the stove, their thin ghosts
unable to hold onto the dear bodies they had played in
in kindergarten under gentler protocols.
Night on night, the men would cleave themselves a row nearer,
drawn by the trace-memory of that warmth,
                              fleeting and indelible,
knowing that when they held it full and close
it would let them go but once.

Funeral

I too know it, the charm of funerals in the rain.
The ferocity of a veil in daylight,
or the studied black suit and millinery:
disremembered rituals of the tribe.

The portals of the mausoleum lean
as if having suffered break-ins
by morbid archangels;
its columns evince a certain verticality,
each finding itself unable to fall
into that abstraction
known as giving up the ghost.

Wreathes sadden in a damp mode.
I smoke an ugly brown cigarillo;
its liverous wisps swell the nose.
We shall float up, a grey twist of smoke.
Are you with me, yourselves, at the rendezvous.

Testimony

You guided me through Dublin and Derrida
and I went along with you though you told me
that one could not be 'wrong' or 'right',
that these were 'words'. You stressed
there was no such thing as *the* canonical text,
nor even the next best thing. You drew me
into Bewley's Oriental Café standing cloned
in its own postmodern pastiche
and Grafton Street. There, over sticky buns
interpolated with glacé cherries that pressed red imprints
into the buns' white substance, you somehow de-conjured up
the self-styled 'writer'
of the *Codex Ulysseus*
so that when he put in a radical failure of appearance
you were able to sever any connection
between author and *oeuvre*,
'What is it, after all, that is *authorised*?',
you said, and gave an allusive nod,
with your feathered black fringe and Irish-blue eyes,
to Althusser whilst continuing to assert
recondite doctrines through unpursed lips
pinkened with cerise so that I tumbled
headlong into ideological concurrence with you:
I knew what you were talking about and I didn't care.

From there we pursued a line of argument
along the General Post Office where I read the proclamation
In the Name of God and the Dead Generations
leaded into the brass plaque beneath Cúchulainn
and I inserted an interpretative finger into bullet holes
typed there on the wall in belt-fed lines;
the beautiful stone, the terrible queerness
of just standing there with the paths the bullets had taken
passing right through me. So we were pleased
to walk the free streets and follow
our merely quodlibetical ratiocinations
in the sight of dead heroes and live tin-whistlers.

But, when we crossed the singular Trinity quad
and perused the Book of Kells
etched forever on the stretched skin of unknown dead sheep,
I felt a revision begin.
There were its principal letters lit up
like O'Connell Street on Paddy's Day night,
knocking seven bells out of itself,
fiddling and chanting and beating the bodhrán
to the infinite glory of God
and the resurrection, with its parchment
grey from multifarious eyes draining the light from it
in rays, surveying its apostolic dogmas inscribed there
by quills snug against ink-stained finger calluses,
the nibs screeching like peewits
against the manuscript's interface, relentless,
taking pains and decades
to give the work the full weight of God's law.

So it was that I saw two sides of an antinomy take hold
and go to undo me like a zip
and I saw that it was writ
that we should be the critics of our own juxtaposition,
to deconstruct what there was between us
and discover if it was all just so much periphrasis
or something more.

Therefore when we found ourselves
beneath the spiral staircase
at the hub of the circular bookshop, in Tomes St
I think it might have been,

with the steeped banks of shelves in aisles that receded
on all points of the compass like the world itself, I delved
into the shelf labelled *Poetry / Irish / in English*,
came up with *The Collected* of yer man,
unread and silent straight from his tongue,
which I held out to you and you took hold of
so it spanned our two hands like an arc of electric
that cracked and spat between us,
both wanting to let go, each unable to.

Black Dog

From the inward night of the unconscionably tall, arched doorway,
the shadows commence a faint unnerving undulation;
they wear an awful sheen, as if the shade has been interminably brushed
after being treated in some scienty new conditioner.
The aperture takes on shape: the hard sway of a long, high neck,
and the absurd tiny slope of what, in another creature,
might have been its shoulders.
                                        Black Dog,
some animal trader's corrupt attempt at a half-understood Swahili term;
his name is inked into him like a torturer's signature mark.
The single specimen they ever found, a male giraffe
black as the whitest sunlight, blacker
than the white crocuses in the ornamental flower-beds,
or the ultra-white of the open-eyed woman's white crêpe blouse.
It is merely a matter of waiting and everything happens:
the chimpanzees write *Titus Andronicus* on their toy typewriters;
the sea-lions bring down a gazelle;
the eels walk on two legs to the north gate and go home.
I feel a sensation of overwhelming disgust.
I make myself turn and leave the side of the enclosure.

GRETA STODDART

Greta Stoddart was born in Oxford-shire in 1966 and grew up in Belgium and Oxford. She trained as an actress in Paris and Manchester before moving to London and starting to write. She now lives in East Devon and is a tutor in Creative Writing at Bath Spa University and for the Poetry School in Exeter. Her first collection *At Home in the Dark* was published by Anvil Press in 2002 and won the Geoffrey Faber Memorial Prize, and her second, *Salvation Jane* (Anvil), was shortlisted for the Costa Poetry Award in 2008.

Stoddart's narrative poems record often fragile relationships between near strangers, lovers, family members. The theme of darkness – both its danger and its anonymity – runs through her earlier work. Childhood, her own and that of her young children, is also a central concern. A formal poet, with a subtle touch in her use of half-rhyme and other sonic effects, she writes with a certain effective detachment from these subjects which might otherwise beckon sentimentality.

Salvation Jane

What is Salvation Jane?

> *Little purple sturdy thistle,*
> *dicot weed of the Boraginaccae*

'But it's beekeepers' gold,
      a sun-chopped sea of violet trumpetheads
         – a god's bright nodding flock!'

And Paterson's Curse?

> *Little purple sturdy thistle,*
> *dicot weed of the Boraginaceae*

'But it's a noxious rough hairy-leaved herb,
    a chemical-resistant infester of cereals;
        it chokes pastures, poisons cattle.'

Who gives these names, who tends them?

    Men and women who look up at the dark
        gold-tinted clouds and mouth 'Heaven',
            who run for their lives shouting 'Storm!'

The Crossing

The sun was setting as the Karoa sailed
into harbour – from the limo I sat
and stared out at the South China Sea
flat as peace itself. I was all in.

At the gangplank they pressed me with the usual
blaze of cameras, name barked out
so I twirled the cane, walked the walk,
got away with a quick pirouette.

There was a boy outside my cabin with a card.
Seeing the famous signature I took it
as some kind of joke but I had to be sure
so I called up the bursar for the list.

And there he was in a peignoir with Pilou
his pet cricket chirping on one finger.
Flicking it gently back to its cage he turned,
'Charlot, mon hero! Venez tout de suite dans mes bras!'

We swapped theories of life and art all night
through his interpreter who sat, po-faced:
'Meester Cocteau ...'e say you are a poet
of ze sunshine ...'e a poet of ze night.'

Next thing I knew it was dawn,
the cage under a towel had gone quiet.
The linguist snored. No witness then
to our warm embrace, the pledge to meet at noon.

Midday. The deck damp and grey.
Neither show but at our desks compose
near identical notes of apology
that cross. We pace our rooms.

All week we're ducking into broom-cupboards,
engrossed in menus, conversations with bores.
Nights we stand alone in our cabins
gazing out at the fixed and brilliant stars.

By the time we got to Hong Kong we could handle
a doffing of hats, brief, despairing smiles
but the days grew fierce and hot, the nights froze
and (dear God!) four more to go till Tokyo.

Verfremdungseffekt

Our budget got the biggest laugh.
We blew half of it on a fat hack in a Chinese
'All You Can Eat for a Tenner!'

We sat and watched as he helped himself to thirds
of Ham Foo Yung – next day we read his piece
on a local midwife's prize ornamental cabbage.

We pulled out all the tricks: natty flip
of a baking sheet for thunder, our hero walking
away to a pair of hand-clopped brogues.

Pulled them out literally, you understand.
We'd read our Brecht and were completely sold;
no bourgeois suspension of disbelief for us!

So really the conditions couldn't've been better
that July evening in Speke Youth Club where,
impossible to get a black-out – the sun, the skylights –

we still crept on 'stage', careful not to follow
the shredded pitch-markings nor make eye contact
with the audience we outnumbered five to three

(had we an ounce of common decency
we'd've pulled the show and paid their refund
in the pub but we were young, and all that mattered).

I've forgotten every word of *Kleines Organon für das Theater*
but not how it ended that night:
our final dramatic pause filling

with the chittity-chit of swallows, the M6's rivery hum,
our faces lifting their faces up
not to some fusty old gods but a heaven

of swing ropes and gym ladders suspended there
like something unbelievable that did once and would,
with faith enough or a full house, happen again.

Greece

Afternoons we have to hide from the heat
where the dog drags his ragged shadow
along the walls. Knives are clean and quiet,
pillows cool, rain remote as tragedy.
In the drawn room as we lie on the verge
of sleep or sex, zapping bad TV,
Chelsea appear and it's like old footage –
men we thought we'd lost forever, a field,
big-dropped Summer rain and that semen
sweet smell that heaves off a certain shrub.
My heart thumps obscurely at the thought of London
as if of a not quite forgotten lover;
and the old song-swell carries from the pitch
like the approach of a massive storm, or myth.

Object

Her eyes were fixed on the horizon
when the man beside her broke out,
'Sometimes when I think of the Earth
spinning I have to grab hold
of something – in my case usually
railings, the solid helm of a bar –
once I clung to a parking meter
till it passed, or I was moved on.'
She stared out at the still water
where a chough was wheeling like a demented clock
and turning he took and held her
fast in his arms till it stopped.

SANDRA TAPPENDEN

Sandra Tappenden was born in 1956, grew up in South East London and moved as a teenager to Devon, where she still lives. She has worked in various professions and has been a Creative Writing tutor at Exeter College of Further Education. A regular performer of her work, she often collaborates with musicians and visual artists. Her collections are *Bags of Mostly Water* (Oplus, 2003) and *Speed* (Salt Publishing, 2007).

For Tappenden, the commonplace contains the extraordinary, where everything mundane is by turns comic, dark, curious and surprising. Her work is refreshingly hard to place. She might be compared to Selima Hill in her digressive and unexpected turns of phrase and extended images and metaphors, but her work is also transgressive, poking into the corners of a collective psyche deploying what one critic called 'manic sanity'. The poems in *Speed* address her feeling that the breakneck speed of today's world leads us to think about and comprehend less of what we encounter.

Promise

I've found it helps to carry an egg in my pocket.
In the past I tried using stones, and lay
amphetamine-eyed on the river bed
in a suitably heavy coat. I believe
I was waiting for obduracy to change
colour, texture, or shape, but it didn't.
Why this surprises me is another mystery.

Poor Arabella. She put an egg down her blouse.
It could only end in tears, although it was an option
I often considered, like the dream of removing
the egg from the dark on my hip to find
the shell had turned lavender, pink, or
transparent, and whether it was even there
when I didn't actually have my hand on it.

Sometimes my fingertips feel a contained world
moving slow as ocean beneath finite sky.
It is happiness, or misapprehension
no one can fault. And when blizzards come,
or drought which threatens to crack
the surface of what I call 'getting on with it',
my hand checks back in, okay, and it is.

Bells

Patterns are transported across the river
in complicated ripples, like the river
on a windy day of confused reflections.

I know someone is pulling a rope
attached to a promise. I know
my heart is in the right place.

It's just the way they come to my ear,
one second hidden in cloud, the next,
take care, take care. Do I ever.

All this knowledge of being in debt
they carry over; the explicable grief
their airborne phalanxes even up.

Waroirrs of the Whiled West

Once were sovereign shilling water magpies
season savvy salt and soil tillers

Once were Godsown downhome educations
mutant cattle auction pirate poets

Once were belt and braces stiff lip adepts
starve march beri beri drop dead bleeders

Once were prefab deadbeat chaos merchants
oily comb back flick knife alter egos

Once were velvet primp sex freedom footpads
thrusty hello dope dupe flower fellows

Once were wa wa wireless techno boomers
sovereign teenage manufactured off cuts

Once were blue screech limb thrash baldy milk lumps
mottled rage flush gully gully suckers

People who are drawn to take free stress tests

The high street is a picture of anywhere
this side of salt water, although there's
a shiny sculpture with old riddles on it
where people tidy their reflected hair.

(I like back streets, where butchers
are selling their hacking kits on-line
and you can buy out-of-date chocolate
in the spooky mini-mart.)

The checkout girl in Boots
wears a scarf arranged over her head
which means she belongs to
something I don't.

A chance encounter with Elizabeth
was the exact missing thing;
hugging and theology in the alley
behind that weird little factory.

Where does anyone live nowadays?
Certainty is a product like anything else
and poets are not much use are they
I often think I overhear someone say.

TIM TURNBULL

Tim Turnbull was born and brought up in North Yorkshire. He began performing his work in clubs and at slams in the early 1990s. His first full collection *Stranded in Sub-Atomica* (Donut Press) was shortlisted for the Forward Prize for Best First Collection in 2006. In the same year, he was awarded the Arts Foundation's Performance Poetry Fellowship, the first major arts award made in the genre. Turnbull used the award to develop a one-man show, *Caligula on Ice*, which includes music and dance. His second collection, also called *Caligula on Ice*, was published in 2009. A bilingual edition of poems, *Es Lebt!*, was published in the same year by roughbooks in Germany.

Turnbull views poetry as a continuum of styles as opposed to a family of definable genres. For him, the page is a stage, on which to perform pastiche, polemic, new takes on old forms. An often formal poet, fond of long lines, his work is varied, veering from scathing, to tender, to exuberantly comic.

Sea Monsters

Up from the pitsaw they are bringing fresh green boards.
At the window, hand over knotty hand, men pass them in;
each will season for a year. Rain scours the courtyard
as women hurry back and forth in heavy oilskin

capes and hoods. An apprentice shivers by the stable.
The stink of tanning hides wafts down the passageway
from the upholsterer's shop. I will make a table
next. A table so finely jointed, polished and inlaid

it will be a masterpiece. Out on the causeway,
sea serpents attack a cart. Men beat them off with staves.
A comet showed its lustrous tail last night. Some prayed.
Down the coast, another town is ravaged by the plague.

Lullaby for an Alcoholic

Put down your head and flutter into troubled sleep.
Dream parachuting soldiers yanked across the sky

on sudden winds. Fall into darkness, bored on trains
by blethering strangers, or in your bed as from the street

a fire engine dopplers past. Pull up the gritty sheets
and count a million sheep or more. Imagine waves

exploding on the pier or make a mental picture
of a silent kite cartwheeling down an empty beach.

Wake up on a sofa-bed, a silver curry tray
set on the floor, a coat wrapped tight about your head.

Surface from beneath an unfamiliar eiderdown,
a warm body beside you and the stink of sweat and sex

or stir in a dusty meadow on a summer afternoon
and lick your lips and catch a little sour taste of death.

What was that?

Through a whitewashed courtyard bleached by inappropriate,
        nearly Mediterranean sun
then stoop into a musty junkshop presided over by the murderer
        Christie and Ma Broon.
The rooms have a whiff of elderly relations visited on summer
        Sunday afternoons
with Mack Sennett shorts on the telly, cold pork for tea and, for
    afters, butterfly buns.

Move into the makeshift shrine, all glass cases stuffed with papers,
        scrapbooks, photographs,
film posters, pairs of bowlers and bow ties and the actual *Sons of
    the Desert* hats,

and here's some correspondence with a fan, bedridden since her
    unexplained collapse
but delighted they could find the time, and Stan, sick and old
    and tired in a late on-set snap,

bitter since the studio took the writing off his hands, and Ollie
    looking fat, even for him, and used.
Cramp into the makeshift picture-house; a room with a big TV
    and salvaged Wesleyan pews,
where Ma loads a cassette and off you go – *Scram, Blockheads,*
    Laughing Gravy, One Good Turn
and, best of all, *Big Business.* Watch the stupid escalating war
    with boggle-eyed James Finlayson

where they take turns to wreck his house as he wrecks their car
    and the crowd troop back and forth
and forth and back and the cop double-takes. Writhe and hoot
    with laughter, shake with mirth
at the pie in the face, a hoof in the rump, a poke in the eye,
    Sartre in Africa, a scissored-off tie,
the flaming thumb, firestorm on the Ruhr, marines with Zippo
    lighters strolling through My Lai,

Oppenheimer quoting the *Bhagavad-Gita*, saying *I am become*
    death; destroyer of worlds, a horse
on a piano that makes you laugh until you gasp for air and, lastly,
    hear the music. It's 'The Cuckoo Waltz'.

Ode on a Grayson Perry Urn

Hello! What's all this here? A kitschy vase
    some Shirley Temple manqué has knocked out
delineating tales of kids in cars
    on crap estates, the Burberry clad louts
who flail their motors through the smoky night
    from Manchester to Motherwell or Slough,
        creating bedlam on the Queen's highway.
Your gaudy evocation can, somehow,
    conjure the scene without inducing fright,
        as would a *Daily Express* exposé,

338

can bring to mind the throaty turbo roar
    of hatchbacks tuned almost to breaking point,
the joyful throb of UK garage or
    of house imported from the continent
and yet educe a sense of peace, of calm –
    the screech of tyres and the nervous squeals
        of girls, too young to quite appreciate
the peril they are in, are heard, but these wheels
    will not lose traction, skid and flip, no harm
        befall these children. They will stay out late

forever, pumped on youth and ecstasy,
    on alloy, bass and arrogance and speed
the back lanes, the urban gyratory,
    the wide motorways, never having need
to race back home, for work next day, to bed.
    Each girl is buff, each geezer toned and strong,
        charged with pulsing juice which, even yet,
fills every pair of Calvins and each thong,
    never to be deflated, given head
        in crude games of chlamydia roulette.

Now see who comes to line the sparse grass verge,
    to toast them in Buckfast and Diamond White,
rat-boys and corn-rowed cheerleaders who urge
    them on to pull more burn-outs or to write
their donut Os, as signature, upon
    the bleached tarmac of dead suburban streets.
        There dogs set up a row and curtains twitch
as pensioners and parents telephone
    the cops to plead for quiet, sue for peace –
        tranquillity, though, is for the rich.

And so, millennia hence, you garish crock,
    when all context is lost, galleries razed
to level dust and we're long in the box,
    will future poets look on you amazed,
speculate how children might have lived when
    you were fired, lives so free and bountiful
        and there, beneath a sun a little colder,
declare *How happy were those creatures then,*
    who knew that truth was all negotiable
        and beauty in the gift of the beholder.

JULIAN TURNER

Julian Turner was born in Cheadle Hulme, Cheshire in 1955 and educated at New College, Oxford and Goldsmith's, London. He now lives in Otley, West Yorkshire and works in the field of mental health. His first collection, *Crossing the Outskirts* (Anvil, 2002), was a Poetry Book Society Recommendation and shortlisted for the Forward Best First Collection Prize. His second book, *Orphan Sites*, was published in 2006.

The accounts of extreme experiences and our reactions to them can be found in Turner's work, which Ian Duhig has described as being 'distinguished by a compassion as intense as its musicality'. Turner's poetry can be amusing as well as perturbing, and his work reflects the need for courage in facing the adversity which is the subject of many of the pieces. Careful and formal, Turner's peculiar imagination is his trump card, as he concocts modern fables and finds poetry in unexpected corners, unannounced memories and in the tiniest of artefacts.

Bert Haines' Yard

What was it my dad and brother were searching for
those times they dragged me down to Bert Haines' yard,
thistles and groundsel bushing up through floors
of cars, the unhinged gravestones of van doors
tilting towards the sun, their paintwork scarred
by unrecorded bumps and scrapes, a ghost
topography where all things come to rest,

the stripped down bicycles and engine parts,
vast sprockets from the giants' industries,
their magnitude remembering lost arts
of universes smelted and cast in foundries
moving at night to patterns planned by star-charts,
an after-life of objects grassed in dust
and grease, a leaf-soft mall which sells what's lost,

forgotten, repossessed, passed on: cement
statues, wheelless wheel barrows, old machines,
their movements gone? Maybe some link between
two boyhoods, a chain broken by accident
which they must mend but didn't have the means?
To find among the litter of the dead
a golden circlip? Neither ever said.

Penalty of Stroke and Distance

These are the ones whose rules, exact and pure,
remind you poor conditions are no excuse;
who in all weathers will turn out and draw
their pitching irons cold from rusted pools,
who practise after dark their follow-through,
their swing-weight, wrist cock and pre-putt routine
alone with fog or rain in motley shoes
like shadows on the ninth at Halloween.

Have you seen them when snow has turned the links
into a glittercloth of blinding stymies?
Then they cut loose, lost on the fairway banks,
intent and abstract, caddying their dead ponies
through waistdeep drifts across Antarctica.
They shield their faces from the icy sun
in search of pitchmarks on a glacier,
in search of the most extreme hole-in-one.

You must have seen them, in the dead afternoon
returning with their far-off eyes, as touched
as if they were illuminated from within,
the long climb over and their summit reached,
their parka hoods on fire; forgotten ones
who stumble home, their hair as white as snow,
to strangeness at the heart of what they know,
uncomprehending faces, eyes which shun.

A Nightjar

Goatsucker, puckeridge, poisoner-bird, lich-owl,
gabbleratch – these are the names of night-born fear
from far-flung farms and blind lane-ends – Fern Owl:
keep me safe with your wheeze at twilight; birch-black
drifter-between-copses, inoculate me with decoction
of feather, spore-of-the-glades, fragments of meteor;
let me walk under the dew-fall, hold in my traction
the Earth, fly open-mouthed through the mothy dark.

At Walcott

The full moon marooned between
the horns of chimney pots,
the stars fat and sugary;
the Insurance Company massive
and back-lit, its arms crossed –

something about the light tonight
brings back that Norfolk shore,
its cascading zither of stars,
their electromagnetic pulses
crawling across our scalps,

both of us taken by a fever
of wishing to approach
until we almost merged,
so close we seemed to share
the same mind

as the moon silvered the frontal lobes
of thunderheads above the sea,
rising as dirigibles of bliss
over the horizon to hang
an illustration in front of us,

to magnify each glance, each touch,
each preparatory kiss. That night
we began construction on the first
foundations, pouring the Ready-Mix
for our own footings,

to support the clouds and their high lancets.
It's been a good year for skies –
like tonight's thrown-back storm hoods
exposing the moon's mother-of-pearl
and dark winged rafts

break off and drift apart.

MARK WALDRON

Mark Waldron was born in New York in 1960 and grew up in London. He works in the advertising business and lives in East London with his wife and son. He began writing poetry in his early 40s and his first collection, *The Brand New Dark*, was published by Salt Publishing in 2008.

Waldron has a distinctive style and diction. His poems are generally short, curious, built around one idea and often consist of just one extended sentence. Clare Pollard noted that Waldron's work in advertising, far from causing him to write jingle-like poems, has actually led him to create poetry which kicks back against society's tension of surfaces. Reactions to his work differ, some finding it darkly psychological and sinister, others charming and amusingly absurd and both are accurate. Odd locutions, exclamations, asides and unlikely adjectives are tics in his poetry, as are repeated emblems such as eyes, dogs, skin and furniture. John Stammers described him as 'the most striking and unusual new voice to have emerged in British poetry for some time'.

The Brand New Dark is Getting In,

the speedboats are of the sweetest and wonderful knives,
the clouds and the cranes on the docks –

strips of black leather inlaid in the metal green sky,
the whole thing just sitting back there.

She moves her allure across the engine's holler and
touches the man's liquorice carbine.

She speaks to him and the wind pulls back her hair
and her whole baby skin just tugged up by it.

The boats are holding themselves,
they cry like Jesus on a brittle world;

the guns are so inky and homeless and infant;
everything is loving everything else

and the wakes are softly bleating white now,
and letting it go, stone hard and gone.

Sometimes I remember who I am.

He's Face Down in the Lake

arms out as though he's going *Come here
and let me hug you*, or he's asking *Why?*

his arms describing the size of the question,
or he's been crucified and nailed to the sky,

or he's folding an invisible sheet,
or surrendering perhaps, or closing a window,

or conducting an orchestra, holding some piece of quiet
between his fingers, or letting it go,

or he's bowing before an idol,
going *I am not worthy Master.*

Or he's looking for something
down here among the water weeds,

a lost ring his wife gave him,
he's thinking *She'll kill me*

The Well Dressed Street

wears Marcie – an accessory on its blue white noon.
Marcie wears the pressed uniform

of her comeliness over her ludicrous blood
full of its minute wheels.

She wears her smart body over her pocketed self,
her words under her scent,

her breath beneath her clothes, her heat
under the walloping sky. Her self is a long, translucent eel,

over which days pass, its tail at her birth, its brain here,
pushing the look of her along.

The Very Slow Train,

on the downhill stretch,
moves with the speed with which I grew
and with which I will, in my old age, shrink back
towards the warm and waiting ground –
myself a piston on its single push and pull,
among the billions more,
who grind this almost round world round.
And on the flat we slow to an adhered stamp's progress
across its envelope, or so it seems.
Whole yawning generations
come and go between two sleepers here.
And gazing out the window,
I watch a snail dart and flit beside the track.
The snail, which, before we reach our destination,
will have evolved, its descendants inhabiting shells
with living rooms papered in flock.
They'll rest their single feet on poufs.
They'll watch our train pull in
through windows mucus thin.
They'll see ourselves emerge as orbs of shining mind.
Please God, wait for me.

Underneath the Gone Sky

they stood, stretched with relief and fear,
the spilt night over everything.

The wall she was against was on the world's edge,
her back against her shirt, her shirt against her coat,

her coat against the brick, its knuckle grit holding her on.
And beneath unspeaking clothes, he found her

hopelessly bare, peaceful, shocked,
as though her clothes had been her skin

her skin, flesh. I promise
they were absolutely ruined by its magic.

AHREN WARNER

Ahren Warner was born in 1986 in Oxford and grew up in North Lincolnshire. He read English at Queen Mary College and took an MA in Critical Methodologies at King's College London. He is currently pursuing a PhD and living in Paris. His work has appeared in the anthologies *Voice Recognition* (Bloodaxe Books, 2009) and *City State: The New London Poetry* (Penned in the Margins, 2009). He received an Arts Council writers' award in 2008. A pamphlet is forthcoming from Donut Press, followed by his first full collection from Bloodaxe in 2011.

Warner developed a strong interest in poetry in his early teens and published in several leading magazines, who were unaware of his age. He has a continuing interest in philosophy, specifically ontology and aesthetics, and in visual art. Much of his academic work hinges on a coalescence between art, literature and philosophy and this informs his poetry. He has written that he is 'concerned to try and express a kind of affective music, which has led to me to make frequent use of spacing as something that can denote a more subtle variety of pause and punctuation.'

la brisure

each toll sustains itself   as if expecting
its own next sounding   or   another's

to which it will defer   by default   falling
to its own lack   its spacing from the other

each space comes   tactile   as a relief
or   as the rough joint-lines of a bronze

the repetition   of a hollowed   motif
the becoming sound   of the bronze

so each bell seems   to long
for an end   less partition   than party

a silence on which   each sound   hangs
for its self-sameness   its being *partie*

you listen   to the last toll   draining
retained only   in the space   it becomes

you're unsure   if you're still waiting
or hearing   what has come

Legare

This   is what I consign   perhaps   because my hands fall cold
on the keys of a harpsichord   or my right arm fails to bow
a sustained   viola note.   Or   because I do not wear
breeches at the court   of some Germanic state

do not listen   to the latest offering   of a Herr Mozart
eyeing the women   the aristocrats   those in waiting
or catch their eyes   proceed to bed them
the scandal of high societies: Dresden   Vienna   Venice.

Because   I do not mark this world   with pale cottons
and the hues of birthing girls   bastards   who'll grow
to their own actions   and sadness   coaxing warm tears
from other's eyes   blurred   before books whose words

blot and run   so nothing is known
but affect   and afflicted men   holding or held by
women in straw beds;   spare light
from candles near done;   the kestrel   lingering outside.

Near Saint Mary Woolnoth, EC3

I doubt even your authenticity – tree
amongst this boom of tinted glass, landscaped grass
and men whose Windsor-knotted ties shout *phallus*.

We both know these streets feel best long after
the faded linger of a caretaker's patter,
the guard's breath as loud as his lull will allow;

that this city is felt in a drunken swagger,
the hop of a barrier, ascents via shimmy
and slither, that find you high on a balcony.

Teeter, titter through beer, mutter the view
of the river, windows turned baubles, the buzz
of a night-time generator. Shout *bow low*

multitudes. Know that the city has nothing
to offer but loopholes, itself as a playground
adventure, that to find yourself stumped

at the foot of a tree, suspicious of its age
– that its bark's wizened nature was planned –
is to miss the point entirely.

Léman

Here, at the river's kink, southbank and north
are lost to a city slanting towards
some hinter point
where fabled chimneys meet fabled hills.

Here – where sink estates and conurbations
are forgotten
for the cumulus,
the glare of windows, the plated dome,

light cumulative, the air an illuminated cold –
you watch the scurry
trying to divine
the salt glimmer behind each eye;

a scar set as crystalline, and reading:
unhappy child,
languid marriage,
frayed knot of poverty and desire.

TIM WELLS

Tim Wells was born in London in 1966 and has mostly lived in and around Stoke Newington. As a teenager, he began to perform his poems alongside the 'ranting poets' such as Phill Jupitus and Steven Wells. He returned to writing poetry in his late 20s and then founded the small magazine *Rising* which has been running for around 15 years. He works as a business adviser and also as a reggae DJ. After a number of pamphlets, his first full collection was *Boys' Night Out in the Afternoon* (Donut Press, 2005) which was shortlisted for the Forward Prize for Best First Collection. A second Donut Press collection, *Rougher Yet*, followed in 2009.

Although Wells emerged on the live poetry scene, his work sits well on the page, albeit without the props and risqué asides which make him a popular performer. His poetry is often comic, sometimes playfully coarse, and works as an extension of his obsessions with military history, reggae and country music, monkeys, unhealthy foods and more.

My Own Private Ida Lupino

Not even the completeness of rain,
just the languid 'I might or I might not'
indecisiveness of dull, dreary drizzle.
I'm already reconciled to not going out.
There's a Sherlock Holmes film on the telly;
it's not going well for him. Moriarty,
'the very genius of evil',
is about to snatch the crown jewels.

Indeed, Holmes is in a tight spot
but he'll pull through. I'll make do with hot Vimto.
Outside, all I can see is the sky pressing down
and my underpants flapping on the line.
I should go bring them in
but they're only underpants:
clean of me, moist with London.
There they hang – my flag of surrender.

351

The 1980s Are a Long Time Dead

The books in the 'community' bookshop have gathered a lot of dust,
despite being neatly ordered onto Black, Turkish, Lesbian
and Gay shelves. Opposite, Florjan is doing a roaring trade.
Since buying the shop from Mr Choudhury he's added
Polish to the stacks of Caribbean, Turkish, kosher
and English food. The shop is usually busy – busy and noisy.
In the rare moments of calm, Florjan often gazes over
to the faded picture of Maya Angelou in the bookshop window.
He thinks she looks like a nice lady. He wonders who she is,
where she lives, and bets she can put away a lot of salami.

Comin' a Dance

In this Dalston dusk
the lights from
the chicken shops,
minicab offices,
Polski Produckti
and all the bling
crammed on the bus
have dazzled the stars.
The sky is a dark sheet
replete with the stains
of an East London
Saturday night.
That stop near
the bottom of The Waste,
a girl dressed as a flapper,
dress cut from twilight,
boards. The feather
in her hair
punches hard times
smack on the nose.
Her bloke's in a pony suit
and drek trainers.

He carries a white fedora –
not even enough
snap to sport it:
a distinct lack of effort.
I hope tonight
she ends up
with someone else.
It's the dark
that makes
the stars shine.
At the next stop
three dancehall queen dem
fresh from Yard,
each wearing less
than she that precedes.
Oh my days!
So much good times
squeezed into
so small space.

When the bass drops …
Lawd G-d Almighty!

L.A. Rain

you can see the neon and never see the light
the footsteps of all those who can afford not to walk
readily washed away
men's feet in women's shoes

the footsteps of all those who can afford not to walk
water dancing hipshots across the oiled smear
men's feet in women's shoes
the hookers of Santa Monica Boulevard

water dancing hipshots across the oiled smear
water finds its own level
the hookers of Santa Monica Boulevard
the gutters full to bursting

water finds its own level
only cream and bastards float
the gutters full to bursting
fresh water gives life, this beats down

only cream and bastards float
waitresses course through the channels of Chinatown
fresh water gives life, this beats down
dirtiest rain I ever saw

waitresses course through the channels of Chinatown
readily washed away
dirtiest rain I ever saw
you can see the neon and never see the light

MATTHEW WELTON

Matthew Welton was born in Nottingham in 1969 and lives in Manchester. He received the Jerwood Aldeburgh First Collection Prize for *The Book of Matthew* (Carcanet, 2003), which was a *Guardian* Book of the Year. His second book, *We Needed Coffee But...* was published by Carcanet in 2009. He lectures in creative writing at the University of Bolton. He collaborates regularly with the artist Chris Evans and the composer Larry Goves, with whom he was awarded a Jerwood Opera Writing Fellowship in 2008. He is a member of Goves' experimental-classical ensemble The House of Bedlam.

Welton is interested in exploring the properties of language. His writing process is about finding ways of ordering the words, sometimes using musical structures or mathematics as a way of exploring patterns. He has said, 'perhaps I don't write my poems so much as organise them'. Many of his poems employ borrowed structures, taking things like *Roget's Thesaurus*, the stages of the World Cup, or the architecture of an airport to give the work its form.

Poppy

Scout puts a record on. In the kitchen sits Tujiko. Naomi and Damon eat too much rice. I came back from São Paulo expecting twins.

Joanna and Rachid have a feel for the seasons and an amateur interest in entomology. I cycled slowly into the small green field. Somewhere on the tape there's someone singing hymns.

After the sun sets, the sound of a piano is like a gradual fluctuation in the colour of the clouds. The birds were reappearing; the wind is on its way.

Bailey is thought to have abandoned his wife in a house in Manhattan built from small wooden blocks. The store proprietor drove through London. Mika and Philippe are righteous people.

Ursula started to bore me. Thurston started to bore me. Sunlight becomes twilight; flowers bloom and it rains. McGregor restrains his impressive voice.

I never understood my conversation with Didi. I expect Jakob to separate from Yoshimi, his wife. My older brother stood away from my friends. I'm sitting on a sofa with maracas in my hands.

An ABC of American Suicide

Arbus

The skies are stuffed with bread-coloured clouds and huge, huge
          raindrops
spill like peach juice. Anyone who was hurrying to meet
a friend by the Central Park Zoo bird-house might have to stop,
check themselves, and walk right on before hey found they'd just
          spent
one whole hour watching fat cigar-smoke skimming from the neat
nutmeggy mouth of that mud-eyed girls that those two boy-scouts
can't get enough of. They fidget like jumping beans, pout
like movie stars, but sleep like piglets till their parents slam
in, late from some gallery-crowd party in a backstairs
apartment on Fifty-seventh. Through suitcase-cardboard walls
their half-high father grinds on about cocktails and cab fares,
groaning like a gramophone with a faulty repeat-arm.

Brautigan

San Francisco: the morning arriving on Beaver Street
like just-percolating coffee; the early-day sunshine
hanging around like a catchy tune; the afternoon heat
building and building and growing huge like an easy yawn.
In the Ceiling-Fan Luncheonette, quart jars of Mad Dog wine
and half-packs of pocket-crushed Winstons pass from college kid
to college kid and everyone spoons into hot popcorn.
Skinny boys stretch out fudgy stories about what they did
all summer, bumming truck rides south and getting themselves lost.
Evening comes on like a sudden tiredness; the sky becomes
a smear of cinnamon paste. Girls head home to make phone calls
and down by the bay the streets are empty but for the bums
and dogs and wind and litter and dust, American dust.

Cobain

The wow-eyed boy in the horse chestnut shoes tears a grapefruit
to pieces, throws a corncob smile to a nearby stranger,
pulls his pennies-and-dimes bicycle from the ground, and scoots
southwards from the square till the monument he's spent the day
swinging his legs from is half an hour behind him. Later,
sat on the whitewashed window-sill of someone else's room,
clutching the phone, he gives a howl that could scare snakes away
and hangs up. He says something about finding his way home
then laughs himself to the floor. He looks up with a quick smirk
and makes for town to see someone who meets him with a kiss.
By a park that's sprinkled with a doughnut-sugar snowfall,
he turns to his friend and wonders out loud, *With days like this*
as cheap as chewing gum, why would anyone want to work?

The fundament of wonderment

She said her name was little jones
and bended back her finger-bones

and sang a song in minor thirds.
She spilled a smile and spoke her words.

*

Up here the river turns its boats.
she brings out books of pencil-notes,

her letters from, her letters to,
her clarkesville park, her London zoo.

*

And, in the wind and where she walks
above the blue nasturtium-stalks

at London zoo, the smells of apes
are like the smells of table-grapes.

*

The mice and monkeys tell the trees
the wind will end, the worlds will freeze.

She moves herself beyond the grass
the blue boats pass. The blue boats pass.

DAVID WHEATLEY

David Wheatley was born in Dublin in 1970 and educated at Trinity College, Dublin. He has published three collections with the Gallery Press: *Thirst* (1997), winner of the Rooney Prize for Irish Literature, *Misery Hill* (2000) and *Mocker* (2006), and a number of pamphlets, including *Lament for Ali Farka Touré* (Rack Press, 2008). He co-edits the poetry journal *Metre* with Justin Quinn (contemporary at Trinity College, along with Caitríona O'Reilly and Sinéad Morrissey) and has edited the poetry of James Clarence Mangan for the Gallery Press and Samuel Beckett for Faber & Faber. He is also a widely-published critic and lectures at the University of Hull.

Wheatley's work responds to a variety of writerly environments, both urban and rural, real and imagined. While his early work had formalist leanings, a variety of influences, from George Oppen and Roy Fisher to Emil Cioran and César Vallejo, have helped him develop a more open-plan style.

Chemical Plant

'I am pure ohm'

Seventies concept album cover:
green fields round the chemical plant,
a torch flared in the breeze's shiver,
all the crop circles you could want
and two smoke plumes that go on forever.

Wind down your window for a smell
of the muskily igniting beast:
exoskeleton, pure shell
of power that hides no pacing ghost
but only purely living steel

slicing through the riverside view.
Always there but never seen,
let all humanity be the few
hard-hatted shadows that we join
to work this chemistry we do

to feed the fire firing the hum
that rises snaking from each tower
and drives the chain reaction home
that surges when it finds us, lover,
and runs to ground through our pale flame.

A Fret

The coal merchant shoulders a nimbus of smuts
down a street that insists you've been here before
and recognise the urchin, you, that sits
and stares at his shoes in an open front door.

Don't buy it. The air is thick with the sloughed
skin of dead selves: they fall and settle,
a load too imperceptible to shift,
but sickly and adhesive, mute and subtle.

Let them not expect grief. You dodge and move
through liquid fixities of past and present,
steer by a river whose mud banks leave
you tidal, shifty, bogged down and imprisoned.

The sonic boom of the afternoon roar
from the stadium tracks your footsteps, blows
a dull wound in the boulevard's thin air,
and your pulse thuds to its drumbeat, win or lose.

On the up this year then? Play-off places,
blip, slump, plummet, dead in the water:
the mustard cuts like fog. Cut your losses,
a can kicked into the nearest gutter.

Here the last of empire has meandered
past the fag-end of the North Sea fleet
to a scrap yard sculpture park whose remaindered
Edward VII accepts a vain salute

from a yawning Ford Fiesta's bonnet.
The December sun is a lazy eye.
No vistas you can raise will open it
and you thirst for the liquid dark to bleed it dry,

and so comes evening and beer in a backstreet pub
by the bridge, where you bank the coal fire down
and a dog sips a pint, and onto your tab
goes a Schlenkerla, the 'hobbling man';

and fog on the way home, fog all round
so I can't see you who are a shadow away,
and there are no shadows and there is no ground
underfoot for me to feel give way,

and what kind of weather is this when all I want,
all that I imagine, touch and see
finds not loses itself in all I cannot
grasp, in a fog drifted in from the sea?

La Ultima Canción de César Peru

I sought you by night,
when the screech-owl roared,

when, grave as a newborn child,
impulsive as a dying man,

the triplets on the beggar's guitar
sputtered like tachycardia.

Far to the west
guano archipelagos

fall sheer away
to the breakers, but how

much heavier than one
are two shadows thrown

on the same cobbled square,
draping the admiral's statue

here in our landlocked state.
You draw the curtains

and Inti the sun god
disperses his relics among

the peddlers' trinkets
that his mysteries

might hide in plain view,
lurk amid joyous vulgarity

above all suspicion. And so
it is with our sacred things,

parcelled out among conversations
with the road sweeper and milkmaid,

eccentrically calm
as a telephone call taken

during sex. The oxygen
thins out, the faces

in each street redder
than the last until

we scarcely remember
what saint's day we celebrate,

pushing aside a dovecote
of penitents' flapping white hoods

as we pick through
the washing lines on the tight

hillside streets. House
after house the doors grow

smaller, sharp-eyed
women stooping

and squinting as I salute, until
I enter the house of my childhood

down on all fours. Immortal
forgetfulness, immortal

misrecognition, I remember
and know you too well,

with always the kettle come
to the boil as I enter the door.

When will I learn
to roar like the screech-owl?

When you stoop
to my window, dark one,

rattle my walls, and bid me
follow somewhere only

this chosen, narrowest
entrance could lead.

SAM WILLETTS

Sam Willetts was born in 1962 and edu-
cated in Oxford and he has spent most
of his life there and in London. He has
worked as a teacher, journalist and travel
writer. His first collection, *New Light for
the Old Dark*, was published in 2010 by
Cape Poetry.

One main strand of Willetts' poetry is
concerned with making sense of a trou-
bling past: he was deeply affected by the
loss of his mother when he was 19 and
she herself had narrowly escaped the
Nazi terror in Poland, and met Willetts'
father – an academic – while billeted in a
displaced persons camp. His work seeks
to wring positive values – empathy, in-
sight, even humour – from the darkest experiences: loss, bereavement,
addiction and despair. Elsewhere in his work there is a recurring figure
of the traveller abroad, startled and delighted by his new-found sur-
roundings; even his persona pieces retain this sense of the observant
individual, weighing up their purchases and options in situations of one
versus many.

Home

Near night's end on Dover Docks
the Channel meets the wall in white high-fives

while a wind ramping homeward
pinches my ears goodbye. Unslept,

unshaven, I case the quay, find unlocked
a door to Private whiteness: tiles, towels,

squalling vitreous enamel. Hot water
sends my face to cloudy-mirrored heaven.

Already not quite England, here – no cock fun
pleas, no race-fatwahs, no glory-holes; not one

good mark of English bog cacography.
Homesickness meets seasickness halfway;

from a rainy sundeck the Channel's swells
are sharp and smooth and sharp again,

repeating, un-repeating.
France lies, sunlit in the distance

like a tawny crust, but I keep
looking back at England, riding away shawled

in rain. Great white-walled cake, your dull icing
mined with memories. Sweet, unappetising home.

A Child at Their Party

1969 from the sun-branded end
of a Victorian garden. Chestnut shade,

jasmine tea lukewarm in willow-pattern,
yellow wine sun-mulling

on a middle-class Dionysian lawn:
a scene from a children's book written

by adults for themselves. From a hammock
between apple trees, she murmurs

*you're a beautiful child, children are
so beautiful*, laughs *suck!* when I blow

through her cigarette, launching sparks.
Soon, bored of the wrenchable grass

printing my elbows and the sun my eyes,
I open a story-door: out of the heat,

into a kitchen. As it unglooms, the walls
are stencilled always with forget-me-nots.

Truanting

Masculine, feminine, neuter:
beside boyish reaches of the Thames
I watched horses, companionable
strangers to impatience, switch at summer
head-to-tail. By the little-sister river,
spring calves jostled, saint-francissed me
to keep on scratching the pink
and humble itch between their ears.

A pinched-out cigarette stank in my palm
while I sang 'Trouble in Mind' to the mule canal.
At night, I knew the lines shone
like a river of rails under the sidings-lights
and the wake of a train broke gently
through my bed; by day, the sleepers
were steps laid flat to their vanishing-point,
each track a ladderback *A* for *Away*.

Fur-sorting

In the lit corner of this vast shed I work
like the rats by touch and smell as well as sight:

even the best synthetics crunch between
your fingertips, but real fur parts

down to the aromatic hide, spreads
as it would have when the living animal stood

exploring the wind. A low sheen runs across
silk-cursive legends – *Silvermann*

New Bond Street Guaranteed. Revenant
scent trails from collars and linings. Long-forgotten

assignations. The nearest thing to warmth here
is the radio's lost bonhomie, swallowed into

the dark. Sometimes the bad light yields
little shocks, like the dainty snarls on those four

foxes stitched into Siamese-quads; then my
own hide pimples, horripilates in sympathy.

The furs love lapsing from their pallets, to flood
the concrete in a lavish slump; some pieces,

somehow, keep coming back – that whole bear's skin,
macabre, scurfed with grit and sawdust, clacks

its claws like sad maraccas every fucking time.
Darkness of year's end and a mound of rags

remade daily. The radio yatters to the freezing air. Deep
inside the fur mounds pink litters squirm for life.

Detoxing in the French Quarter

As I stepped out of frigid air-conditioning
onto the skillet noon of Bourbon Street
I heard a man's voice *whisht* to me, but turned
to find the sidewalk vacant – nothing there beneath
the balconies but their long griddles
of shadow. Voodoo believers say the dead
may not leave; sunned-up, I spiked cold again
to think of the Quarter still crowded with others –
its sallow caballeros and darktown strutters,
its long-dead browsers in Cohen the Gunsmith's
and Meyer the Hatter's – aunseen watch
of jealous jazz ghosts glimpsed through wrought-iron,
astir with the vines in the sweet-fried breeze.

SAMANTHA WYNNE-RHYDDERCH

Samantha Wynne-Rhydderch was born in Aberystwyth in 1966 and grew up in west Wales before studying Classics at Cambridge University. She then moved to France where she taught English for two years, returning to the UK to complete an MA in Creative Writing at the University of Wales, Cardiff. She won the Redbeck Press Pamphlet Competition in 1996 and the subsequent pamphlet *Stranded in Ithaca* appeared two years later. The same year she received an Arts Council of Wales award to help her complete her first collection, *Rock-climbing in Silk* (Seren, 2001). Her second collection, *Not in These Shoes*, was published by Picador in 2008. She is currently Poetry Fellow at the University of Wales, Lampeter.

Wynne-Rhydderch has been praised for her 'acute and spare verses dealing with loss, betrayal and death'. Mainly a poet of linear narrative, difficult terrains, both physical and emotional, figure in her work, as does water, that very British concern, which is a strong theme throughout the second of her books in the shape of bath, sea, storms and floods.

Stately Home

The one thing I can recall is
the painted Swedish chair in the playroom,
a heart cut out of its back.
Which is how I feel now
as paint flakes off the gate.

There, on the hall table, would be
my mother's sequined gloves
in love with each other in a pool of light,
the faded purple curtains, the sanity
of doilies. Upstairs, my baby dresses

might lie like pressed flowers
under glass, unvisited,
my five-year-old voice trapped
in the cupboard in which I once
whispered a poem.

Round the back you'd see the sundial
pointing up to the Sychnant Mountain
I longed to climb, when every bedtime
I'd check my piece of driftwood,
still safe under the pillow.

A Pair of Antlers

Ride a horse along the trail.
Glimpse
through leaves every tone of rust
and the jackdaws' call,
the towers of Ingledene,
intricate in the cliff,
my hair the colour of sandstone
on your collar,
only the voice of a decanter
and a northerly in the glen:
a language called Bliss.

The white hart caught again and again
on your wallpaper –
at night I'd hear it once more
from your turret bedroom,
a pair of antlers on the wall
adorned with your hat,
your shirt exhausted
on a tartan chair after a day at the axe.

High up in the south wing
I couldn't take my eyes off you
as you fought roots of rhododendrons,
the precipice below,
slow claimer of all our possessions
through a wide-open sash:
six of my books had already
blanched in the textured Esk.

You'd stand with a single malt,
in braces, admiring a Grinling,
while I did a fingertip search of your face,
woodsmoke and heather in the grate,
after leading me all day along the river
in spate, unintentional dancers,
discovering the recesses of baronial you,
lairding it in a rented estate
we were about to lose. So many rooms,
rooms of rooms. I would surprise myself
at dusk in gilded mirrors, disappear
behind an aspidistra the size of a small tree,
the ceilings ornate as my inarticulate heart.

At first just flakes, but as the months
wore on, more plaster started to fall.
Each evening as we read by the fire's soliloquy,
our chairs strident on the flagstones,
another piece of eighteenth century horsehair
and lath would sigh onto the floor.
More Madeira, me dear? and you'd pour.

We'd pretend it wasn't happening, this falling apart:
was *decadence* really bordering on *decay*?
I held the drawing pins and you took white sheets.
We blanked it all out
with interior sails.

Indiscretions

Opposite the Parc St Jacques
each cube of light
invites the evening in.
Henri in his shirtsleeves
soothes a wrought-iron balustrade.
On the second floor Mme Fougères
feeds her poodle with revolting
devotion, ignoring the husband who
wilts behind *Le Figaro*.
Below, Jean-Yves admires his twin
spattered with shaving foam,
turns out the light and crashes
into the *ascenseur*. Next door,
Mlle de Reuilly's shadow pulls out
her pins one by one. Hair falls
to her elbows as Jean-Yves enters
the *Métro*. On the *troisième* Bernard's
come home with someone new.
The way he strips the cuticle
from his garlic tells you his
gratin dauphinois isn't the only thing
that tastes good.

TAMAR YOSELOFF

Tamar Yoseloff was raised in the USA and moved to the UK in her early 20s. Her poetry collections are *Sweetheart* (Slow Dancer Press, 1998), which was a Poetry Book Society Special Commendation and the winner of the Aldeburgh Festival Prize, *Barnard's Star* (Enitharmon Press, 2004), and *Fetch* (Salt, 2007). She is also the author of *Marks*, a collaborative book with artist Linda Karshan (Pratt Contemporary Art, 2007), and editor of *A Room to Live In: A Kettle's Yard Anthology* (Salt, 2007). She is currently the poetry editor of *Art World Magazine* and a tutor for The Poetry School in London. In 2005 she was Writer in Residence at Magdalene College, Cambridge, as part of their Year in Literature Festival. A lot of her work is triggered by the visual arts and she has worked collaboratively with artists and with galleries, such as Kettle's Yard in Cambridge.

Yoseloff's poems are largely concerned with ruin, decay and abandonment and are often gradual and atmospheric, with a Gothic twist and an eye for blood. Another strand of her poetry looks back ambivalently on her childhood America of the 1970s and 1980s.

Barnard's Star

The angels dancing on a pin's head,
the UFO glittering in the night,
the aura left after you have gone –
all of them in my mind.

That faint red dwarf that passes
overhead when I am boiling a kettle
or making the bed
is invisible to the naked eye,

a ball of hydrogen and helium
making for the sun
over eighty miles a second,
certain of its course,

but I know it's there, just as I steer
through a darkened room
by trust, its familiar contours
charted on my fingers.

The Angle of Error

This is a more complex geometry than I had intended

I have charted this on my graph of unease –

your hand in motion –
       push, twist, splay

the arrowed grass in a rain-soaked field, each blade defined –

       the grey stone of disappointment.

Your face picassos –
       I can no longer picture you whole.

An endless spyrograph of a narrow room, an off-season coast –

       my head slanted to catch your mouth
your hand sphering my wrist –

       the gazetteer of hurt.

I think I'm moving forward
       but I'm not

my heart pounding its old song – stop, stop, stop

navigating a tiny circle
       a crutch dragged in the dirt.

The Venetian Mirror

When I first hung it in our bedroom we could not sleep all night,
it was like having the moon for company, so bright it shone.
JIM EDE

1

Silver has its day, recedes
to reveal the surface beneath

gone black –
its own Dorian moment.

It reflects back what we have
not been able to understand,

an abundance lost, just hinted
in the etched leaves, tendrils lacing

the frame. What's inside is
rust, a pox on a lovely face,

still we trade its dimensions
for our own: dumbstruck, vain.

2

The basilica behind a slick
of rain, gold diminished

to dun. The colour of nothing.
The bulk of it jagged

on the darkening sky.
The end of day, odic light

illuminates a shrivelled rose;
all the sadness we contain

in this drop of rain, its
crystallised gloom.

3

The ghost hulk of the palazzo
leans into the canal. Narcissus crazed.

Tarnished jewels, pink marble
dulled to flesh. Shiver of a ballroom

out of season, sliver of broken
glass, the first glistening of frost,

as the campana strikes,
mourns itself in echo.

ACKNOWLEDGEMENTS

Patience Agbabi: 'The Wife of Bafa', from *Transformatrix* (Canongate, 2000); 'Postmod', 'The London Eye' and 'Josephine Baker Finds Herself', from *Bloodshot Monochrome* (Canongate, 2008); all reprinted by permission of the publisher. Photo: Lyndon Douglas.

Jonathan Asser: 'The Birdbath's Saying *Dive*', previously unpublished, by permission of the author. 'Interlude', 'Something To Do' and 'No Mercy', from *Outside the All Stars* (Arc Publications, 2003), reprinted by permission of the publisher.

Tiffany Atkinson: 'Portrait of the Husband as Farmer's Market' and 'Rain', previously unpublished; 'Philology', first published in *Fragments from the Dark: Women Writing Home and Self in Wales*, ed. Jeni Williams (Hafan Books, 2008), all by permission of the author. 'Autobiography Without Pronouns' and 'In This One', from *Kink and Particle* (Seren, 2006), reprinted by permission of the publisher.

Simon Barraclough: 'Frigidaire', 'The Open Road', 'Desert Orchid' and 'Los Alamos Mon Amour', from *Los Alamos Mon Amour* (Salt Publishing, 2008), reprinted by permission of the publisher. Photo: Isobel Dixon.

Paul Batchelor: 'To a Halver', first published in *Poetry London*, reprinted by permission of the author. 'Keening', 'The Secret Papers', and 'Triage', from *The Sinking Road* (Bloodaxe Books, 2008), reprinted by permission of the publisher. Photo: Caroline Forbes.

Kate Bingham: 'De Beers', from *Cohabitation* (Seren, 1998); 'Dalby Bush Farm', 'The Mouths of Babes' and 'The Island-designing Competition', from *Quicksand Beach* (Seren, 2006); all reprinted by permission of the publisher.

Julia Bird: 'Five Years Trying to Win the Flower Show Vegetable Animal Class', 'Your Grandfather Would Have Wanted You to Have This' and 'Breathing Pattern', from *Hannah and the Monk* (Salt Publishing, 2008), reprinted by permission of the publisher. Photo: Caroline Forbes.

Patrick Brandon: 'Mountain Man', 'Dolphin', 'Higgs Bison', 'The Water Cycle' and 'A Sloping Pitch', from *A Republic of Linen* (Bloodaxe Books, 2009). Reprinted by permission of the publisher. Photo: Sarah Harrison.

David Briggs: 'Twenty Below Zero' and 'Winter Music', first published in *Magma*; 'Self-Portrait in a Rear-view Mirror', first published in *Limelight*; 'Asking the Difficult Questions', first published in *Notes from the Underground*. All reprinted by permission of the author. Photo: Jane Wolf.

Andy Brown: 'The Last Geese', first published in *The Storm Bern* (tall-lighthouse, 2008), reprinted by permission of the author. 'Samhain' and 'A Poem of Gifts', from *Fall of the Rebel Angels* (Salt Publishing, 2006), and 'As the Tide Sucks Out at Daybreak', from *Goose Music* (Salt Publishing, 2008), reprinted by permission of the publisher. Photo: Amy Shelton.

Judy Brown: 'The End of the Rainbow', 'The New Neighbours' and 'Unfamiliar Festivals', previously unpublished; 'Peckham Poem(s)', first published in *Magma*. All by permission of the author. Photo: Chloe Barter.

Colette Bryce: 'In Defence of Old Men Dozing in Bookshops', from *The Observations of Aleksandr Svetlov* (Donut Press, 2007), reprinted by permission of the author. 'The Smoke', from *The Full Indian Rope Trick* (Picador, 2004); 'Line' and 'Nevers', from *The Heel of Bernadette* (Picador, 2000); 'Self Portrait in a Broken Wing-mirror', from *Self-Portrait in the Dark* (Picador, 2008); all reprinted by permission of the publisher.

Matthew Caley: 'Acupuncture', '*King Size Rizlas*', and 'Big Sur', from *The Scene of My Former Triumph* (Wrecking Ball Press, 2005), reprinted by permission of the author. 'The Argument', and 'For Howard Devoto', from *Apparently* (Bloodaxe Books, 2010), reprinted by permission of the publisher. Photo: Ian McDonald

Siobhán Campbell: 'Massy Wood' and 'Miner', from *The Permanent Wave* (Blackstaff, 1996), reprinted by permission of the author. 'Almost in Sight', from *Cross-Talk* (Seren, 2009), reprinted by permission of the publisher.

Vahni Capildeo: '*from* Winter to Winter: August – North', first published in *The Undraining Sea* (Egg Box, 2009); 'Vacant Possession', first published in *Dark and Unaccustomed Words* (Egg Box, 2010), both reprinted by permission of the author. 'Lilies', 'White Jasmine' and 'What Is Your Guy Really Like?', from *No Traveller Returns* (Salt Publishing, 2003), reprinted by permission of the publisher. Photo: Nicholas Laughlin.

Melanie Challenger: 'Stac Pollaidh or *Regret*', previously unpublished, by permission of the author. 'Sleeping Beauty', 'Blue Whale', and 'Pygmalion', from *Galatea* (Salt Publishing, 2006), reprinted by permission of the publisher. Photo: Aleksandar Sepi.

Kate Clanchy: 'Patagonia' and 'Poem for a Man with No Sense of Smell', from *Slattern* (Picador, 2001); 'Love', 'Dark, Dark' and 'Scan', from *Newborn* (Picador, 2005); 'Bridge Over the Border', from *Samarkand* (Picador, 1999), all reprinted by permission of the publisher.

Polly Clark: 'Women' and 'Nibbling', from *Take Me With You* (Bloodaxe Books, 2005); 'South Uist', from *Kiss* (Bloodaxe Books, 2000); 'Dog Opera' and 'Thank You' from *Farewell My Lovely* (Bloodaxe Books, 2009); all reprinted by permission of the publisher. Photo: Simon Hollington.

Julia Copus: 'A Soft-edged Reed of Light' and 'Raymond, at 60', previously unpublished, by permission of the author. 'Love, Like Water', 'In Defence of Adultery' and 'Topsell's Beasts', from *In Defence of Adultery* (Bloodaxe Books, 2003); all reprinted by permission of the publisher. Photo: Nigel Gallear.

Sarah Corbett: 'Taking the Night Train', 'The Dog's Kiss', and 'Kisses', from *Other Beasts* (Seren, 2008), 'Shame', from *The Red Wardrobe* (Seren, 1998); all reprinted by permission of the publisher.

Claire Crowther: 'Open Plan' and 'Summerhouse', from *The Clockwork Gift* (Shearsman Books, 2009); 'Investigating the Easter Issue', 'Lost Child', and 'Next Door Moon', from *Stretch of Closures* (Shearsman Books, 2007); all reprinted by permission of the publisher. Photo: Tony Frazer.

Tim Cumming: 'Snow', from *Apocalypso* (Stride, 1999); 'Days' and 'Foreign News' from *The Rumour* (Stride, 2004). 'Danebury Ring' and 'Late Picasso', previously unpublished. 'Following the Bloom', first published in *Limelight*. All by permission of the author.

Ailbhe Darcy: 'Swan Song', 'The Art of Losing', 'The mornings you turn into a grub' and 'Crossing', all first published in *A Fictional Dress* (tall-lighthouse, 2009), by permission of the author. Photo: Conor Friel.

Peter Davidson: 'Of Death, Fame and Immortality', previously unpublished, by permission of the author. 'The Englishman's Catechism' and 'Concerning Stillness and Distance' from *The Palace of Oblivion* (Carcanet, 2008), reprinted by permission of the publisher.

Nick Drake: 'Babylon' and 'Sea Change', from *From the Word Go* (Bloodaxe Books, 2007); 'Eureka', 'The Hunt By Night' and 'The Ghost Train', from *The Man in the White Suit* (Bloodaxe Books, 1999); all in later versions than those in the original collections and reprinted by permission of the publisher. Photo: Lisa Tomasetti.

Sasha Dugdale: 'Ten Moons', first published in *Poetry*; 'Maldon', 'Moor' and '*from* Red House', previously unpublished, all by permission of the author. 'Carnation, Bible' from *The Estate* (Oxford Carcanet, 2007) and 'Stolen', from *Notebook* (Oxford Carcanet, 2003), both by permission of the publisher. Photo: Paul King.

Chris Emery: 'Carl's Job', and 'The Destroyer's Convention', previously unpublished, by permission of the author. 'The Lermontov', from *Radio Nostalgia* (Arc Publications, 2006), reprinted by permission of the publisher. Photo: John Wilkinson.

Bernardine Evaristo: excerpts from *Lara*, chapters 2 & 12 (Bloodaxe Books, 2009), reprinted by permission of the publisher. 'The Language of Love (II)' and 'Epilogue: Vivat Zuleika', from *The Emperor's Babe* (Hamish Hamilton/ Penguin, 2001), by permission of the publisher. Photo: Katie Vandyck.

Paul Farley: 'Newts', first published in *Poetry Review*, 98, No. 3 (Autumn 2008); 'North Atlantic Corridor', first broadcast on BBC Radio 4's *Front Row*, and published in *Field Recordings: BBC Poems 1998-2008* (Donut Press, 2009), both reprinted by permission of the author. 'Dead Fish', 'Diary Moon' and 'An Interior', from *The Ice Age* (Picador, 2002); 'Keith Chegwin as Fleance', from *The Boy from the Chemist is Here to See You* (Picador, 1998); 'The Scarecrow Wears a Wire', from *Tramp in Flames* (Picador, 2006); all reprinted by permission of the publisher.

Leontia Flynn: 'The Furthest Distances I've Travelled' and 'By My Skin', from *These Days* (Jonathan Cape, 2004); 'Airports' and 'Belfast', from *Drives* (Jonathan Cape, 2008); all reprinted by permission of the Random House Group Ltd. Photo: Caroline Forbes.

Annie Freud: 'Daube', previously unpublished, by permission of the author. 'The Study of Disease', The Symbolic Meaning of Things', 'A Scotch Egg' and 'A Canaletto Orange', from *The Best Man That Ever Was* (Picador, 2007), all reprinted by permission of the publisher. Photo: Chloe Barter.

Alan Gillis: 'Whiskey', published in *The Green Rose* (Clutag Press, 2010), by permission of the author. 'The Ulster Way', from *Somebody, Somewhere* (Gallery Press, 2004); 'Harvest', from *Hawks and Doves* (Gallery Press, 2007), by permission of the publisher.

Jane Griffiths: 'Epitaph for X', previously unpublished, by permission of the author. 'Valediction', 'Clairvoyance', 'Travelling Light' and 'On Liking Glass Houses', from *Another Country: New & Selected Poems* (Bloodaxe Books, 2008), all by permission of the publisher. Photo: Nigel Smith.

Vona Groarke: 'To Smithereens', 'Ghosts' and 'The Return', from *Juniper Street* (Gallery Press, 2006); 'Bodkin', from *Sprindrift* (Gallery Press, 2009), all reprinted by permission of the publisher.

Jen Hadfield: 'The Blokes and the Beasties', previously unpublished, by permission of the author. 'Melodeon on the Road Home', 'Unfledging', 'Full Sheeptick moon' and 'Thrimilce, Isbister', from *Almanacs* (Bloodaxe Books, 2005); 'Hedgehog, Hamnavoe' and 'Prenatal Polar Bear', from *Nigh-No-Place* (Bloodaxe Books, 2008); all reprinted by permission of the publisher. Photo: Caroline Forbes.

Sophie Hannah: 'Long for this World', from *First of the Last Chances* (Carcanet, 2003); 'The Bridging Line', from *Leaving and Leaving You* (Carcanet, 1999); 'No Ball Games etc', from *Pessimism for Beginners* (Carcanet, 2007); all reprinted by permission of the publisher. Photo: Mark Mather.

Tracey Herd: 'Spring in the Valley of the Racehorse', previously unpublished, by permission of the author. 'Sir Ivor', and 'Coronach', from *No Hiding Place* (Bloodaxe Books, 1996); 'Black Swan', from *Dead Redhead* (Bloodaxe Books, 2001); all reprinted by permission of the publisher. Photo: Moira Conway.

Kevin Higgins: 'Almost Invisible', from *The Boy With No Face* (Salmon, 2005); 'From the future, a postcard home', 'Shapeless Days Shuffling', 'The Great Depression', 'The Candidate' and 'The Couple Upstairs', from *Time Gentlemen, Please* (Salmon, 2008); all reprinted by permission of the publisher. Photo: Mark Higgins.

Matthew Hollis: 'Hedge Bird', from *Trees in the City* (Axon, 2007); 'Diomedes', broadcast on Classic FM and published by The Royal Philharmonic Society 2008; both by permission of the author. 'The Sour House', from *Ground Water* (Bloodaxe Books, 2004), reprinted by permission of the publisher. Photo: Claire McNamee.

A.B. Jackson: 'Foxes', first published in *The Wigtown Poetry Competition 2005: winning and commended poems* (Galloway Gazette, 2006); '*from* Apocrypha: Adam lay miraculous', first published in *The Dark Horse*; '*from* Apocrypha: Abraham' and '*from* Apocrypha: Daniel's ear', first published in *Magma*; '*from* Apocrypha: Gethsemane', previously unpublished; all by permission of the author. 'A Ring', 'Lauder's Bar' and 'Star', from *Fire Stations* (Anvil Press Poetry, 2003), reprinted by permission of the publisher. Photo: Susan B. Breakenridge.

Anthony Joseph: 'The Cinema', 'Conductors of His Mystery', 'The Myst', and 'Folkways', from *Bird Head Son* (Salt Publishing, 2009), reprinted by permission of the publisher. Photo: Aiste Leipute.

Luke Kennard: 'The Forms of Despair', from *The Migraine Hotel* (Salt Publishing 2009), reprinted by permission of the author. 'Chorus', 'Daughters of the Lonesome Isle' and 'Instrumental #3', from *The Harbour Beyond the Movie* (Salt Publishing, 2007), reprinted by permission of the publisher. 'Scarecrow', from *The Solex Brothers* (Stride, 2007), reprinted by permission of the publisher. Photo: Esther Kennard.

Nick Laird: 'Adeline' and 'Donna', both first published in *The Manchester Review*, by permission of the author. 'Pug' and 'The Hall of Medium Harmony', from *On Purpose* (Faber & Faber, UK; W.W. Norton & Company, USA, 2007); 'The Eventual', from *To a Fault* (Faber & Faber, UK; W.W. Norton & Company, USA, 2005), all by permission of the publishers.

Sarah Law: 'Phase transitions', first published in *Ascension Notes* (Shearsman, 2009); 'Breathing', 'Easy Posture' from 'Stretch: A Yoga Sequence' and

'A Gem for Women' from 'Stretch: A Yoga Sequence', from *The Lady Chapel* (Stride, 2004), all by permission of the author. 'Parisian', from *Perihelion* (Shearsman Books, 2006), reprinted by permission of the publisher. Photo: Kevin Dwyer.

Frances Leviston: 'The Zombie Library', first published in *Tower Poetry Review*, reprinted by permission of the author. 'Sight', 'The Gaps', 'Moon' and 'Scandinavia', from *Public Dream* (Picador, 2007), reprinted by permission of the publisher.

Gwyneth Lewis: 'Memorial Sweater', and 'Prayer for Horizon', previously unpublished, by permission of the author. 'A Golf-Course Resurrection', and 'Night Passage to Nantucket', from *Chaotic Angels: Poems in English* (Bloodaxe Books, 2005), by permission of the publisher. Photo: Alexandra Cool.

John McAuliffe: 'Tinnutus' and 'The Electric Jar', from *Next Door* (Gallery Press, 2007); 'Flood' and 'You Can See', from *A Better Life* (Gallery Press, 2002), reprinted by permission of the publisher. Photo: Brian McAuliffe.

Chris McCabe: 'Lemon Blue', first published on *Poetry International Web*, by permission of the author. 'Radio', 'The Essex Fox' and 'Poem in Black Ink', from *Zeppelins* (Salt Publishing, 2008), reprinted by permission of the publisher. Photo: Jack Goffe.

Helen Macdonald: 'Poem', previously unpublished; 'MIR', 'Jack' and 'Earth Station', from *Shaler's Fish* (Etruscan Books, 2001), all by permission of the author.

Patrick McGuinness: 'Montreal' and 'Age of the Empty Chair', first published in *19th Century Blues* (Smith/Doorstop, 2007), and 'Blue', previously unpublished, by permission of the author. 'Heroes' and 'Dust', from *The Canals of Mars* (Carcanet, 2004), reprinted by permission of the publisher. Photo: Geraint Thomas.

Kona Macphee: 'Pheasant and astronomers', from *Perfect Blue* (Bloodaxe Books, 2010), and 'Melbourne, evening, summertime', 'Shrew', 'Terminus' and 'Waltz', from *Tails* (Bloodaxe Books, 2004); all reprinted by permission of the publisher. Photo: Patrick Andrews.

Peter Manson: 'Hymn to Light', 'In Vitro', 'Poem' and 'Four Darks in Red', from *For the Good of Liars* (Barque Press, 2006), reprinted by permission of the author. 'Familars', from *Between Cup and Lip* (Miami University Press, 2008), by permission of the publisher. Photo: Tom Raworth.

D.S. Marriott: 'Tap', from *Incognegro* (Salt Publishing, 2006), reprinted by permission of the publisher. 'The Day Ena Died' and 'Over the Black Mountains', from *Hoodoo Voodoo* (Shearsman Books, 2008), reprinted by permission of the publisher.

Sam Meekings: 'Migration', previously unpublished, by permission of the author. 'Describing Angels to the Blind', 'Bees' and 'Depth', from *The Bestiary* (Polygon, 2008), all reprinted by permission of the publisher. Photo: Xue Lian.

Sinéad Morrissey: extract from 'China', from *The State of the Prisons* (Carcanet, 2005); 'Shadows in Siberia According to Kapuscinski' and 'Love, the Nightwatch...', from *Through the Square Window* (Carcanet, 2009); 'On Waitakere Dam', from *Between Here and There* (Carcanet, 2001); all reprinted by permission of the publisher.

Daljit Nagra: 'This Be the Pukka Verse', previously unpublished, by permission of the author. 'Look We Have Coming to Dover!', 'University' and 'Our Town With the Whole of India!', from *Look We Have Coming to Dover!* (Faber, 2007), all reprinted by permission of the publisher. Photo: Sarah Lee.

Caitríona O'Reilly: 'Octopus' and 'Pandora's Box', from *The Nowhere Birds* (Bloodaxe Books, 2001); 'Calculus' and 'The Lure', from *The Sea Cabinet* (Bloodaxe Books, 2006); all reprinted by permission of the publisher.

Alice Oswald: 'Field', 'Shamrock Café', and 'Woods etc.', from *Woods etc.* (Faber & Faber, 2005); 'A Greyhound in the Evening after a Long Day of Rain', from *The Thing in the Gap-stone Stile* (Faber & Faber, 2007); all reprinted by permission of the publisher and United Agents.

Katherine Pierpoint: 'Waterbuffalo', first published in *Wild Reckoning* (eds. John Burnside & Maurice Riordan (Calouste Gulbenkian Foundation 2004); 'Burning the Door', previously unpublished, both by permission of the author. 'Cats Are Otherwise' and 'Plumbline', from *Truffle Beds* (Faber & Faber, 1995), by permission of the publisher. Photo: Jon L. Bird.

Clare Pollard: 'The Panther', first published in *Poetry International*, by permission of the author. 'Puppetry' and 'Fears of a Hypochondriac Insomniac', from *Bedtime* (Bloodaxe Books, 2002), reprinted by permission of the publisher. Photo: Jayne West.

Jacob Polley: 'The Bridge', previously unpublished, by permission of the author. 'Rain' and 'The Turn', from *Little Gods* (Picador, 2006); 'The Crow' and 'The North-South Divide', from *The Brink* (Picador, 2003); all reprinted by permission of the publisher. Photo: Sandi Friend.

Diana Pooley: 'The Bird', 'Listen Amelio', 'Inscriptions', 'Back at Pathungra', and 'King', from *Like This* (Salt Publishing, 2009), all reprinted by permission of the author. Photo: David Barnett.

Richard Price: 'Wake Up and Sleep' was commissioned by the Calouste Gulbenkian Foundation and first published in their anthology *Signs and Humours* in 2008; 'Languor's Whispers' was first published in *Earliest Spring Yet* (Landfill Press, 2006); both appear in *Rays* (Carcanet, 2009) and are reprinted by permission of the author. Poems from 'A Spelthorne Bird List' from *Lucky Day* (Carcanet, 2005), reprinted by permission of the publisher. Photo: B. Kemp.

Sally Read: 'Fog', 'Mastectomy' and 'Mafia Flowers', from *Broken Sleep* (Bloodaxe Books, 2009); 'Instruction' and 'The Death Bell', from *The Point of Splitting* (Bloodaxe Books, 2005); all reprinted by permission of the publisher.

Deryn Rees-Jones: 'My Father's Hair', from *Signs Round a Dead Body* (Seren, 1998); 'A Visitation', from *Quiver* (Seren, 2004); both reprinted by permission of the publisher. 'Trilobite', from *Falls & Finds* (Shoestring Press, 1998), reprinted by permission of the author.

Neil Rollinson: 'Dreamtime', 'Constellations', and 'Long Exposure', from *Spanish Fly* (Jonathan Cape, 2001); 'Between Bradford and Pudsey', from *A Spillage of Mercury* (Jonathan Cape, 1996); all reprinted by permission of the Random House Group Ltd. Photo: Sheila Deegan.

Jacob Sam-La Rose: 'The Beautiful', 'Blacktop Universe', 'A Life in Dreams', and 'Plummeting', all by permission of the author.

Antony Rowland: 'Lésvos', 'Damrak', 'Pie' and 'Golem', from *The Land of Green Ginger* (Salt Publishing, 2008), reprinted by permission of the publisher. Photo: Emma Liggins.

James Sheard: 'Four Mirrors', 'Cargo Cult', 'The Lost Testament of R. Catesby' and 'Café Verdi', from *Scattering Eva* (Jonathan Cape, 2005), all reprinted by permission of the Random House Group Ltd. Photo: Barney Jones.

Zoë Skoulding: 'History', first published in Agenda, reprinted by permission of the author. 'Trappist Brewers', from *The Mirror Trade* (Seren, 2004); 'New Year', 'Docks', and 'Preselis with Brussels Street Map', from *Remains of a Future City* (Seren, 2008); all reprinted by permission of the publisher.

Catherine Smith: 'The Set of Optics You Wouldn't Let Me Buy in Portobello Road Market, September 1984', previously unpublished; 'Wonders', from *The Butcher's Hands* (Smith/Doorstop Books, 2003); 'Picnic' and 'The Fathers', from *Lip* (Smith/Doorstop Books, 2007). All reprinted by permission of the author. Photo: Derek Adams.

Jean Sprackland: 'The Way Down', 'Bracken' and 'Hands', from *Tilt* (Jonathan Cape, 2007); 'An Old Friend Comes to Stay', from *Hard Water* (Jonathan Cape, 2003); all reprinted by permission of the Random House Group Ltd. Photo: Caroline Forbes.

John Stammers: 'Funeral' and 'Black Dog', previously unpublished, by permission of the author. 'Mary Brunton' and 'A Younger Woman', from *Stolen Love Behaviour* (Picador, 2005); 'Testimony', from *Panoramic Loungebar* (Picador, 2001); reprinted by permission of the publisher. Photo: Derek Adams.

Greta Stoddart: 'Verfremdungseffekt', and 'Salvation Jane', from *Salvation Jane* (Anvil Press Poetry, 2008); 'The Crossing', 'Greece', and 'Object', from *At Home in the Dark* (Anvil Press Poetry, 2001); all reprinted by permission of the publisher. Photo: Manuel Harlan.

Sandra Tappenden: 'Promise', 'Bells', 'Waroirrs of the Whiled West', and 'People who are drawn to take free stress tests', from *Speed* (Salt Publishing, 2009), reprinted by permission of the publisher.

Tim Turnbull: 'Sea Monsters', 'Lullaby for an Alcoholic', and 'What was that?', from *Stranded in Sub-Atomica* (Donut Press, 2005); 'Ode on a Grayson Perry Urn', from *Caligula on Ice and Other Poems* (Donut Press, 2009); all reprinted by permission of the publisher. Photo: Shiona McArthur.

Julian Turner: 'To a Nightjar', previously unpublished, by permission of the author. 'Bert Haines' Yard' and 'Penalty of Stroke and Distance', from *Crossing the Outskirts* (Anvil Press Poetry, 2002); 'At Walcott', from *Orphan Sites* (Anvil Press Poetry, 2006); all by permission of the publisher.

Mark Waldron: 'The Brand New Dark is Getting In', 'He's Face Down in the Lake', 'The Well-Dressed Street', 'The Very Slow train' and 'Underneath the Gone Sky', from *The Brand New Dark* (Salt Publishing, 2008), reprinted by permission of the publisher. Photo: Julie Hill.

Ahren Warner: 'la brisure', first published in *Poetry Review*; 'Legare', first published in *Magma*; 'Near Saint Mary Woolnoth, EC3' and 'Leman', previously unpublished; all by permission of the author. Photo: Nathan Penlington.

Tim Wells: 'My Own Private Ida Lupino' and 'L.A.Rain', from *Boys' Night Out in the Afternoon* (Donut Press, 2005); 'Comin' a Dance' and 'The 1980s are a Long Time Dead', from *Rougher Yet* (Donut Press, 2009); all reprinted by permission of the author. Photo: Sara Leigh Lewis.

Matthew Welton: 'Poppy', previously unpublished, by permission of the author. 'An ABC of American Suicide' and 'The fundament of wonderment', from *The Book of Matthew* (Carcanet, 2003), reprinted by permission of the publisher. Photo: Laurette Evans.

David Wheatley: 'A Fret', first published in *Drift* (Hull City Council, 2008); 'La Ultima Canción de César Peru', previously unpublished, both by permission of the author. 'Chemical Plant', from *Mocker* (Gallery Press, 2006), reprinted by permission of the publisher. Photo: Aingeal Clare.

Sam Willetts: 'Seasickness', 'A Child at the Party', 'Truanting', 'Fur-sorting' and 'In the French Quarter', from *New Light for the Old Dark* (Jonathan Cape, 2010), reprinted by permission of the Random House Group Ltd. Photo: Flora Botsford.

Samantha Wynne-Rhydderch: 'Stately Home' and 'A Pair of Antlers', from *Not in These Shoes* (Picador, 2008), reprinted by permission of the publisher. 'Indiscretions', from *Rockclimbing in Silk* (Seren, 2001), reprinted by permission of the publisher. Photo: Keith Morris.

Tamar Yoseloff: 'Barnard's Star', from *Barnard's Star* (Enitharmon, 2004), reprinted by permission of the publisher. 'The Angle of Error' and 'The Venetian Mirror', from *Fetch* (Salt Publishing, 2007), reprinted by permission of the publisher. Photo: Derek Adams.